Great
Sewn
Clothes

from

Threads
MAGAZINE

Great Sewn Clothes

from *Threads* MAGAZINE

The Taunton Press

Cover photo by Nancy Ney

First printing: May 1991
Second printing: February 1992
Printed in the United States of America

A THREADS Book

THREADS magazine® is a trademark of The Taunton Press, Inc.
registered in the U.S. Patent and Trademark Office.

The Taunton Press
63 South Main Street
Box 5506
Newtown, CT 06470-5506

Library of Congress Cataloging-in-Publication Data

Great Sewn Clothes from Threads magazine.
    p. cm.
  "A Threads book" — Copr. p.
  Includes index.
  ISBN 0-942391-82-9 : $16.95
  1. Sewing.   2. Clothing and dress.   I. Threads magazine
II. Title: Great Sewn Clothes
TT705.G74   1991   90-23608
646.4'04—dc20   CIP

Contents

Introduction

really great clothes are a perfect blending of fabric, cut and finish: a creation that functions perfectly, falls gracefully and fits fabulously. When we look at masterful garments created by great couturiers and custom tailors, we're awed and inspired. But when we examine these garments closely, we also learn what makes them great.

In this collection of articles from *Threads* magazine, sewers, teachers and designers give us a close look inside some fine garments. Underlinings, handstitches and clever details are revealed; cut, drape and fabric grain are explored along with ideas about image and how clothes should function. There's much to learn from the women and men whose designs and techniques we explore, from Coco Chanel to Rei Kawakubo.

Betsy Levine, editor

The Comfortable Side of Couture

Practical techniques of Coco Chanel

by Claire Shaeffer

When Coco Chanel reopened the House of Chanel in 1954, she was already a legend. Between the wars, her innovative designs had included comfortable, easy-to-wear clothes frequently inspired by menswear, children's school blazers, working-class garments, and sailors' uniforms. Chanel turned ordinary fabrics—wool tweeds, mottled wool flannels (kasha), and nubby linens—into luxury garments; and she used luxury laces to create understated shirtdresses. Chanel made it chic to look poor and charged outrageously for the privilege. Compared with Dior's collection of heavily structured garments, which often required waist cinchers, the clothes in Chanel's '54 collection fit the body easily. Older women looked younger and slimmer, while young women looked sophisticated and elegant. The Chanel suit dominated fashion in the early '60s. Thousands of women wore them, including America's trendsetter, Jacqueline Kennedy.

Although the influence of the couture house faded after Chanel's death in 1971, in 1983 Karl Lagerfeld was installed as couture designer to rejuvenate the Chanel collections. He boldly introduced wit and youth to the Chanel look, creating clothes Chanel herself might have designed. This year, the

Coco Chanel, facing page, relaxes in one of her signature suits. Designers like Adolfo are still being influenced by Chanel's distinct use of such details as fabrics with a handwoven texture, gold buttons, jewelry chains, and lots of trim. (Photo by Cecil Beaton, courtesy of Sotheby's, London)

Chanel influence on designers such as Carolyn Roehm, Ralph Lauren, Bill Blass, Yves Saint Laurent, and Adolfo is particularly strong. Lightweight jackets with chain belts, gilded buttons, and bold fake jewelry saturate the luxury ready-to-wear market.

The not-so-basic suit—At first glance, the Chanel suit merely looks like a boxy jacket with a matching skirt and well-coordinated blouse. When we closely examine it, however, we realize that nothing has been left to chance, either in the way it is worn or in its construction and fit. The suit was a well-planned ensemble. The jacket and skirt linings matched the blouse so that wearing the suit with another blouse was almost impossible. A blouse was often sewn to the skirt, resulting in a "dress" whose blouse always remained properly tucked in.

Many Chanel techniques, such as quilting the lining to the jacket shell and stitching gilded chains to the hem, control the set of the garment on the body or prolong its pristine appearance. Functional buttons and buttonholes adhere to the design principles that Chanel set for herself. Many of these "Chanelisms" are labor-intensive techniques, but home sewers can apply them to enhance a special jacket, just as I did when I made my jacket (photo below), using a commercially available pattern.

Chanel designed suits for comfort and mobility. Extremely narrow-cut shoulders and small, high armholes (almost 1 in. higher than normal) let the wearer raise or cross her arms without having the jacket lift or bind across the back (drawing below). A narrow, straight side panel creates a slight indentation at the waist and a slim silhouette. The three-piece sleeve, which

conforms to the natural curve of the arm, seems to have a life of its own.

Chanel suits are lightweight, which adds to their comfort, because they're assembled without traditional interfacings, underlinings, facings, and heavy linings. The jacket has only two fabric layers: the shell, or fashion fabric, and a blouse-weight lining. Shell fabrics are often soft, loose, and textured handwovens; many are Scottish wools or Linton tweeds, while others are guipure lace (embroidery on a background that's dissolved), chenille, or sequin embroideries.

Linings of silk gauze, China silk, silk foulard, silk satin or shantung, and wool jersey often contrast with the shell fabric in color, design, or texture. Most linings are luxurious, delicate materials that feel wonderful next to the skin. Few are suited to hard wear. Linings extend to the shell's edge and can be completely hidden, can peek out as a subtle trim, or can be boldly exposed on flipped-back collars and revers.

The linings were machine-quilted to the shell so the loose structure of the outer fabric wouldn't sag and bag and the garment would maintain its shape. The quilting is almost invisible, since the stitching thread often matches the color of one of the shell-fabric elements.

It isn't a bit unusual to find Chanel suits sporting ten or more buttons. Buttons were often custom-made, dyed to match, or painted to accent the fabric design. Some are simple fabric buttons encircled with large or small gold rings; one of my favorites features a small gilded button encircled with fabric.

The hand-worked buttonholes on the original suits were hand-stitched on the shell fabric and finished with a bound but-

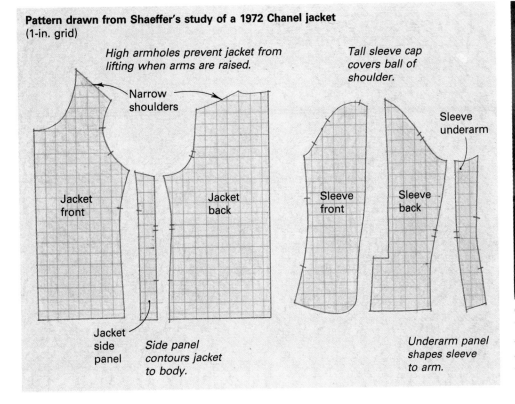

Pattern drawn from Shaeffer's study of a 1972 Chanel jacket
(1-in. grid)

High armholes prevent jacket from lifting when arms are raised.

Narrow shoulders

Jacket front

Jacket back

Tall sleeve cap covers ball of shoulder.

Sleeve front

Sleeve back

Sleeve underarm

Jacket side panel

Side panel contours jacket to body.

Underarm panel shapes sleeve to arm.

Claire Shaeffer wears a princess-line jacket that she made, using Chanel's techniques and slightly modified Vogue pattern #1919. Horizontal rather than vertical quilting works with the princess seams and cross-rib fabric. (Photo by Steve Medd)

tonhole on the lining. This technique actually solves two problems: The loosely woven fabric is too unstable to support bound buttonholes; and hand-worked buttonholes are relatively unattractive on the wrong side, which is accentuated when the silk thread doesn't match the lining.

The "Chaneliest" Chanels are trimmed at jacket edges, pockets, and sleeve vents. A great deal of imagination and ingenuity went into these trims. Some of my favorites include rows of topstitching, plaited yarns on top of grosgrain, selvage or selvage combined with braided bands, and linings extended to look like pipings.

Quilted lining—The parts of the jacket are quilted to the lining before the side, shoulder, or sleeve seams are stitched. The pieces are pinned to the lining, then basted and stitched along the quilting lines. The shell is basted together, fitted, and stitched at the side seams and shoulders; then the lining is hand-stitched together.

The quilting pattern—vertical, horizontal, or rectangular—is determined by the shell fabric and garment design. Examine the shell fabric to decide where the quilt stitching will be placed. The quilting rows should be inconspicuous and parallel to grain lines and stripes. Generally, tweeds

and fabrics without prominent fabric patterns are quilted vertically; however, when designs have princess seams, horizontal quilting rows, perpendicular to the seamline, may be less conspicuous. Quilted rectangles are inconspicuous on plaids (photo inset at left). When you're quilting lace or large prints, hand-quilt around the motifs.

Lining tends to shrink when quilted. Instead of cutting the lining exactly to the shape of the jacket pieces, I cut rectangular pieces with little or no shaping (top drawing, left). On both the shell fabric and the lining, first stitch and press any vertical seams (princess, center-back, etc.) on the front and back sections. Lay the lining section wrong side up on a table. Cover it with the shell fabric, right side up. Pin the layers together, matching the grain lines so the lining will remain smooth without shifting when you baste. Using white cotton basting thread, baste the shell to the lining so the basted lines are parallel to the planned quilt stitching; remove the pins.

With the shell fabric on top, machine-quilt each section with silk floss, machine-embroidery thread, or mercerized cotton. Stop and start about 2 in. from the edges so you can complete side seams, trims, and buttonholes; leave the threads long. Pull the threads into the space between the shell and lining; knot and trim the ends.

Complete the side, shoulder, and sleeve seams of the shell fabric (bottom drawing). Fold and pin the lining fabric out of the way. With the right sides of the shell sections together, baste the seams. Then check the fit—the quilting may have caused the sections to shrink. Stitch, remove the basting, and press the seams open.

To stitch the lining seams, fold one raw edge under so that the folded edge touches the seamline; pin and baste approximately ¼ in. from the folded edge. Repeat for the corresponding edge. Slipstitch the lining edges together.

Chanel buttonhole—The Chanel buttonhole (drawing and photo, facing page) has a fan instead of an eyelet to accommodate the shank of the button and a bar at the other end. The buttonholes are worked before the lining is stitched down at the edges of the jacket.

Pin the lining fabric out of the way. Interface the buttonhole areas in the shell with preshrunk muslin or firmly woven lining fabric; baste the rectangular interfacing to the wrong side with diagonal stitches.

Carefully mark the buttonhole positions with white basting thread. So that the layers won't slip while you're working and the fabric won't fray, stitch around each buttonhole with short stitches, overlapping the stitching on one long edge by three or four stitches. Pull the threads through to the wrong side; then knot and trim them.

Cut the buttonholes with a mat knife or single-edge razor blade. To create a more

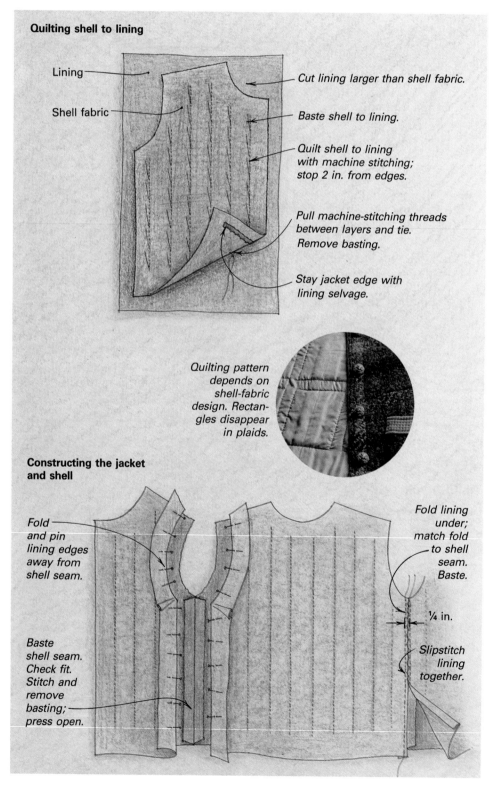

Quilting shell to lining

Lining

Shell fabric

Cut lining larger than shell fabric.

Baste shell to lining.

Quilt shell to lining with machine stitching; stop 2 in. from edges.

Pull machine-stitching threads between layers and tie. Remove basting.

Stay jacket edge with lining selvage.

Quilting pattern depends on shell-fabric design. Rectangles disappear in plaids.

Constructing the jacket and shell

Fold and pin lining edges away from shell seam.

Baste shell seam. Check fit. Stitch and remove basting; press open.

Fold lining under; match fold to shell seam. Baste.

¼ in.

Slipstitch lining together.

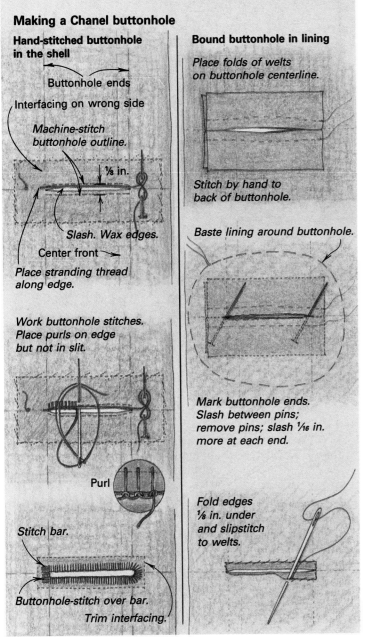

Making a Chanel buttonhole

Hand-stitched buttonhole in the shell

Buttonhole ends

Interfacing on wrong side

Machine-stitch buttonhole outline.

⅛ in.

Slash. Wax edges.

Center front

Place stranding thread along edge.

Work buttonhole stitches. Place purls on edge but not in slit.

Purl

Stitch bar.

Buttonhole-stitch over bar.

Trim interfacing.

Bound buttonhole in lining

Place folds of welts on buttonhole centerline.

Stitch by hand to back of buttonhole.

Baste lining around buttonhole.

Mark buttonhole ends. Slash between pins; remove pins; slash ¹⁄₁₆ in. more at each end.

Fold edges ⅛ in. under and slipstitch to welts.

A hand-stitched buttonhole in this jacket's shell stabilizes the loosely woven fabric, while a bound buttonhole in the lining hides the back.

attractive fan, insert an awl into the end near the garment opening before making the slit. To prevent fraying, cut precisely along the thread of the material, and seal the buttonhole slit with beeswax. To apply the wax, fold the buttonhole slit lengthwise, wrong sides together. Heat the blade of a small paring knife, rub the blade over the wax, and rub the raw edges of the slit with the waxed knife. Repeat as needed.

Tailored buttonholes are worked on the right side of the fabric. To create a purl (knot) with a figure-eight shape and produce an identical knot each time, wrap both threads from the needle's eye under the point of the needle. You can work the buttonholes from right to left or left to right. Loop the thread from the needle under the needle in the same direction.

Work the purls over a strand of silk floss, machine-embroidery thread (size 30), or topstitching thread in a matching color to raise the texture. Wax the strand thread to strengthen it and to reduce knotting and twisting. Press the thread with a warm iron

between sheets of paper so that the wax melts into the plies. Thread a needle and knot one end; if the fabric is heavy, strand the buttonhole with two plies instead of one ply. Place the knot about ½ in. from the end of the buttonhole slit; bring the thread out at the end of the slit. Lay the stranding thread along one edge of the buttonhole; secure the other end by wrapping it around a pin. After you've worked half of the buttonhole, strand the other half.

Using machine-embroidery thread or waxed silk floss and a small needle, make the buttonhole stitches around the slit. Cut the thread long enough to complete the buttonhole without cutting a second piece; generally, a ¾-in. buttonhole can be worked with ¾ yd. of floss.

Pull the thread straight up from the fabric so the knot or purl is on top of the fabric at the edge; it shouldn't be inside the buttonhole slit. If the purl isn't exactly where you want it, use your thumbnails to position it correctly. Place stitches so there is one thread of fabric between each stitch.

When you reach the fan of the slit, release the stranding thread from the pin and hold it in place with your thumbnail around the fan. Work five to nine evenly spaced stitches around the fan over the stranding thread, with one stitch in line with the buttonhole slit. Keep the purls close together so the buttonhole will be strong enough to withstand the wear from the button shank. Count the stitches so you can make all buttonholes the same. Work down the other side of the buttonhole to the end.

Finish the buttonhole with a bar—two or three stitches across the end of the buttonhole. Work several stitches over the bar. Knot the thread and pop it to the underside. When you've completed the buttonhole, cut off the stranding-thread knot; pull the thread to the underside at the end of the buttonhole; and cut the ends close to the material. Trim the interfacing approximately ⅛ in. from the buttonhole.

For each bound buttonhole in the lining, cut two welts 1 in. wide and 1 in. longer

Topstitching, around the collar and down the front of the jacket above, is the simplest trim. (Suit courtesy of the Victoria and Albert Museum.) Grosgrain ribbon hand-stitched to the edge of the jacket below brings out the pattern of plaited yarn.

The selvage from the shell fabric is basted, then machine-stitched to this jacket's edge. Braid or woven tape is hand-stitched to the outside edge of a selvage trim, leaving openings for buttonholes.

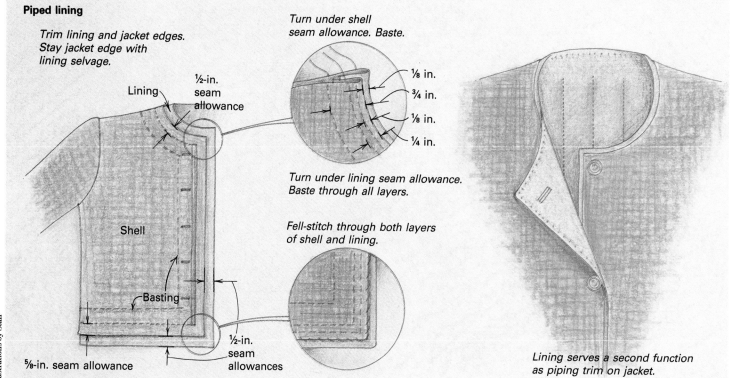

Piped lining

Trim lining and jacket edges. Stay jacket edge with lining selvage.

Lining

½-in. seam allowance

Shell

Basting

⅝-in. seam allowance

½-in. seam allowances

Turn under shell seam allowance. Baste.

⅛ in.
¾ in.
⅛ in.
¼ in.

Turn under lining seam allowance. Baste through all layers.

Fell-stitch through both layers of shell and lining.

Lining serves a second function as piping trim on jacket.

than the buttonhole. Cut the welts on the lengthwise grain unless the lining has horizontal stripes that are to be matched. Fold the welts lengthwise, wrong sides together, and press. Pin the welts to the back of the buttonhole, and secure them permanently with a short running stitch.

You can finish the lining now or wait until you finish the jacket edges. Baste the lining around the buttonhole. Carefully mark the ends of the buttonhole with pins; clip between the pins, and another 1/16 in. at each end. Using a small needle with thread to match the lining, begin in the center of the buttonhole. Turn under a scant 1/8 in. and slipstitch the folded edge to the welts. I prefer to sew around the buttonhole twice instead of making tiny stitches. When you reach the ends, use the needle point to shape the opening into a rectangle. Overcast the corners firmly to make them square.

Trims—Apply trims after the jacket is quilted but before stitching the lining to the jacket edge or making the buttonholes. While some trims are stitched on top of the jacket edge, others are attached to the outside edge, so adjust your pattern accordingly.

The House of Chanel frequently has a fabric manufacturer provide it with matching yarns or fancy, wide selvages and companion trims. Knitters and weavers can create one-of-a-kind bands and yarn trims. Weavers can custom-weave strips or decorative selvages or use matching yarns. The rest of us will have to be content with combining purchased braids, ribbons, and yarns that we've unraveled from the fabric.

I rarely use gilded braids and lace, which look great on after-five jackets, but are too glitzy at lunchtime. Generally, shiny rayon braids are more suitable for dressy jackets, while dull-wool or polyester braids look better on sportier designs; but, when placed on a grosgrain base, even shiny braids can look sporty.

Topstitched trim, one of my favorites, features many rows of topstitching on the overlap, collar and flap edges, and sleeve placket (top-right photo, facing page). Using a regular stitch length (1.75 mm or 15 stitches/in.), edgestitch 1/16 in. from the edge. Stitch 8 to 12 parallel rows, spacing them 1/16 in. apart. Don't worry if your topstitching isn't perfect; the Chanel topstitching isn't either.

Grosgrain and plaited-yarn trims were often used to trim tweed fabric (bottom-right photo, facing page). The grosgrain-ribbon base frames the plaited yarns so that the trim is highlighted against the fabric. Use a steam iron to shape the grosgrain to fit curves. Imported grosgrain, marked by tiny scallops at the edges, is easier to shape than the straight-edge American grosgrain. Beginning at a side seam, sew the grosgrain to the garment by hand with small running stitches placed in the center of

the ribbon. Miter the ribbon with a fold at the corners as needed. Narrow ribbons are easier to shape at curves and corners; you can use two ribbons placed side by side instead of a single wide ribbon.

To make the plaited strips, cut four to eight strands of yarn twice the finished length of the ribbon needed. Knot or sew the strands together at one end; pin the knotted end to your ironing board. Hold the strands taut while you plait. Secure the other end of the plaited strip with machine stitching. Center the plaited strip on the ribbon and sew it in place with hand running stitches.

A *selvage strip combined with a narrow woven band* (left photo, facing page) has in-seam buttonholes. You'll need a fabric selvage about 1 in. wide and a narrow, plain-woven band the same width. (Braided bands tend to ravel and flair at the cut edges.) Add a 1/4-in. seam allowance to the finished selvage width, and cut the strip from the fabric. Cut the seam allowances on the jacket edges 1/4 in. wide. With right sides together, hand-baste the selvage to the jacket, mitering the corners of the selvage when you reach a corner. Stitch, and then press the seams toward the jacket. Mark the buttonhole placement with a temporary marking pen. Butt one edge of the band to the selvage and sew them together by hand. Fasten the thread securely at the ends of each buttonhole. To finish the jacket, fold under the raw edges of the lining so that it covers the trimmed edges of the selvage. Slipstitch the lining in place.

Piping that is actually an extension of the edge-to-edge lining was used to trim many Chanel jackets. If there are buttonholes, finish them before proceeding with this trim.

Use a 1/4-in. selvage strip cut from the lining fabric to stay the edges of the opening and neckline of the shell. Baste it to the wrong side where the finished edge of the jacket will be (drawing, facing page); use a small whipstitch to secure the outer edge permanently. Lightly catchstitch the inside edge of the strip.

Pin the shell and lining fabrics together at the edges. Trim the shell fabric so the seam allowances around the neck and opening are no more than 1/2 in. wide; trim the hem allowance to 5/8 in. Trim the seam allowances on the lining fabric so they extend 1/2 in. beyond those of the shell fabric. (If you don't want piping, trim the lining even with the shell edges.) Baste the layers together about 3/4 in. from the finished edges of the garment.

Fold under the seam allowances of the shell fabric. If necessary, miter the corners and trim away the excess seam allowances so that the edges are finished neatly. Baste 1/4 in. from the folded edge; press. With the garment right side up, fold under the raw edges of the lining fabric so that the lining looks like a narrow piping and the folded

Making a Chanel button: Stitch a gold button in the center of a fabric circle, wrap the fabric around a curtain ring, and stitch the fabric closed.

edge extends 1/8 in. from the folded edge of the shell fabric; baste. Since the lining fabric is lightweight, you can fold the corners neatly without stitching miters. (If you don't want piping, fold the lining even with the edge.) Fell the shell fabric to the lining, making sure you catch both layers so the "piping" won't vary in width.

Chanel buttons—Encircled by a ring of fabric, this novelty button is easy to duplicate (photo above), or you can have special buttons made by Fashion Touches (Box 804, Bridgeport, CT 06601; 203-333-7738).

To make your own buttons, first choose a small (3/8-in. to 1/2-in.) gold-colored button with a shank that will fit comfortably inside a plastic curtain ring. Cut a circle of shell fabric slightly more than twice the diameter of the curtain ring. Using an awl, work a hole into the center of the circle. Insert the button shank into the hole and sew the shell-fabric circle securely to the fabric. Place a row of gathering stitches around the edge of the circle; then place the ring on the wrong side of the circle, and pull the gathering stitches taut so that the button fits snugly inside the ring and the fabric fits smoothly over the ring. If you pull the stitches too tight, the button won't fit inside the ring. Flatten the raw edges on the back of the button by sewing back and forth over them several times. Cover the raw edges with a circle of lining fabric. Sew the button to the garment with a thread shank. □

See Claire Shaeffer's article, "Clothing Connections," on pp. 74-79. Shaeffer teaches clothing-construction techniques at College of the Desert in Palm Desert, CA. Her latest book on specialty fabrics is Claire Shaeffer's Fabric Sewing Guide *(Chilton Book Co., 1989). Garments and details on pp. 10-12 are from the collection of The Edward C. Blum Design Laboratory at the Fashion Institute of Technology in New York City, except where noted.*

The Garment Within the Garment

Why couturiers love underlinings and how they use them

by Elizabeth A. Rhodes

the finest couture clothes are commonly thought to be distinguished by such beautiful inside finishing that "you could wear them inside out!" For many sewers, this legend implies that all fine clothing needs a lining in order for the inside to really be finished. In the realm of couture, this assumed connection between fine workmanship and linings does not exist. Of course, couture garments are beautifully finished inside and out, and many are lined, but a great many are underlined instead. Why, and when, is one method preferred over the other, and what does underlining do for a garment?

In classic couture, more so than in any other type of clothing construction, the ultimate questions behind the design and construction choices are: "How will the garment look when the client wears it?" and "How will the client look in it?" No effort or expense is spared to ensure that the answer to both questions is "fantastic." For a variety of reasons, underlining often creates a garment that hangs better and looks better on the figure than the same garment would if it were lined.

Linings vs. underlinings—Linings differ from underlinings primarily in that linings hang separately inside the fashion shell. Lining is cut from a pattern that's similar to, but not identical to, the main garment, and it's usually assembled separately, then attached to the garment, wrong sides together. Underlining is cut from the main-garment pattern pieces. It is applied to each fashion-fabric piece separately. When the garment is assembled, the two fabrics are treated as one.

The greatest advantage of lining is the finished interior it provides. Because all

For this 1905 bodice, from the Parisian couturier Doucet, underlining was a perfect choice. It offsets the embroidered lace and completely conceals all seam allowances.

seams are enclosed, less stress is put on seam edges, and there's less risk of raveling. Garments like jackets and coats, which are removed in public, are the best candidates for linings because both the interior and exterior are visible during normal wear.

The greatest disadvantage of linings is that the grain seldom can be aligned perfectly or held in alignment with the grain of the fashion fabric. This can interfere with the intended hang of the garment. Another disadvantage of linings is that imprinting of seam bulk to the surface from both the fashion fabric and the lining fabric can easily occur unless additional layers are built in. An underlined fashion fabric has two extra layers of buffer between the seam-allowance edge and the outer fabric—the underlining layers on both the seam allowance and garment. For total protection when pressing, you still need to use strips of paper under the seam allowances, but at least with underlining you can get to them. Underlinings also work well for layers of sheer fabric because the seams and other construction details are concealed behind all the layers.

The more seams in a garment (couture garments tend to have many seams because each seam is another opportunity for refined shaping), the more obvious the imprinting of lining seams becomes when they're offset from garment seams during normal wear. With underlining, this isn't an issue, because the garment seams and the underlining seams are one.

Linings have to be carefully fitted to the garment, and a successful fit can be hard to achieve. Underlinings merely need to be the same size as the garment and are fitted to it piece by piece.

Many couture garments, particularly clingy evening wear, are intended to be worn with just a few undergarments or none at all, so that yet another source of imprinting bulk is removed. Underlining is ideal for providing maximum privacy, while ensuring a smooth flow of fabric.

The inner fabric usually bears the brunt of the stresses on a garment. Both linings and underlinings can provide support and stability for fashion fabric, but underlinings do a better job than linings because the support for the fashion fabric is attached directly to that fabric. When underlinings are used, seams are more stable, grain lines are less likely to shift during wear, and fabric abrasion is reduced.

Underlinings have some limitations, the most obvious of which is that seam allowances and construction details aren't concealed. Underlinings are nearly impossible to remove and replace, while linings can be taken out and redone if the garment shell is in good condition. The counteradvantage is that underlined garments are easier to alter than lined garments. If quality choices are made for underlining fabrics, replacing them usually isn't a problem.

The traditional methods used to underline garments are admittedly painstaking and time-consuming, as you can see from Charles Kleibacker's step-by-step instructions on pp. 18 and 19, but all things considered, for fine garments that are not going to be removed in public, like dresses, skirts, trousers, and blouses, underlining usually is the treatment of choice.

Choosing underlining fabrics—The fabric you choose for underlining must be considered as carefully as the fashion fabric. Think of the finished garment on the figure. Use a dress form or a friend, and drape fashion fabric into the general idea of the garment. What do you need to make that fabric take on the desired look?

Compatibility is the key word. Look for fabrics that are compatible in hand, drape, weight, care, fiber characteristics, and reaction to stress. Compatibility needn't always be exactly the same, but the two fabrics must work together to produce the desired look. This look can't be accomplished by either fabric alone. If it could, there would be no need for two fabrics. Let's

From *Threads* magazine (December 1989) 20:58-63

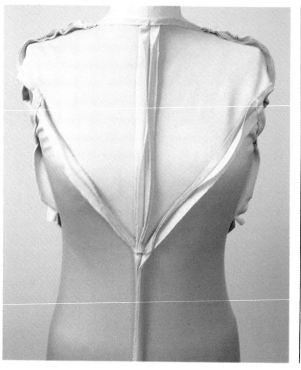

Charles Kleibacker's silk-rep bodice (top left) was not a good candidate for self-underlining because of the weight of the fabric. Inside the top (above), a silk shantung matched the silk-rep outer fabric in drape but was sufficiently light to make a good underlining. With the exception of the band of blue at the waist, all its facings were cut in one with the outer fabric. All of the edges of the bodice were hand-overcast and tacked to the underlining. At bottom left, Kleibacker's Qiana dress from the 1970s is completely underlined in self-fabric to ensure a smooth drape and to minimize imprinting of the seam allowances. An interior view of it (bottom, right) reveals the double seam allowances, which are the only clues that this garment is constructed in two layers.

The silk snakeskin print in this 1986 Galanos outfit was perfect for smocking after being underlined in a sheer, firm silk chiffon. Anything less would have been too flimsy; anything more, too bulky. At right, the seams of the Galanos bodice have been bound with the underlining fabric in a Hong Kong finish, an alternative to hand-overcasting in this case because the binding is very thin.

look at some compatibility problems and examine a few couture garments that exemplify their solution.

Drape, weight, and care—The biggest concern in the selection of underlining fabric is the compatibility of drape with the outer fabric. If the two fabrics don't hang in a similar manner, the underlining technique is doomed from the start. Over time and during wear, the difference in drape will be accentuated. If a lot of garment bias is involved, the problem will be much worse.

For fabrics that aren't too thick or too heavy, the best choice for underlining may be the fashion fabric itself. It's certainly the easiest-to-find compatible fabric. The search for truly compatible underlining fabrics can be time-consuming, so weigh the value of your time against the expense of twice as much fashion fabric.

The gray jersey dress pictured at bottom left on the facing page) is an example of a garment successfully underlined in the fashion fabric. In the early '70s, the Ameri-

can designer Charles Kleibacker was employed by Dupont to develop designs, using their new fabric, Qiana; this dress was one of those designs. Qiana's hand, like that of other jerseys, makes imprinting a serious problem. That issue, and the design statement he wanted, led Kleibacker to underlining. Locating an underlining to match the drape of the jersey was critical. A woven fabric would move completely differently than the Qiana. A knit underlining that stretched in a different way would be equally disastrous. So, the obvious choice for underlining the jersey was the fashion fabric. You can see the double fabric in the interior close-up of the dress at bottom right on the facing page. Because the jersey didn't ravel, a seam finish wasn't necessary. If this were a woven fabric, both pieces of the seam allowance would have been hand-overcast as one. Because the Qiana clings to itself, and the dress clings to the wearer, it wasn't necessary to tack down the allowances against shifting, and they don't imprint through two layers of Qiana.

When fabrics lighter than the fashion fabric are desired for underlining, the tendency is to go too light. Fabrics labeled "lining fabric" may not have enough body. Consider other fashion fabrics for underlining. A silk shantung that is medium weight to lightweight, for instance, may be the best choice for a wool-crepe dress. Don't be afraid to break rules; fabric doesn't have to be called lining to be used as such.

A good example of a nonlining fabric providing the most compatible underlining is shown in the Kleibacker design in the top-left photo on the facing page. The bodice is of silk rep, characterized by defined warp ribs. The fabric weight, as well as its inherent crispness, make it a poor choice for self-underlining. The silk shantung Kleibacker selected is a stable, tightly woven silk with a drape similar to that of rep. Notice in the interior close-up (top-right photo, facing page) that all seams are hand-finished with the layers as one. The self-facings also are underlined and hand-finished at the edges and loosely attached

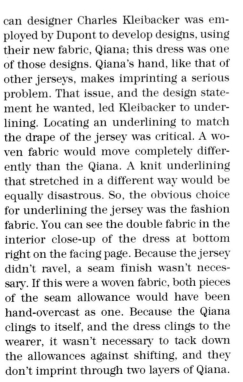

to the bodice underlining. Stitches to secure facings, hems, etc., can be made through the underlining only, so no stitches are visible on the face of the fashion fabric.

Since both fabrics are silk, garment care is easy. A garment made of two fibers that require very different care can make it almost uncleanable. I once owned an expensive ready-to-wear handkerchief-linen skirt that was lined with polyester. Both fabrics were washable, but the ironing temperature needed to remove the wrinkles from the linen melted the polyester.

Stress-resistance and breathability — Certainly the comfort of many a natural-fiber garment has been compromised by unbreathing synthetic linings. A related problem is perspiration. Whatever fabric is closest to the body must be able to absorb and vent perspiration without substantial fiber damage. China silk, for example, which is often used as a lining fabric, is highly susceptible to deterioration from perspiration.

An unfortunate combination I once created myself was a wool suit that I carefully tailored and underlined with cotton batiste. The breathability of the cotton and wool was quite compatible, but the drape was very different, and so was the resistance to stress from wear. The wool, being very resilient, could be worn almost wrinkle-free, and certainly any wrinkles would hang out between wearings. The cotton, however, being next to the body, received heavy stress and, being low in resiliency, wrinkled madly. The wrinkles didn't hang out at all; they imprinted into the wool, so the suit looked unpressed as soon as I put it on. A silk underlining would have worked better.

The underlining fabric needs a substantial thread count and the strength to withstand stress. If the underlining breaks down, then the additional stress is passed immediately to the fashion fabric.

The 1986 Galanos bodice in the photos on p. 17 is a smocked, snakeskin-print silk underlined in a sheer but firm silk chiffon with high dimensional stability due to the thread count of the fabric. This acts as a reinforcement behind the smocked areas of the sleeve and bodice without adding weight or bulk. Smocking has a certain amount of give built into the stitch. By being underlined, the two pieces are smocked as one, and the ease of the stitch is preserved. A very sheer underlining was essential so as not to interfere with the hang of the smocking. Lining would have prohibited the movement of the fashion fabric and interfered with the design.

For the seams and hems Galanos used a Hong Kong finish made of the underlining fabric, which was perfect for the task. This technique, in which a strip of bias fabric is stitched over the raw edges, is quite workable for very ravelly fabrics or for seams that are exposed in wear. When using the Hong Kong finish, the sewer must evaluate the weight it adds in the seam area and its effect on imprinting. Galanos was successful with the Hong Kong finish for this bodice because of the texture of the fashion fabric, which resisted imprinting, and because the underlining was very light.

Color and feel — Color statements also can be accomplished with underlining layers. Paris couturier Doucet was known for his facility with fabric layers, as shown in his 1905 bodice pictured on p. 14. The fashion fabric is a silk lace, brought to life by the blue-gray underlining, which also conceals the seam allowances from admiring viewers.

Layered fabrics can produce colors that are softened and enhanced beyond the abilities of one layer. A white Stavropoulos gown from spring 1984 is mysteriously warmed by alternative layers of pink and white silk chiffon under the white outer layer. The two bottommost layers are sewn together as one layer, while the top three float freely.

Another essential criterion for the underlining fabric is how it will feel against the skin. This must be evaluated in relation to the undergarments that may also be worn. What will touch your skin? How will your skin feel? Is the underlining adequate for both the privacy and the imprint buffer desired? What else do you want it to do?

Finding inspiration — If garment engineers are to successfully create a total, unified look, serious investments in time, energy, and money are usually required. Inexpensive fabrics are tempting to use as underlinings where they don't show. However, they do show — in the drape, wearability, and grace of the garment on the body.

The need to envision a garment and plan its every detail from conception to completion can't be stressed enough. The designer must know the materials available for construction. They must be carefully analyzed in relation to the desired end product, and choices must be made. When compromises occur, they should be intentional, and the engineer should have thought through the consequences. But, alas, the best laid plans.... When a plan ceases to work, stop right then and experiment with solutions.

Look carefully at what others have done, but also think critically about your design. The one rule is that the garment and the anatomy must be mutually enhancing to each other. After that, you, as the designer, set all the rules for your own creation.□

Elizabeth A. Rhodes is head of the Department of Human, Environmental and Consumer Resources at Eastern Michigan University in Ypsilanti. She wrote an overview of Charles Kleibacker's sewing techniques on pp. 24-29. All the garments pictured here are from the Historic Costume and Textile Collection at Ohio State University. Many thanks to Mr. Kleibacker and his staff and students for their help.

Charles Kleibacker's underlining technique

Charles Kleibacker, a widely recognized master of underlined garments, outlined his method for me and offered these procedures for underlining any garment.

For the utmost accuracy, all Kleibacker's marking and cutting are in relation to the seamline instead of the cutting line. Once that is established, he is unconcerned with the exact cutting line so long as it allows room for alterations. All seamlines are thread-traced to the face of the fashion fabric so the garment can be slip-basted together from the outside, ensuring that the desired finished effect is visible throughout this basting process.

The most critical aspect of cutting and using underlinings is preserving perfect grain compatibility with the outer fabric throughout the process. To ensure this, Kleibacker first transfers his pattern, developed by draping, to a length of uncut muslin, making sure each piece is exactly aligned with the muslin's grain and allowing plenty of room for 1- to 2-in. seams around each piece. Then he can trace off the pattern on underlining fabric as often as necessary without reestablishing the grain, especially useful if there are many pieces. All he has to do is align the selvage of the muslin with the selvage of the other fabric.

Overlapping basting

Start with a knotted thread, make about 2 in. of running stitches along seamline; then cut thread. Baste another 6 in., overlapping last few stitches. Cut and repeat.

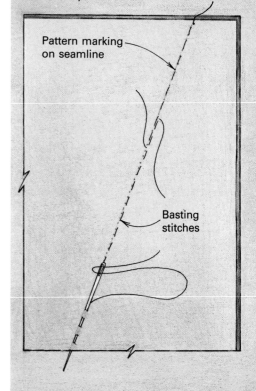

Pattern marking on seamline

Basting stitches

Admittedly, some complex decisions must be made if your muslin, underlining, and fashion fabric are all significantly different in width.

The entire method works best when all the fabrics being used are in reasonable lengths. To determine where to cut, Kleibacker places all his pattern pieces on the fabric to find natural breaking points. He cuts the fabric into 1½- to 2-yd. lengths and works only with these pieces one at a time.

Then, *before* he cuts the underlining, he pins it on top of the fashion fabric so that those selvages are aligned; therefore, the grainlines throughout are in compliance with each other. He thread-traces all his marking lines through to the garment fabric. This serves to hold the two fabric pieces together and also to mark the fashion fabric for basting and stitching. His thread-tracing is in a contrasting color, so it is easily distinguishable for removal. Only then does he cut the fashion fabric and underlining together as one; he treats them as one throughout the remainder of the process.

If bias seams are involved, before doing any cutting, he carefully places the two underlined pieces to be seamed one atop the other and then uses overlapping basting (see drawing, facing page) through all four layers. This technique can be used for identical center-front, center-back, and side seams that can be basted before cutting. With bias seams this approach is critical because it stabilizes the inevitable stretching of the fabric. Until the fabric

is cut, bias-seam areas are no different from any other part of the weave. When it's finally cut and sewn, the overlapping basting allows Kleibacker to stretch the bias seam as hard as he can as it goes under the needle, removing any possible further stretch.

When the garment is basted together and before it's permanently stitched, he puts the garment on the figure. If it hangs improperly anywhere, he releases the basting in the problem areas and manipulates the seams and layers to achieve the desired drape; then he rebastes for final stitching. Here are the steps in his procedure:

1. Select the pattern pieces you plan to underline, usually all the major pieces.
2. Divide the fabric into 1½- to 2-yd. lengths for ease of handling. Cut all fabric on the cross grain, marking each piece so you won't ever reverse the nap. You can use the edge of the table to establish the cross grain. Don't try to straighten the grain; you'll probably do more harm than good.
3. Thoroughly steam-press each length, ideally with a professional steam iron.
4. Cover the table with large face-up sheets of dressmaker's carbon paper.
5. Put two lengths of pressed underlining fabric together, wrong sides facing, on top of the carbon paper with their selvages aligned to each other and the table edge.
6. Align your pattern muslin on top of all layers, matching selvages (left drawing, below).
7. Pin all three selvages together, at 2-in. intervals, taking a tiny bite with the pin at right angles to the edge, for the least distortion of the fabric.

8. With a toothed, but not pointed, tracing wheel, trace all the stitching lines.
9. Unpin and remove the pattern. Then turn the layers of underlining over onto the carbon paper, realigning their selvages. Retrace over the carbon lines you just made to mark the second layer.
10. Align, with wrong sides together, one piece of marked underlining on top of a piece of fashion fabric, match selvages, and pin.
11. Using a contrasting color of thread, thread-trace all the stitching lines marked on the underlining through the underlining and fashion fabric for all pattern pieces (right drawing, below).
12. For those seams that can be basted without being cut (usually only center-front, center-back, or sides seams), arrange together matched pairs of pattern pieces, with fashion fabrics right sides together.
13. Hand-baste these seams. Baste bias seams with overlapping basting.
14. Cut out all the pattern pieces through all four layers, allowing large seam allowances, as much as 2 in., so there'll be plenty of room for alterations.
15. Slip-baste all seams and parts of seams that you couldn't baste flat before cutting.
16. Try on the basted garment, checking the fit and hang of the garment and all layers. If there are any bubbles or bumps, release the basting and smooth the fabric until the layers hang as one.
17. Throughout the rest of the construction, treat both underlining and fashion fabric as one. All hand-stitching for hems and facings goes through the underlining only. Hand-overcast through both layers as one to finish edges. −E.A.R.

Layout for marking underlining layers

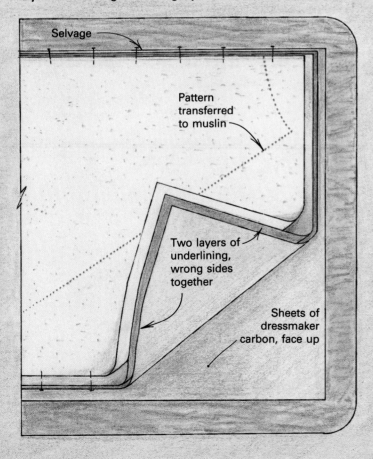

Selvage

Pattern transferred to muslin

Two layers of underlining, wrong sides together

Sheets of dressmaker carbon, face up

Thread tracing through underlining and fashion fabric

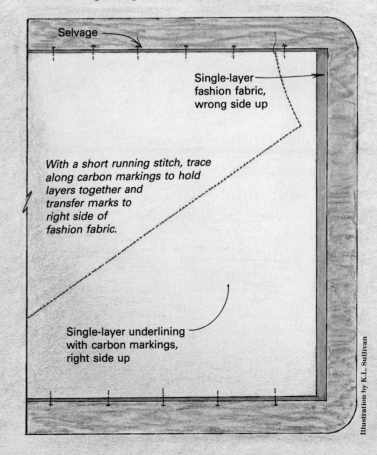

Selvage

Single-layer fashion fabric, wrong side up

With a short running stitch, trace along carbon markings to hold layers together and transfer marks to right side of fashion fabric.

Single-layer underlining with carbon markings, right side up

Illustration by K.L. Sullivan

Making Sense of Interfacing

Clothes stretch in different ways—so do interfacings. How to match the inside to the outside.

by Margaret Deck Komives

*a*n interfacing is a layer of fabric between the facing and outer layer of a garment. Its purpose is to add any needed firmness, strength, or stability, while adding as little bulk as possible.

Interfacings are used on collars, necklines, hems, facings, cuffs, pockets, button or buttonhole areas, waistbands, or on any other area the sewer chooses to reinforce. Any fabric can serve as an interfacing if it helps achieve the desired results, but in most cases it pays to take advantage of the lower cost and special properties of products designed specifically to be interfacings. These are either fusible (attached by steam and pressing) or sewn in place. They're available in four basic fabric structures.

Woven interfacings feel good to the touch, drape well, are strong and resilient, and stretch most in the bias direction. Readily available brands are Acro, Veriform, Shapewell, and Armo Press, and there are fusible and sew-in versions of some of these.

Nonwoven interfacings are fiber webs, similar to paper or felt. If the fibers are laid parallel to each other, the fabric is stable along that grain; in the other direction, it is less stable and will stretch (second photo, facing page). Examples of this structure are fusibles like Easy-Shaper, Stretch-Ease, and Pellon Sheer Blenders, and sew-in Pellon for sheers. If the fibers are strewn helter-skelter, the result is an all-bias interfacing (third photo), which can be cut and stretched in any direction. Examples of this are all-bias sew-in Pellon and fusibles, Pel-Aire and Sof-Shape.

Knit interfacings (fourth photo), most of which are fusible, are softer and more flexible than wovens or nonwovens and can stretch in all directions—mostly in the crosswise direction. Every fusible knit purchased should be tested on a swatch of garment fabric, as lots vary. Even within the same brand some will add more firmness than others. Easy-Knit is the best known, and my students and I have often used it on loosely woven, extremely ravelly fabrics by fusing it to an entire piece of fabric before cutting. This results in a bonded, but still flexible, fabric.

Weft-insertion interfacings (fifth photo) are relatively new and could be described as woven knits, as they consist of crosswise (weft) yarns held together by lengthwise lines of warp knitting. This structure combines the softness of knitting with the stability of weaving: lengthwise stability, some crosswise give, and bias stretch. They are more supple than wovens when fused, yet give a surprising feeling of substance to the fabric to which they are applied. Armo Weft and Suit-Shape are the best-known brands. Whisper Weft is lighter in weight than either of these but gives a firmer hand because of the closeness of its fibers.

Basic rules—When you're using interfacings, there are a few rules you should follow:

Preshrink all interfacings. (I'm from Missouri.) To find out which interfacings to preshrink, one of our instructors conducted a controlled experiment with large samples and made up a table listing the results. Almost all shrank. She then repeated the tests, and the next group shrank differently. Some that hadn't shrunk the first time did so the second time. Don't take any chances—preshrink all interfacings.

Fusibles can be placed folded in hot water, left to soak about half an hour, and then drained on a towel and laid out on nylon carpeting to dry. Handle gently so the fusing agent isn't dislodged, taking care not to wrinkle them too much. Fusibles can be further shrunk if an iron is held about an inch above the interfacing and the entire piece is steamed. You can preshrink sew-ins by hand- or machine-washing them on the delicate cycle. If you plan to have the garment dry-cleaned, you just have to steam-press them, but I give mine the same treatment as fusibles.

It is important to remember that both cotton fabrics and interfacings can continue to shrink by small amounts even after several washings. To avoid "bubbling" (the result of different shrinkage rates between fabric and fusible after fusing), don't use fusibles on 100% cotton fabrics, and use caution with 100% cotton fusibles, like Shape-Flex, Shapewell, Fusible P-91, and Kuffner, avoiding them entirely with smooth, closely woven fabrics, which will reveal the slightest change.

The interfacing shouldn't alter the characteristics of the fashion fabric. Smooth

fabrics must remain smooth. Except for detail areas (buttonholes, pockets, etc.), stretchy fabrics should retain their stretch. Soft fabrics should not become crisp.

The interfacing shouldn't interfere with the fabric's care requirements. If the fabric is permanent-press, the interfacing should be too, but we also use permanent-press interfacings in 100% cotton or linen fabrics.

Interface the outer layer of fabric—an upper collar, outer cuff, etc.—for a smoother result and to prevent the seam allowance from shadowing through. Fuse to the whole piece; the interfacing should end at a seam or fold line, not short of it, to prevent shadowing where the interfacing ends. It is almost always apparent when a fusible stops in the middle of a garment section, if only because the two parts move differently.

Seam allowances in nonwovens can be trimmed more closely than in wovens. If a woven is trimmed to much less than ⅛ in., it is likely to pull loose unless it is handled carefully and then topstitched.

Always test a fusible on a swatch before fusing it to a garment section. The fusing process itself generally adds firmness beyond the weight of the interfacing.

Keep a record of your finished garments. I use 3 x 5 cards, on which I place a swatch of fabric and indicate the interfacing used, the fiber content, care instructions if needed, and comments. If the interfacing proves the test of time, or fails it, I won't have to take the garment apart to see which interfacing I used. A set of test swatches of basic fabrics fused to a variety of appropriate interfacing is also helpful to have on hand. See drawing on p. 23.

If the fashion fabric is sufficiently firm and the design doesn't require additional support, don't interface. Small pieces of interfacing can be placed behind button and buttonhole areas; any excess can be trimmed away after these are complete.

How to apply interfacings—A fusible requires heat, moisture, and very firm pressure applied with an iron with a metal soleplate. After carefully positioning the interfacing on the fashion fabric, wrong sides together, we use a double layer of white wrapping tissue as a press cloth. We then spray a good mist of water over the paper and press with the iron on a wool setting. It is important not to slide the iron and to hold it in each position for 15 full seconds.

When the interfacing is entirely fused, with the tissue still in place, smooth the area by gently sliding the iron over it. Then press again from the fabric side. We mark "UP" on the tissue so it won't get reversed later and transfer any resin that has seeped through to the iron, though it's easily removed with denatured alcohol. Allow the fabric to dry and cool thoroughly before removing it from the ironing board.

Knit interfacings present fusing problems, but they are worth dealing with for the sake of the soft, flexible effects they provide. If you want to try bonding to a ravelly fabric, do so before cutting, piecing the narrow interfacing carefully as necessary. One of our students fused knit interfacing to two jacket fronts after cutting and found they varied in length by an inch when finished. Because of this irregular shrinkage and because the flexibility of knits can make them difficult to handle, we avoid fusing to any large areas after cutting. You can deal with small cutout pieces by aligning the fabric and interfacing underneath the actual pattern, correcting the grain and shape before you fuse. Dry-press through the pattern to hold in place, and then remove the pattern and fuse permanently.

Sew-in interfacings are applied to the garment by some form of basting until permanent stitching fastens them securely. Speed-basting notions like glue stick or basting tape can be used if desired. We'd rather hand-baste than machine-baste. The time you save machine-basting you later spend removing the stitches, and while you're hand-basting, you can shape the fabric by letting it and the interfacing fold over your hand or knee as you baste the layers together. Actually, by fusing over a ham or a seam roll, you can also shape while fusing. You can establish lapel rolls by fusing flat up to the roll line, folding the lapel and interfacing over at the roll line, and fusing in the new position.

Making the choice—Sew-in interfacings do take more time to apply, but they may hold up better than fusibles after many washings and wearings. On the other hand, on topstitched garment details like pocket flaps, fusibles will usually give better results because fabric distortion and puckering are eliminated. Some fabrics, such as velvets, velveteens, and corduroys, can be beautifully fused if pressed on a needle board. We have had good results with weft insertions on the these fabrics.

Whether or not you're fusing, here are several considerations that are applicable to every choice:

First of all, the stretch capability of the interfacing should be matched with the need for stretch in the garment. I refer to it as the need for flex. The front band of a blouse or shirt needs no flex, because it lies flat against the body. A cuff needs one-way flex around the arm, as does a collar stand around the neck. A collar or French cuff, which will bend around and over as well, will require a two-way flex, as you can see in the drawing at top left, page 22. These requirements correspond neatly with the kinds of stretch found in interfacings. In other words, no flex requires the stable

Six interfacing structures are shown at right, two times actual size. Lengthwise grain is top to bottom. Arrows indicate direction of greatest flexibility. The structure of the material determines how each type of interfacing will stretch.

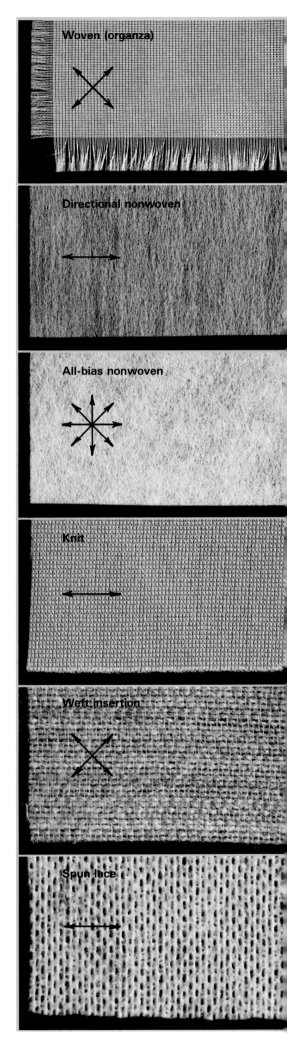

Woven (organza)

Directional nonwoven

All-bias nonwoven

Knit

Weft insertion

Spun lace

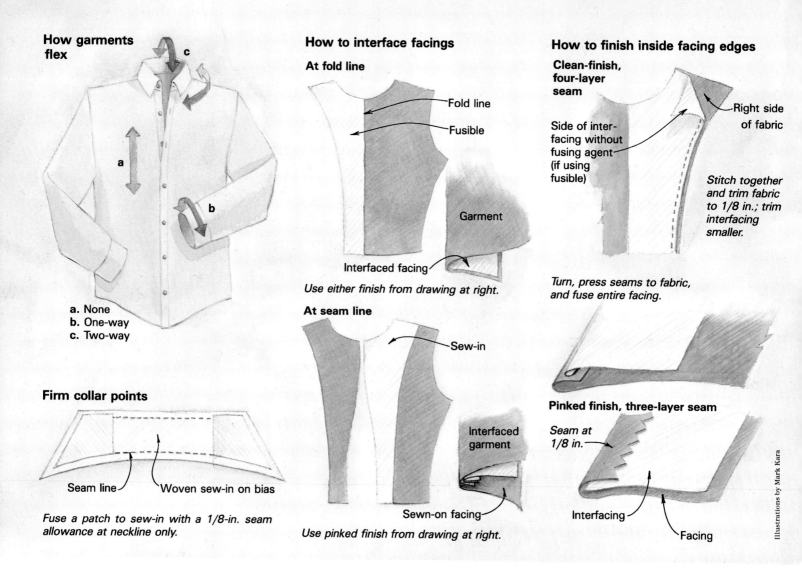

How garments flex

a. None
b. One-way
c. Two-way

Firm collar points

Seam line — Woven sew-in on bias

Fuse a patch to sew-in with a 1/8-in. seam allowance at neckline only.

How to interface facings

At fold line

Fold line
Fusible
Garment
Interfaced facing

Use either finish from drawing at right.

At seam line

Sew-in
Interfaced garment
Sewn-on facing

Use pinked finish from drawing at right.

How to finish inside facing edges

Clean-finish, four-layer seam

Side of interfacing without fusing agent (if using fusible)
Right side of fabric

Stitch together and trim fabric to 1/8 in.; trim interfacing smaller.

Turn, press seams to fabric, and fuse entire facing.

Pinked finish, three-layer seam

Seam at 1/8 in.
Interfacing
Facing

Illustrations by Mark Kara

grain of the interfacing; one-way flex needs a little stretch, such as in the cross grain of a woven or a knit; and two-way flex should always be cut in the direction of the greatest stretch so it will flex smoothly. For wovens and weft insertions, this is on the bias. Fusible interfacings that allow a generous two-way flex are Sof-Shape and Pel-Aire—both all-bias—and Easy-Knit. A medium weight all-bias Pellon will also work well. If more firmness is desired, as in a shirt collar, a woven sew-in like Veriform or Sta-Shape, cut on the bias, could be the answer. For even more stiffness Shirt-Fuse or Shirtailor can be applied just to the collar points of the sew-in interfacing, as shown in the above drawing at bottom left. This will provide the stiffness desired in the points without the danger of bubbling and leave the rest of the collar flexible.

Second, consider the "see-through" problem. Some fabrics, because of either their construction or color, will alter in appearance when interfaced. There are a few colored fusibles, called Sheer Blenders, that work well but are not all-bias. Polyester organza is more flexible and is available in a wider array of colors. It is permanent-press and can be cut on the bias for collars. We use it for voile, chiffon, and georgette. If organza seems too heavy, there's chiffon. For more body, polyester or nylon organdy

can be used. Our experience has been that nylon fabrics wrinkle more than polyester fabrics of the same type; check before you buy. For batiste, we've used the lightweight Armo Press. A double layer of net or tulle can also be used if their structure does not show through. This has worked well on button-down collars for my husband, particularly in summer-weight fabrics. For silks, silk organza gives beautiful results. Finally, don't ignore the possibilities of the fabric itself as an interfacing if there is no pattern to shadow through. Extending a seam allowance can serve nicely to interface an area, especially if it's not very large, like a front band or a narrow cuff.

Third, the weight and drape of the interfacing should be compatible with the fabric. You can determine this by draping the fabric over a variety of interfacings, remembering that fusing will add firmness.

Last, consider the appearance of the fabric surface. A very smooth-surfaced fabric makes the choice of an interfacing more difficult because it is not forgiving. Run a test; then examine the results in a variety of lights. A crinkled fabric will probably be better interfaced with a sew-in so the surface will not be flattened, but a soft fabric, like crepe de chine, can also have its surface distorted by a sew-in interfacing that's too firm.

Seam allowances—The more bulk we can eliminate in the construction of a garment, the smoother the results will be. The entire seam allowance of an interfacing can be eliminated if the seam is to be topstitched or if the interfacing is fusible and is placed just up to the stitching lines. However, often in handling, the carefully cut interfacing will fall slightly off the intended line.

In my classes, I suggest to students that they leave the seam allowance on fusible interfacing and pull it away after fusing and stitching, except in the case of corners, which can be cut off at an angle. This may sound like heresy, but it's safe and usually works, especially if the interfacing is pulled away before it is trimmed. We've found that this technique works fairly well with weft insertions and fusible knits, depending on the fabric fused to, and we have no problems at all with fusible nonwovens. Trim seam allowances to ¼ in. for the layer just under the outer part of the garment, ⅛ in. for the next layer, and trim just less than ⅛ in. for woven sew-ins. Trim fusibles and nonwovens to the stitching. If you choose to remove the interfacing seam allowance before you do the fusing, lay the semitransparent interfacing over the pattern before cutting, and trace the desired cutting line from the pattern with a soft-lead pencil.

Construction details—Most garments have facings. Their construction usually determines how they should be interfaced. If the interfacing is to lie up against a fold of fabric, as in an attached facing, there will be no seam allowance to conceal—no shadowing to prevent. In this case, a fusible applied to the facing will give very satisfactory results and is the easiest to use (see drawing at top center, facing page).

If you prefer a sew-in, apply it to either the facing or the garment proper, basting to the fold line. When the garment is finished, the buttons and buttonholes can be depended on to hold it in place. Tiny, permanent hand stitches are often recommended, but these invariably show on fine fabrics.

If there is a separate facing, a sew-in applied to the garment proper would be a wiser choice, as fusing to the facing wouldn't cover the seam bulk, and, in most cases, fusing to the garment would require the whole front to be interfaced. Lying between the outer layer of fabric and the seam allowances, a sew-in will prevent any shadowing and give a smooth surface (see drawing at bottom center, facing page).

For a lapel, where both garment and facing should be without shadowing, the solution often is to interface both with a layer of lightweight, probably sew-in, interfacing. A textured or print fabric probably wouldn't show as much seam shadowing as a smooth, solid color, so an all-bias fusible might work well on the lapel side. See right-hand drawings on the facing page for ways to finish the inside edge of the facing.

To back an entire one-piece cuff, we use a sheer-weight sew-in, and since the interfacing folds right along with the cuff, it stays in place nicely. With a two piece cuff, we baste a sew-in, or, if we can safely do so, apply a fusible to the outer layer.

There are many interfacings that have not been mentioned here, and new ones are always appearing. Test them for stretch, see-through, and compatibility with your fabric, and compare them with the more familiar ones. That's how we discovered Shape-Up. Among the newest products, it's a nonwoven structure referred to as spunlace, fusible, very supple and surprisingly smooth after application to the fabric (see bottom photo, page 21). Tailor's Touch is another spun-lace product.

Quality is important. Compared with the total fabric cost, the cost of interfacing will be minimal, even if it's silk organza. A poorly interfaced area can severely detract from an otherwise beautiful garment. Keep experimenting, file those experiments, save test swatches, be flexible, and the compliments will keep coming in.

Margaret Deck Komives taught sewing techniques in the St. Louis public schools before moving to the North Campus of the Milwaukee Area Technical College. She and her sewing students don't believe anything until they've tested it.

When fusing fails

by David Page Coffin

Fusing interfacings is an industrial technique that home sewers have borrowed. The problems started right there. Factories can set their precise, consistent fusing machines for exactly the right temperature, pressure, moisture, and time, while home sewers can be sure only about how long they try to fuse. A 90-lb. sewer who is using a new steam iron will inevitably get different results than a 180-lb. sewer who is using an old, inaccurate dry iron and a wet press cloth. If the heat's too low, the time needs to increase, vice versa, and so on.

The solution? The same one industry relies on: careful testing. Make a swatch, as shown in the drawing below. What to look for when testing? A fusible should be hard to pull off. If it's not, your technique is at fault. Insufficient pressure is the most common problem. Try lowering your ironing board so you can really lean on it, but don't put more pressure on the heel than on the toe of the iron. Home economists who work for interfacing companies favor heavy-duty steam irons like the VaporSimac and the Hi-Steam, and they think press cloths are likely to be too wet or too dry, but an evenly damp cloth is better than erratic steaming. Surprisingly, some find that the small presses, like the Elnapress, provide inadequate pressure, though the large area is a plus. If resin comes through the front, either the heat's too high or the interfacing's too heavy. Bubbling? Preshrink, as described on page 20. All instructions say "preshrunk" because manufacturers are afraid you'll mishandle their products. The last resort, and a good place to start, is to write or call the interfacing manufacturers for information. Here are their addresses, along with those of two mail-order sources:

Crown Textile Company
Armo Division
1412 Bdwy.
New York, NY 10018
(212) 391-5880

Pellon Company Limited Partnership
Consumer Products Department
119 W. 40th St.
New York, NY 10018
(212) 391-6300

Stacy Industries Inc.
Consumer Products Division
Box 395
Wood-Ridge, NJ 07075
(201) 779-1121

Staple Sewing Aids
141 Lanza Ave.
Garfield, NJ 07026
1-800-631-3820

Newark Dressmaker Supply
Box 2448
Lehigh Valley, PA 18001
(215) 837-7500
Good mail-order source. Call or write for free catalog.

G Street Fabrics
11854 Rockville Pike
Rockville, MD 20852
(301) 231-8998
Send $1 and a large, self-addressed envelope for their interfacing list.

How to make a test swatch

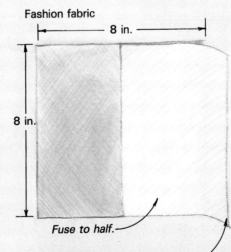

Fashion fabric

8 in.

8 in.

Fuse to half.

Leave a few inches of unfused interfacing hanging free for easy identification in the future.

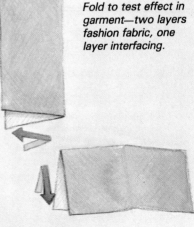

Fold to test effect in garment—two layers fashion fabric, one layer interfacing.

Fold in opposite direction and bend to test flexibility. If you get sharp folds instead of a smooth bend, try a lighter interfacing; also bend on bias.

Techniques of Haute Couture

Designer Charles Kleibacker teaches fundamentals, from fabric to finish

by Elizabeth A. Rhodes

*h*aute couture, which means "high sewing," is exactly what designer Charles Kleibacker teaches. When we began working together five years ago, he stressed, "A beautiful garment is forever. The design idea and its careful, dedicated construction go hand in hand to bring a fine garment to reality. Design is engineering...fitting on human anatomy...to bring a garment to the comfortable perfection of couture. The designer-engineer researches fabric; he or she understands the value of a good iron; and, early on, realizes that a designer's work is ninety-nine percent sweat and one percent glamour."

The following sampling of Kleibacker's couture techniques are not for everyday dresses. They're for the special occasions when you really want high sewing.

Fabric

Fit is the real secret of couture, and fabric is the starting point for achieving it. That's why Kleibacker advises, "Explore your fabric!" Always start with the best quality. His preference is for natural-fiber fabrics that can be molded.

Consider the fiber quality and the yarn and fabric construction. The length, diameter, and regularity of fibers vary with the weather, the animal's diet, or the soil in which the plant grows. Consult a good textile book for details on the qualities to look for in various fibers (see "Resources," page 29). Yarn is a group of fibers twisted together. The greater the twist, the stronger, duller in luster, and more costly the yarn. To determine the amount of twist, count the revolutions in an inch. Evaluate the yarn construction with the purpose of the garment in mind. Often drapability may be sacrificed for strength or durability.

Fabric is a combination of yarns interlaced at right angles (wovens), interlooped (knits), or intermeshed (nonwovens). Check the woven fabric's construction for flaws—is the grain straight and the thread count consistent?—and consider the amount of fiber and yarn packed into an inch of fabric. Again, decide what will work best for the intended design. Kleibacker recommends using a "gutsy" fabric—one with sufficient fiber to make a statement.

Explore the fabric's personality. Pull on it and check its stability in horizontal, vertical, and diagonal directions. The vertical grain is made up of yarns that are placed on the loom as warp. Warp yarns must be exceptionally strong to survive the weaving process. Because they are held under tension during weaving, they're often rigid in the finished fabric. In general, warp yarns are used vertically on the body so areas that flex, such as elbows and knees, have stronger yarns in the flexing direction. Filling, or weft, yarns, which cross the warp in weaving (and make up the cross grain of the fabric), do not have to be strong, as less tension is placed on them in processing. They are often more relaxed in the finished fabric, and perhaps more drapable.

Examine the yarns and fibers in the vertical and cross grains and evaluate each. Don't be a slave to rules such as always cutting garments on the vertical grain. Check the drape, or hang, of the fabric on all grains. Where does the fabric look fullest and richest? Stitch the fabric on the cross grain, vertical grain, and bias. Look at the stitching and analyze the results. Many times Kleibacker finds fabric at its drapable and stitchable best on the cross grain, so he does bias cuts, placing the crosswise grain in the vertical direction. A further advantage to the cross grain, he points out, is that it is often more economical.

Underlining

Once you have chosen a fashion fabric, you must decide whether it can stand alone or whether it must be combined with another fabric beneath it, either for visual reasons or structural support. If the fabric needs an extra layer, Kleibacker recommends the use of an underlining rather than a lining. The underlining (cut the same size and shape as the fabric, placed back-to-back with it, and sewn as one with it) has many advantages. Dressmaker's carbon markings can be made on the underlining rather than on the face fabric; the underlining reduces imprinting from pressing; and hand stitches can be taken in the underlining only so that they won't show on the face. An underlining provides the wearer with greater privacy, especially in a case where undergarments would spoil the outer appearance. Underlining also tends to improve the drapability of a garment.

Kleibacker recommends using fashion fabric for underlining whenever possible (in other words, double fashion fabric). Decide if two thicknesses of the fabric will hang well; some fabrics are too heavy for this treatment. However, even fabrics with as much weight and body as silk linen (a medium-weight pure silk in a linenlike weave) can be treated this way with great success. For heavier wovens, silk shantung often works well. Kleibacker points out that whatever the underlining, it must be compatible with the fashion fabric: The more these two layers can act as one fabric, the better the hang of the finished garment.

To prepare all fabrics for the needle, Kleibacker suggests a heavy steam pressing on the wrong side of the fabric with an industrial iron like the Sussman, which is heavy and provides regular blasts of steam. After you've steamed and pressed all fabrics, let them dry well before proceeding.

Pattern layout

A pattern of your own design or one you use repeatedly, Kleibacker advises, should be drawn and stored on muslin without seam allowances. Experiment with the pattern pieces and fabric to determine the most economical layout. Measure the amount of fabric needed for one pattern piece, and cut two lengths, one each for the left and right sides. Place them right sides together, with the nap running in the same direction. All fabric has some nap; for compatibility of color and drape, identify the "top" of the fabric with a thread tack each time you cut the lengths for a pattern piece. If you're using an underlining, cut two lengths of that as well, and with corresponding

Charles Kleibacker

Kleibacker, who was literally brought up in women's ready-to-wear at his family's department store in Cullman, AL, began his career as a reporter for the *Birmingham News*. Next he wrote copy for Bernice Fitz-Gibbon at Gimbels, NY, where he extolled automobile tires and garden accessories. When a fashion copywriting job opened, Fitz-Gibbon chose him. "He was horrified. We talked him into it," Fitz-Gibbon recalled. (As a designer, Kleibacker is "right up there next to Norman Norell, maybe alongside Norell," wrote Fitz-Gibbon in her book, *Macy's, Gimbels and Me*.)

While at Gimbels, Kleibacker did graduate work in retailing at NYU. Three years later he took a job writing advertising and promotion copy for DePinna, a Fifth Avenue specialty store.

After many visits to the house of Dior in Paris (where singer Hildegarde, his next promotion-writing charge, was a client), Kleibacker realized that women's fashion had always been his first love. Returning to New York, he and two partners opened a women's custom and limited-edition ready-to-wear business. He eventually sold designs through Hattie Carnegie, Bergdorf Goodman, Bonwit Teller, and Neiman-Marcus to celebrities such as the late Gertrude Lawrence and Lady Iris Mountbatten.

In 1953 he closed up and went to Paris to work as a designer for Antonio Castillo in the house of Lanvin. He found this a great experience. He admires Paris designers. Alix Grés, who does "beautiful, lyrical, lilting, soft body clothes," is one of his favorites. But he says, "I feel what keeps me in business is what I have to offer as an entity...not something taken from here, there, and everywhere and not a garment watered down for production purposes." Kleibacker has also worked in Italy. He did two small collections on his own in Rome before returning to this country in 1957.

After three years of designing for Seventh Avenue's Nettie Rosenstein, he opened his own business in 1960. His designs are usually on-the-bias soft body shapes in silk. The clothes are painstakingly made, individually cut, and supervised by Kleibacker in his studio in the Hotel Park Royal on New York's West 73rd St. They sell for $950 to $2,500. Kleibacker believes in simplicity, fit, and comfort. His designs may be dramatic, but they are never flamboyant in silhouette or color.

In recent years, Kleibacker has entered the entertainment field—as lecturer/showman. With his collection of vintage clothing from the 1870s on, he narrates two fascinating programs: "Trends: Then and Now," a lighthearted fashion-history lesson, and "Designs Worn by Famous People." He also serves as designer-in-residence for the Department of Textiles and Clothing, College of Home Economics, Ohio State University, Columbus, OH.   —E. R.

This luxurious skirt gathers 12 yd. of silk crepe de chine on a hip-clinging band. It's paired with a bias silk-crepe top, whose bias sash wraps the waist three times. From design to execution, it's Kleibacker's brand of haute couture. Photo courtesy of Kleibacker.

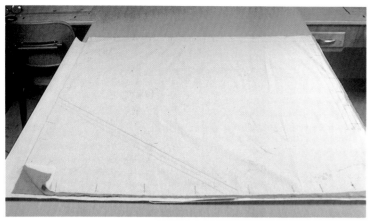

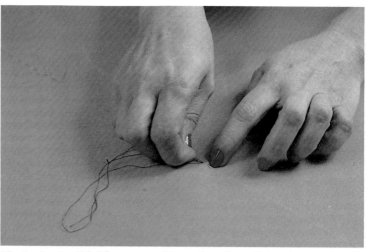

Two pieces of face-to-face fashion fabric, positioned with the same nap, are laid over large sheets of dressmaker carbon. The muslin pattern is on top, and the three layers are pinned at the selvages, ready for Rhodes to wheel the pattern markings onto the fashion fabric.

Rhodes bastes this bias seam with overlapping stitches before she cuts the fabric so she can stretch it to the maximum as she machine-stitches.

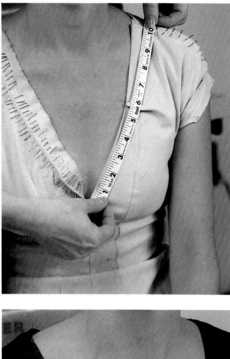

A deep V neckline often sags and gaps when a woman sits or stoops. To prevent this, Rhodes eases the excess fabric against a bias tape by pinning the bodice front closely to the tape (muslin, top). With natural fibers, up to ⅞ in. may be eased out. After easing and pressing, the neckline of the finished garment adheres to the body. White slip basting is in place for the first fitting (bottom).

lengths of outer fabric and interlining back-to-back, align the grain. The two layers will be treated as one.

With the two lengths of fabric right sides together, pin the selvages together with the pins perpendicular to the selvage and taking up only the smallest amount of fabric. Place large sheets of dressmaker carbon (26 in. by 39 in. is best) underneath the fashion fabric, and position the muslin pattern on top, aligning the grain. Use a tracing wheel (one with teeth but not spikes, please!) to transfer all pattern markings for stitching lines to the bottom piece of fashion fabric (or to the underlining if you use one). For accuracy, push forward—if you are holding the wheel with your right hand, use the index and middle fingers of your left hand to secure the fabric in front of the wheel. Carefully remove the muslin pattern, and turn the fabric over onto more sheets of dressmaker carbon. Wheel along the carbon lines you just made to transfer the markings to the other piece of fashion fabric. Transfer all markings to the face of each fabric layer by thread-marking—baste along the carbon markings with a contrasting color thread. (If you use an underlining, align its grain with that of the face fabric before you baste through both layers.) You're now ready to cut the fabric, using about 2-in.-wide seam allowances for fitting purposes. Some seams may be stitched before cutting, as I'll explain.

Seams

Seams may be placed on the straight of grain, on garment bias (an angle other than straight or 45°), or on true bias (45°). The closer the angle of the seam is to true bias, the more the fabric will stretch and "drip."

When possible, hand-baste bias seams together before you cut out the garment. Use overlapping basting stitches, which will stretch with the fabric as you machine-stitch. Begin with a knot in the thread and baste about 6 in. Then cut the thread and, without knotting the end, baste another 6 in., overlapping the last few stitches of the preceding basting. Repeat, starting anew

about every 6 in. Then, when machine-stitching a bias seam below the bust, stretch the seam fully and stitch as far as possible before stopping the machine. This will remove all the stretch in the seam and prevent it from shifting with every wearing.

If possible, also baste the straight-grain seams before you cut them. Since there will be little stretch in them, you needn't use overlapping basting. Simply stretch the seams as you machine-stitch. The stretch will be nominal, but the seams are usually smoother if some tension is used.

A seam that can't be basted *before* the garment is cut should be slip-basted before it is permanently stitched. Slip basting is worked from the right side of the garment so that you can see the finished product. Then you turn the garment inside out and machine-stitch on top of the basting—the ultimate in accuracy! Fold one seam in on the stitching line and match it to the stitching line of the other side. Pin in place. Then slip a hand needle, threaded in a contrasting color, into the fold of fabric exactly on the stitching line. Slide the needle about ¼ in. to ½ in. and pick up fabric on the matching stitching line of the corresponding piece. The contrasting thread can be picked out easily once the permanent stitches are in place. The technique is demonstrated in the drawing on page 28.

Holding in a seam—To mold flat fabric to the curved body, you must hold in some seam areas to fit the body. This technique is useful for fitting a plunging neckline.

Here's what you do. Ask the person wearing the dress to sit. Pin a fold into the neckline to take up any gap. In general, for a nice finished look, ⅞ in. is about the maximum that can be taken up. If the fold is bigger, a fitting dart or seam starting at the neckline may be needed. The fullness must be eased onto a piece of fabric tape. Cut the tape a bit longer than the desired length of the neckline edge, and mark it in five places: at the beginning and end of the desired length, in the middle, and halfway between these marks. Remove the pin that takes up the excess fabric, and divide and mark the neckline edge in the same way. Match the tape markings to the neckline markings and use five pins to attach the tape to the wrong side of the fabric, centered on the seam line. Divide each section in half and pin at these points. Continue to further divide each area in half as the fabric rolls over your finger—pinning as you progress until all the excess fabric has been eased in. At this point, pins will be about as close together as they can be. Baste the tape along its center, with the tape facing up, and remove the pins. Hand-stitch down the middle of the tape, just to the inside of the basting line, with the fabric facing up. Use a short needle and single-ply size A silk thread to make tiny running stitches (the thread is three ply, so separate it as you would embroidery floss). Remove the basting; the fabric will look gathered.

Press the stitches on the wrong side of the fabric. Then place the garment right side up over a curved surface, such as a tailor's ham. Use a damp cotton press cloth and apply pressure with the point of the iron to shrink out the fullness. As you work, move the iron out to the edge to smooth in the fullness. Keep the garment over the ham until the garment is dry. When pressing is finished, the fabric should be smooth. Fullness is held in at the neck and eased out in the bust area, giving a beautiful fit in all positions.

Seam finishes—Once they have been permanently stitched, seams should be trimmed to ⅝ in., or up to 1 in. in areas where further fitting may be needed. Seam edges on woven fabrics must be finished to prevent raveling. Kleibacker recommends hand overcasting, which is secure and creates a smooth edge without adding bulk.

Hand-overcast seams (photo, below left) are stitched with cotton sewing thread and a No. 8 or No. 10 needle. Insert the needle in the fabric parallel to the seam edge and about 1/16 in. away. If the needle is in your right hand, move from right to left, and control the fabric by rolling it over your left index finger. Stitches, made about ⅛ in. apart, appear slanted on the surface. Make them deeper and closer on more ravelly fabric. In very ravelly fabric it may be necessary to "cross your hand," overcasting in both directions to form an X stitch.

Where seams cross—When a seam crosses another seam, take care to avoid a tight, bulky point. Stitch the seam until you approach the crossing seam. Lift its seam allowance and stitch to the seam line. Stop machine-stitching, leaving a 6-in.-long thread. Pull the bobbin thread through to the top side and tie a tailor's knot, as shown in the drawing below. Don't be tempted to cheat and tie a square knot; it will not be nearly as secure. Begin stitching again on the other side of the seam allowance. Begin and end all seams with tailor's knots instead of backstitching, which is frequently inaccurate and always causes a heavy area.

Tailor's knot

To make a tailor's knot where seams cross, wrap top and bobbin threads around forefinger and pull ends through to make a knot. Slip knot smoothly down thread. With the help of a needle, snap the knot in place right on top of fabric.

Facings and hems

Whenever possible, advises Kleibacker, use self-facings, generally about 1-in.-wide extensions of seam allowances at the garment's edge. They're comfortable, and they lie neatly. Near strong curves, facings can gap in a V-neck garment; sometimes making a clip, or cut, in the seam allowance will allow for fit. At the point of the V, a bar tack will secure seams.

Facings may need to be stayed on the underside at the garment edge. Just inside the roll of the facing and centered on the seam line, sew a piece of fabric tape, making tiny stitches with a fine, short needle and single-ply size A silk thread. The work should be nearly invisible. Finish the facing's raw edge with hand overcasting, and secure the facing to the garment loosely, and only at seam intersections.

Bias bands—A garment edge may be finished with a decorative bias band rather than a facing. Bias bands vary in width, but not in method of application. They're cut on true bias, the diagonal line that bisects the right-angle intersections of warp and filling threads. The easiest way to establish true bias for cutting and sewing purposes is to measure down the selvage a given amount, then across a filling thread the same amount, and to connect the two points with a straight edge.

To determine the width to cut the bias strip, decide how wide the finished band should be. Neckline bands can't be as wide as hemline bands. (Kleibacker achieves interesting designs with bias bands varying from 6 in. to 15 in. at hems.) Cut bias strips four times the desired width of the finished band plus twice the seam allowance.

If you don't have enough fabric for the entire length, don't panic. Bias strips can

To hand-overcast fabric edges (above), Rhodes works from right to left, using cotton thread and rolling the seam edge over her left forefinger. This results in slightly slanted parallel stitches that bind the raw edge without adding bulk, as seen in the finished garment at right.

The bias band

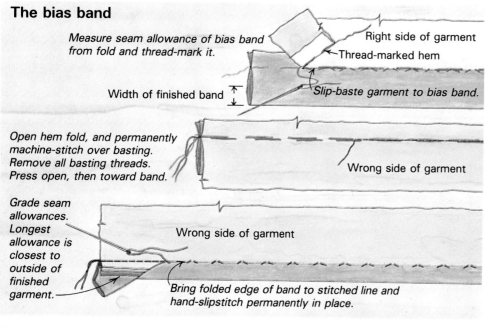

Measure seam allowance of bias band from fold and thread-mark it.

Right side of garment

Thread-marked hem

Width of finished band

Slip-baste garment to bias band.

Open hem fold, and permanently machine-stitch over basting. Remove all basting threads. Press open, then toward band.

Wrong side of garment

Grade seam allowances. Longest allowance is closest to outside of finished garment.

Wrong side of garment

Bring folded edge of band to stitched line and hand-slipstitch permanently in place.

Illustrations by Barbara Snyder

Before sewing a tailor's hem, Rhodes hand-overcasts the cut edge of the hem, bastes it, and folds back about ¼ in. of fabric. The hem itself is stitched with a light hand, size A silk thread, and a No. 10 needle. Rhodes alternates from folded edge to face fabric, catching only one thread of the face fabric (demonstrated on muslin, left). The overcast edge is visible on the inside, but not on the outside, and bulk is avoided (right).

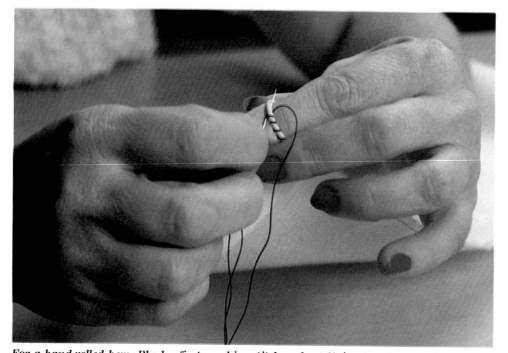

For a hand-rolled hem, Rhodes first machine-stitches about ¼ in. from the fabric edge and trims close to the stitching. She moistens her fingers and rolls the fabric over the machine stitching. Then she whipstitches over the roll, as shown. The stitches of the finished hem slant parallel to each other. The sizes of the roll and the stitches are exaggerated here for clarity. Aim for a tiny roll, and make stitches with a No. 10 needle and one strand of size A silk thread.

be joined together with little difficulty. Cut the ends of the pieces to be joined on straight grain and stitch (the cut ends will look diagonal, as will the seam).

The garment is applied to the bias, not vice versa. Neither side needs stretching or shrinking. To illustrate, let's assume you want a 3-in.-deep bias band rather than a traditional hem at the bottom of your skirt. The skirt is completely finished, except for the hem, which has been thread-marked.

Cut a (3 in. x 4) + (⅝ in. x 2) = 13¼-in.-wide bias band as long as the circumference of the skirt plus the seam allowances to join the ends. Fold the bias band in half lengthwise, and 6 in. from the fold thread-mark the seam allowance through both layers. Check the consistency of the seam allowance and adjust.

Fold the skirt hem under on the thread-marked line, and bring the folded edge of the skirt over the cut edge of the bias band, matching thread-marked lines. Slip-baste the two together and check width for consistency. Open the seam allowance on the wrong side of the garment and permanently machine-stitch directly on top of the basting. Remove all the basting, and press the seam allowances open. Then press all layers down toward the hem. Grade the seam allowance so that the layer nearest the outside of the garment is longest, as shown in the drawing at left.

Fold the bias band in half toward the wrong side of the garment, matching the folded edge to the machine-stitching line. Permanently hand-slipstitch the band to the stitched line. (The same technique works for a ¼-in. band at the neckline.)

Hems—Before a hem can be stitched, the garment's finished length must be determined. Kleibacker advises measuring from the floor so that the center back is ½ in. longer and the side areas are about ¼ in. longer than center front. This is the look he feels is flattering to most women.

Thread-mark the fold line for the hem. Measure from the fold line and cut the hem's width. The straighter the skirt, the deeper the hem can be. The hem of a straight skirt can be 2½ in. wide, whereas a bias skirt that is very full may be best with a ½-in. hem.

Hand-overcast in matching cotton thread to finish the hem's raw edge. The hem itself is done in size A silk thread. Baste the hem up on the fold line. Then fold the top of the hem back on itself about ½ in. or less and sew a tailor's hem, which crosses back and forth from the garment to the hem. When the stitch is made in the garment, only *one* thread of the fabric is picked up—or if the fabric is lined, only the underlining is caught. When the stitch is made in the hem, several threads are caught. The secret is to keep the stitches as loose as possible, but tight enough to hold the hem in place. If the hem has bias folds because of flare, loosely stitch them and al-

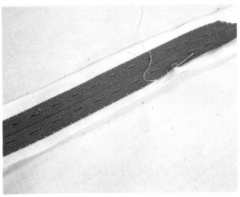

Rhodes hand-bastes the zipper in place (above) so the teeth are slightly more than covered and the basting fans out sufficiently to cover the tab. Then she zips the zipper to check that a tiny overlap occurs in the center of the slot.

Rhodes permanently stitches the zipper (red) with tiny running stitches equidistant from the folded edge, using one strand of size A silk thread and a No. 10 needle. The stitches fan out at the top to cover the zipper tab (top right).

After stitching the front of the zipper, Rhodes slipstitches (white) the edge of the zipper tape to the seam allowance (near right).

When the zipper is complete, the base of the zipper needs a bar tack for security. Rhodes whips several stitches and works a buttonhole stitch over them (far right).

low them to fall in place. Don't try to nail them down or control them in any way—the inside of the hem may look prettier, but the garment's outer appearance and hang won't be nearly as satisfactory. Press the hem lightly, using a press cloth, leaving a roll at the bottom edge.

Hand-rolled hems can finish any edge on lightweight fabrics. To achieve a good rolled hem, keep the roll tiny and the stitches fine. To ensure the evenness and stability of the garment edge, machine-stitch about ¼ in. from the fabric's cut edge with a normal stitch length and cotton thread. Next, trim the fabric as close as possible to the machine stitching, but trim only as much of the hem as you can expect to complete in one sitting. Roll the fabric on the edge, moistening your fingers to help get the roll started. Whipstitch the roll in place with a fine, short needle and single-ply size A silk thread. The needle enters the roll parallel to the edge, and the stitch comes forward. The stitches should have a slight, but consistent, slant. Don't pull the stitches too tight, unless you want a scalloped edge. If you hold the needle in your right hand, you can hold the roll, which is ready to be stitched, over the index finger of your left hand (see bottom photo, facing page).

The zipper

Kleibacker's choice is a centered slot zipper. Aesthetically, this is the most balanced and least bulky application possible on the side or center of a garment.

Leave the zipper area of the garment unstitched, and press back the seam allowances. Place the open zipper in the garment opening. With the face of the fabric up, position the folded edge of the opening so that it just barely covers the teeth of the open zipper. Baste the zipper in place, as shown in the top photo at left. When the zipper is zipped, the folds overlap a shy ¹⁄₁₆ in. When the garment is worn, the zipper slot lies flat, with enough fabric to conceal the teeth.

At the top of the zipper, let the basting fan, or angle, out so the zipper pull is covered by the lap of the zipper slot. Permanently stitch the zipper by hand, using a fine, short needle and matching size A silk thread. Sew tiny running stitches, not backstitches, about ⅛ in. from the folded edge. (They also fan out slightly at the top of the zipper, just enough so that the folds cover the zipper tab.) The backstitch, often taught for hand-applied zippers, creates "nails" that secure the fabric to the zipper and hold them together when the body moves. Kleibacker feels that the garment needs to move with the body, and the running stitch allows that flexibility in the zipper area.

After you've stitched the zipper on both sides, work a bar tack at the bottom of the zipper by whipping a small area across the zipper's end and then working a buttonhole stitch over the whipped stitch. On the inside of the garment, trim the zipper bottom into a V-shape before slipstitching the edge of the zipper to the seam allowance. □

Resources

These textile references are available through interlibrary loans.

American Fabrics. *A.F. Encyclopedia of Textiles,* 2nd ed. Englewood Cliffs, NJ: Prentice Hall, 1973.

American Home Economics Association. *Textile Handbook,* 4th ed. Washington, D.C.: AHEA, 1970.

Hollen, M., and J. Saddler. *Textiles,* 5th ed. New York: Macmillan, 1979.

Linton, George E., ed. *The Modern Textile and Apparel Dictionary,* 4th ed., 1975. Distributed by State Mutual Book and Periodical Service, New York.

Tortora, Phyllis G. *Understanding Textiles,* 2nd ed. New York: Macmillan, 1982.

Wingate, Isabel B., ed. *Fairchild's Dictionary of Textiles,* 6th ed. New York: Fairchild Publications, 1979.

Wingate, Isabel B., and June F. Mohler. *Textile Fabrics and Their Selection.* Englewood Cliffs, NJ: Prentice Hall, 1984.

Here's a mail-order and walk-in source for the Sussman iron, large sheets of dressmaker carbon, cotton and silk threads, and other sewing supplies: *Greenberg and Hammer,* 24 W. 57th St., New York, NY 10019; (212) 246-2836.

For information on workshops by Charles Kleibacker, contact Dr. Elizabeth A. Rhodes, head of Human, Environmental, and Consumer Resources, Eastern Michigan University, Ypsilanti, MI 48197; (313) 487-1217. Photos pages 54-57 by Roger McLeod.

Class All the Way

Norman Norell's garments, entirely ready-made, rivaled the best of couture

by Mary C. Elliott

imagine the perfect suit–the perfect coat. It has everything you associate with impeccable craftsmanship and quality: welt pockets lie on the garment as if woven into the fabric, bound buttonholes march in uniform precision up the cuff, the fabric is sumptuous, the proportions are perfect, the fit is supreme.

For over 40 years Norman Norell made this fantasy a reality for many women by producing the finest clothing the American fashion industry could offer. Norell's quest for excellence ended in 1972 with his death, but his work still serves as an inspiration for creators of fashion who seek to refine their craft.

In the fall of 1988, I helped curate a retrospective show of Norell's garments at Mount Mary College in Milwaukee, WI, and was able to see firsthand, and in detail, just what Norell's achievement was.

Picking couture apart–Norell grew up in a family of haberdashers and theater lovers and studied costume design at Pratt Institute in New York City. His first job was with Paramount Pictures, designing for silent-screen stars, but it wasn't until he joined Hattie Carnegie in 1928 (then the most famous design house in America) that he really began learning the craft of garment-making. Miss Carnegie, the first American designer to have a ready-to-wear label, bought Paris originals in volume to translate for the U.S. market. Norell's job was to literally take apart the clothes and copy them for mass production. It was through this experience that he learned the techniques of French couture and developed his exquisite taste for the best fabrics and fit.

In 1940, Norell joined forces with Anthony Traina to form the Traina/Norell design house. Their sophisticated sequin-encrusted designs were an immediate success, despite wartime rationing. In fact, Norell's extensive use of sequins can be linked to the rationing laws; sequins were exempt! Norell

From 1940 to 1972 Norman Norell, shown here with actress Lauren Bacall, dressed America's most prominent women in superbly made clothing. (UPI/Bettmann News photo)

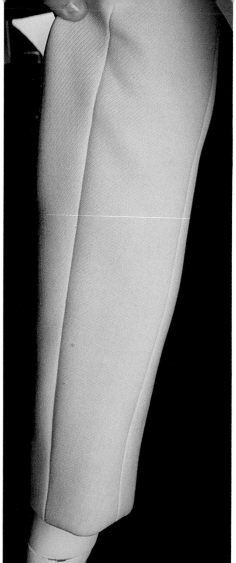

The cream wool suit at left from Norell's 1970 collection is a showcase of Norell signatures: The narrow, slightly gathered skirt and cropped jacket, with raised and sloped waistline, and the deft balance of prominent accessories. Norell devised a unique two-piece sleeve (above) with a narrow, slightly bias underarm strip to eliminate the need for an elbow dart on such a slender sleeve.

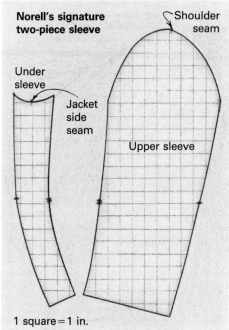

Norell's signature two-piece sleeve

Shoulder seam

Under sleeve

Jacket side seam

Upper sleeve

1 square = 1 in.

opened his own salon in 1960 with an established reputation for quality and for the next 12 years delighted his loyal clientele with refinements on his trademark clean silhouette, from sultry evening gowns to impeccably tailored suits and coats.

Daywear fabrics—Norell achieved his signature look with a combination of fabric, proportion, fit, and technique, but his first step was always selecting the fabric—a task he never delegated to others. He said, "I close my eyes, squash a piece of coating around in my hand, feel its heft, solidness. Good fabric has good weight. It has a reason."

Norell suits and coats have such substance and shape that they appear to have a form within them, even on a hanger. To achieve this, one would think that Norell needed an abundance of interfacing, underlining, and padding, but he used only a lightweight linen wigan for the shoulder yoke, front, lower lapel, and hemline, which added stability rather than shape. He used hair canvas only for the upper collar, where the pad stitching was surprisingly widely spaced. It was the wool fabric—spongey double cloth, melton, gabardine, and heavy cavalry twill—molded to shape with a flat iron wrapped in damp linen towels, which gave Norell coats and suits their distinctive resilience. Long-time client and friend Betty Furness says of her Norells, "The ones I have kept are remarkable, still as fresh as when I bought them. Class will tell—and Mr. Norell was class all the way."

Norell's day dresses were most often worked in wool jersey. Fluid, yet with a definite character, the fabric conformed to his premise that a woman's body movement should be seen under the dress, but any hint of tightness was unacceptable. Once again Norell achieved his shaping with the lightest interfacings—linen or silk organza—for which he sometimes paid up to $20/yd. To achieve the proper weight for an elegant drape in these jersey dresses, he didn't hesitate to use 10-in. interfaced hems. When asked about the extravagance, Norell replied, "It's terrible, but it's the way I am, and it's too late for me to change."

Proportion and fit—Norman Norell's eye for proportion was legendary. Years spent ripping apart and mimicking couture designs at Hattie Carnegie had so fine-tuned his sense of scale that even his suit (left photo, page 31) with 12 working buttons and bound buttonholes, a bow and a 5-in. belt does not overwhelm.

This suit, from 1970, is a superb example of one of Norell's favorite silhouettes: the short, cropped jacket over either a narrow or bouffant skirt. The cropped jacket is set solidly on the figure, neither so tight as to appear pinched nor so loose as to be boxy. The sleeve, as on all Norell suits and coats, has a narrow, slightly bias piece (see pattern and photo above it, page 31) set

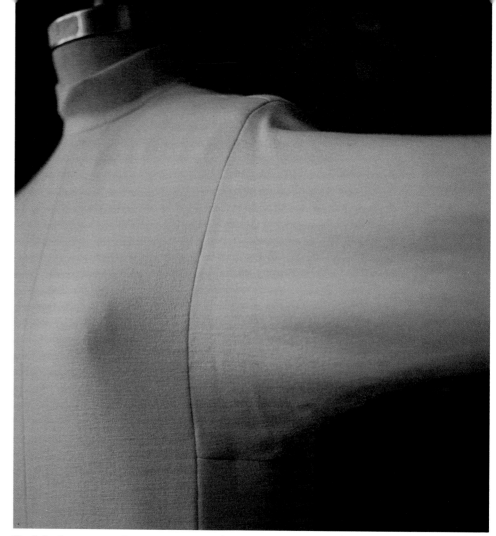

Bust darts were anathema to Norell; this dolman-sleeve design incorporates dart shaping into the armhole seams by easing the front between the shoulder and the side panel.

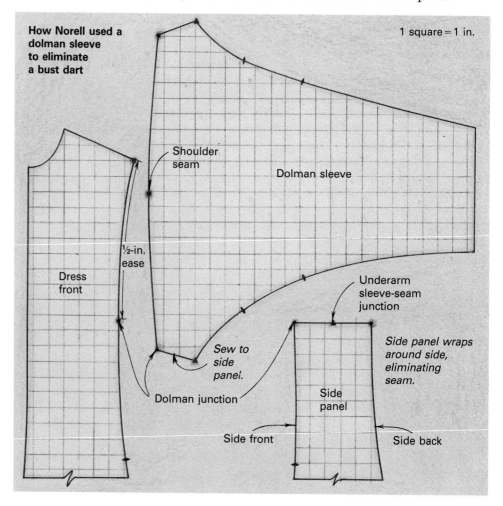

How Norell used a dolman sleeve to eliminate a bust dart

1 square = 1 in.

Shoulder seam

Dolman sleeve

½-in. ease

Dress front

Sew to side panel.

Dolman junction

Underarm sleeve-seam junction

Side panel wraps around side, eliminating seam.

Side panel

Side front

Side back

The handworked buttonholes on the cuffs cross over checks, so Norell insisted on changing threads in the middle.

From 1968, a cream wool-twill bolero jacket (left) over a sleeveless black wool dress, scene of the amazing double zipper shown below. (Illustration by David Page Coffin)

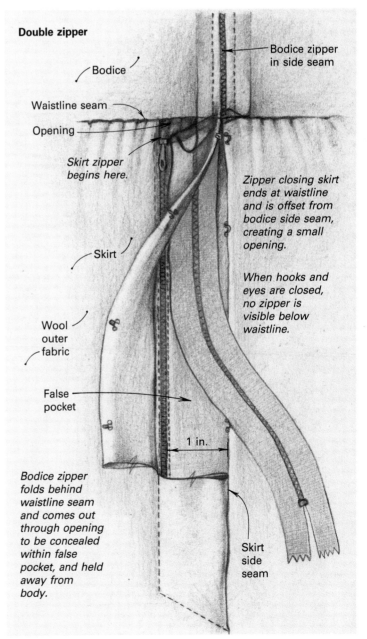

Double zipper

Bodice

Bodice zipper in side seam

Waistline seam

Opening

Skirt zipper begins here.

Zipper closing skirt ends at waistline and is offset from bodice side seam, creating a small opening.

When hooks and eyes are closed, no zipper is visible below waistline.

Skirt

Wool outer fabric

False pocket

1 in.

Bodice zipper folds behind waistline seam and comes out through opening to be concealed within false pocket, and held away from body.

Skirt side seam

directly under the arm, to eliminate the need for an elbow dart and to keep the sleeve slender. It isn't the traditional two-piece suit sleeve; it's neither as wide nor set back so far on the arm. The jacket length is a bit longer in back to enhance a woman's spinal curve—another Norell trademark.

The skirt, though pencil thin, still has fullness over the hip and stomach. This is not a design statement; it's Norell's acknowledgment of the shape of a woman's body, and it's part of most of his skirt designs, including all those shown here. Norell loathed tight, ill-fitting clothing that was uncomfortable. He said, "If you plan to accommodate the human body, you can't miss."

One never finds bust darts in Norell dresses. He called them "home-madey looking, graceless things...an easy way out." Instead, he created shaping with square-set dolman sleeves, underarm side panels, pin tucking, or with the natural elasticity of the wool jersey. An example of Norell's square-set sleeves is shown in the photo on page 32, along with a drawing of how the armhole seams incorporate dart shaping. Virtually no Norell garments make use of true bias grain, so their superb fit without darts or intricate seaming is even more impressive.

Perfect details—For we seamstresses, Norell's wizardry is most apparent in the technical expertise with which his designs were made. The first glance is chicanery; they look so simple, but as the eye is drawn to the details, the implications of that simplicity are revealed. The tomato-red wool cavalry-twill suit in the top photo at right is a prime example. The parabolic cut of the jacket is effortless; it flows to a perfectly dipped center back without distortion of any kind. Following the curve draws your eye to those pockets (bottom photo at right): curved, single-welt, working pockets set in on the bias. The tiny rib on the twill is matched. There is no distortion of shape, no puckering, no room for error. It is perfect. And one layer of this fabric is more than $\frac{1}{16}$ in. thick!

The black wool raised-waist dress with bolero jacket (left photo, page 33) is another example. Here is Norell's astonishing double-zipper system in action. At first glance the side-seam bodice zipper looks well-made but perfectly ordinary, ending at the waistline with scarcely a ripple. A closer look (drawing, page 33) reveals two zippers. The first zipper, a 7-in. one, is set into the lining and into a false pocket extension on the skirt, 1 in. or so in front of the side seam. The second zipper is 16 in. long and closes the bodice along the seam, but it hangs freely beyond the bodice/skirt junction, allowing it to open as wide as the shorter, lower one. The skirt is then fastened with hooks and eyes, concealing both the first zipper and the unattached portion of the longer zipper. The results? No visible zipper to interrupt the design of the skirt,

the appearance of matching side-seam pockets (there's a working pocket on the other side), and a snug-fitting bodice.

Zipper ingenuity continues on suit skirts where, rather than using one 7-in. or 8-in. center-back zipper as a closure, Norell used two 4-in. hip-dart zippers. As a result, no zipper is visible beyond the hemline of the suit jacket when it's worn.

Every Norell button and buttonhole (invariably bound on suits and coats) works—even those on sleeves. When handworked buttonholes were used, the results could be even more amazing. The suit blouse of black-and-wine-colored checked silk in the top photo on the facing page has cuff buttonholes that horizontally cross both colors. Not content with selecting one color, Norell worked it in two colors on each buttonhole—wine silk buttonhole twist on the wine portion of the check and black on the black portion.

Almost everything by Norell is lined with magnificently supple China silk gently slip-stitched in by hand. Many woven fabrics have Hong Kong finishes at the hem, unless, like the wool jersey dresses, the fabric was so thin that this finish might leave a visible line on the outside.

Such attention to detail is expected in the custom-made segment of the industry, but one must remember that Norell clothes were *not* made to order. These were ready-made garments sold through quality department stores like Bergdorf Goodman, Henri Bendel, and Nan Duskin. The fact that, right off the rack, they fit so many women is the ultimate tribute to Norell's understanding of fit and proportion and his respect for a woman's body structure.

Norell's legacy—Fortunately, Norell's loyal clientele did not part company with their treasured suits, coats, and dresses in a hasty manner. Many women are still wearing coveted pieces or are savvy enough to donate them to costume collections, where the Norell tradition can be appreciated by a new generation. The collection of Norells at Mount Mary College now includes more than 30 pieces, dating from the late 1940s through 1972. Student designers study the clothes and absorb details in workmanship, fabric, and fit with which they have little familiarity. As the students develop and refine their skills, their appreciation of Norman Norell invariably grows deeper. Always a generous man who shared his ideas (he once published his culotte pattern in *Woman's Wear Daily,* free for the taking so that ill-fitting examples wouldn't be produced) he would, I'm sure, take great satisfaction in knowing that his designs are being used to teach and inspire the next generation of designers. ☐

Mary C. Elliott is an instructor and the Curator of Historic Textiles at Mount Mary College in Milwaukee, WI.

Above, in heavy cavalry twill, a suit with no straight lines, from the 1967 collection. At first glance, the single-welt pocket below seems ordinary; a closer look reveals the subtle curve, the careful grain matching, and the thickness of the fabric, which makes the perfect finish a minor miracle.

Patch Pockets: Plain, Fancy, and False

A tailor's guide to bagging them on

by Stanley Hostek

*t*he U.S. government once forbade tailors to make patch pockets. A World War II edict, intended to conserve fabric, banned patch pockets, along with vests for double-breasted suits, vents on coats, pleats and cuffs on pants; and it put limits on coat lengths and pant-leg sizes. Custom tailors didn't think much of this law, because they bought fabric by the suit length (usually 3½ yd.), so even if there was enough fabric for patches, they couldn't use it, and it became scrap. But manufacturers were able to save thousands of yards of precious wool.

Patch pockets resumed their popularity immediately after the restrictions were lifted (vests took a little longer). But despite the extra fabric and sewing time that they require, patch pockets are more decorative than practical: Any content of consequence is immediately obvious from the outside and spoils the effect. A partial solution to this dilemma is to add tucks and pleats, with a binding, or "cord," at the opening to hold them all in place, as in the photo at left. This provides a little flexibility so the pocket can expand, but a complete solution requires more elaborate measures. I've devised a pocket in which the patch conceals an opening through the coat, from which a set-in pocket hangs. I call it a false patch pocket (see description, p. 39).

With careful marking and a reasonably sure hand at the machine, you can attach all types of patch pockets (tailors call it "bagging on") entirely by machine, from the inside of the pocket, so no machine stitches are visible from the coat front, and all stripes and plaids match. Once you're comfortable with it, you'll find the machine method much faster and stronger than handsewing.

The methods I describe in "Bagging on a patch" (p. 37), while based on men's custom-tailored coats and overcoats, are applicable to any garment, man's or women's, made of lightweight to heavyweight woollike material. They also apply to virtually any type of patch pocket, except one with square corners, as machine-bagging requires a curve to negotiate a change in direction.

Using tailor's chalk—To bag on successfully, you need clearly marked lines so you can accurately position the pocket while you're sewing it, as I'm doing at left. Most tailors use three types of marking chalk: lead, wax, and clay, available from tailor's supply houses like Banasch's (2810 Highland Ave., Cincinnati, OH 45212; 800-543-0355). Lead

Following carefully marked outlines, Stanley Hostek attaches a prepared patch pocket to the front of a woman's coat entirely by machine. The completed breast pocket gives no hint of the manipulations Hostek requires to align marks on the pocket and coat as he machines around the pocket's ¼-in. seam allowance from inside the patch.

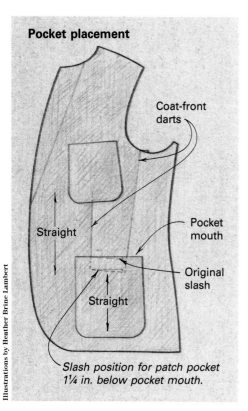

Pocket placement

Coat-front darts

Straight

Pocket mouth

Original slash

Straight

Slash position for patch pocket 1¼ in. below pocket mouth.

Illustrations by Heather Brine Lambert

(sold as Dixon's Crayons) sharpens easily and holds an edge well. It's used for drafting patterns and sometimes for marking critical and precise, but hard-to-remove, outlines that won't show on the finished garment. It isn't used in making patch pockets.

Wax chalk can make a sharp, fine line, but it dulls quickly, and the marks will not easily brush off. Heat from an iron will melt the marks; and on thick, soft fabrics, like tweeds, the marks will disappear. On thin, hard fabrics, like gabardine and tropicals, a grease mark will remain. This can be easily removed by dry cleaning, but a garment shouldn't require dry cleaning before it's worn. Wax chalk is appropriate for cutting and interior lines, but these lines may melt through to the front of thin fabrics. You should test your materials before using any chalk.

Clay chalk can't be sharpened to as fine an edge as wax (like wax, you sharpen it by scraping it with a pen-knife blade—lead chalk is sharpened on sand paper), but it doesn't dull as quickly. Clay lines tend to blur and rub off. I use clay chalk for the front-surface marking when I'm making patch pockets, and I brush off the lines with a whisk broom held tight near the working end of the bristles so they remain stiff.

Tailors slide chalks forward and backward along their edges with sure, definite strokes, never rubbing back and forth to strengthen a line. After you make your first mark, you can make another one on top of it if necessary, or you can use a ruler to perfect and reinforce a line marked with short dashes. When you're marking next to a soft edge of fabric or paper, as you'll need to do when you trace the patch shape onto the garment front, place your fingertips on the edge and run the chalk along your nails. Mark curves with short, straight lines, moving both fingertips and chalk to the next spot as you move around the curve.

Handling fabric at the machine—After marking, your main challenge when bagging on pockets by machine is to exactly match marked lines while the machine foot is pushing the fabric toward you, and the feed dogs are pulling the bottom layers away. You can't baste or pin the seams, because they curve in opposite directions. So, as you shift the seams together under the presser foot, push the pocket edge slightly with your left hand while you pull the coat slightly with your right hand. The curves are the toughest parts, of course, and if the marks fail to line up, you have no choice but to rip back and try again. But even with a few false starts, I find this method faster and more accurate than methods that require the pocket to be first formed with an iron and then basted in place.

When I'm sewing seams that can be basted and that need to go together without ease, like the lining/pocket-facing seam (step 3 of "Bagging on a patch," facing page), or when I'm machine-basting the lining to the patch, I try to overcome the action of the machine by placing a folded edge of paper (usually an 8½-in. x 11-in. piece folded in half) under the presser foot to the left of the needle. This also acts as a guide, ensuring straight seams.

Placement of the patch—On the front pattern that I draft for a man's traditional coat there are two vertical side darts connected by a horizontal, V-shaped slash, as shown in the drawing at left. The slash serves as a fitting dart, but it must be positioned before the cutting stage so that whatever the desired pocket style (patch, slanted, or piped), it can incorporate or conceal the slash.

The usual position for the slash when you want a patch pocket is 1¼ in. (the width of an arm of the tailor's L square) below its normal position at the mouth of a horizontal piped or flap pocket. The patch is centered over the slash, with the pocket opening at the same level as the piping would have been, so that the slash is well within the pocket, as shown at left.

When garments deviate from standard, the eye of the tailor or the choice of the wearer determines where the pockets go. But, despite the fact that pocket placement has absolutely no effect on fit, if the pockets seem to be in the wrong place, the wearer will often perceive that the coat itself is ill-fitting, so the proper position is worth some thought.

Matching stripes or plaids—Once the position of the patch is established, lay the patch pattern in place on the coat front; the darts and slash should be closed. With a pencil, mark on the pattern where the dominant lines must fall. Because of the darts, it will be impossible to match a design along the entire pocket mouth, so mark the pattern up to the first dart, along both sides and at the bottom. The breast patch is designed with its front edge on the straight grain; all the other edges are angled slightly (see "Patch-pocket patterns," facing page).

Lining and topstitching—I have two sport coats that I made 30 years ago with unlined patch pockets that still look new. Lining contributes luxury more than strength if the garment fabric is good quality. A lined pocket is also easier to clean and is virtually lint-free. The lining can be a single layer (just the back of the patch) or two layers (coat and pocket), which conceals raw edges. If I were making a sport coat for myself today, I'd choose a false patch, which requires no lining. For pleated pockets, I'd probably choose a double lining but wouldn't pleat the pocket lining so the pleat would hold its shape. In "Bagging on a patch" (facing page), I describe two layers of lining. If you prefer one layer, or none, omit what doesn't apply. For an unlined pocket on a pattern with a horizontal slash, cover the slash with a 1-in.-wide strip of bias lining, which you machine-stitch in place before you attach the pocket.

Most fine-tailored garments are hand-topstitched ¼ in. or so in from the front edges and around the pockets. On pockets that aren't double-lined this serves to enclose the raw seam edges on the inside of the pocket. If no lining or topstitching conceals the exposed seam, serge or overcast it.

Materials—Besides a well-shrunk (steamed or dipped and drip-dried) lightweight lining, you'll need enough ⅜-in. thoroughly shrunk edge tape (available at William Wawak, Box 59281, Schaumburg, IL 60159; 800-654-2235) to reinforce the pocket mouth. Soak the tape in cold water, squeeze out the excess, and iron it dry on both sides. Straighten the tape while ironing to remove any curve it developed when it was rolled. You'll also need two reinforcing scraps of lightweight pocketing, called silesia (also available at Wawak's), about 1½ in. x 1 in. to support the pocket mouth at the corners.

The lower-right coat pocket usually contains a small ticket pocket. This is nothing more than a 4-in.-sq. patch of silesia, preferably cut so the opening is on the selvage and won't need hemming. It is machine-topstitched into place about 1¼ in. below the pocket mouth. On a double-lined pocket, it is sewn in place after the pocket is attached so it gets sewn to the coat and not just to the lining. ⇨

Stanley Hostek has taught tailoring for 32 years. Custom patterns, tailoring supplies, and four books on tailoring techniques are available from him at 4003 W. Armour, Seattle, WA 98199.

From *Threads* magazine (August 1988) 18:59-63

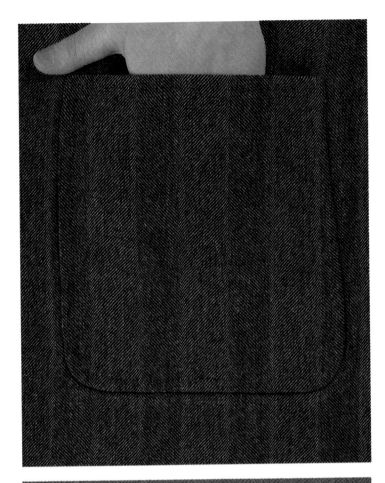

Bagging on a patch

The order of construction for the following three pockets is the same: Prepare the patch (with tape, lining, pleats, etc.), mark its location on the garment, machine-stitch it on, and hand-finish as needed. I'll describe a plain patch pocket, a fancy one, and a false patch pocket. It's usually most efficient to make all the pockets for your garment at the same time, rather than one after the other.

Plain patch pocket

1. Cut and shrink enough edge tape to reach from *a* to *b* for each pocket (see patterns below). This will be used to keep the opening from stretching. Trim silesia 4½ in. x 4½ in. for the ticket pocket in lower-right pocket if desired. Trim two pieces of lining for each pocket if both sides are to be lined, one piece for each pocket if one is to be lined, or skip it if you don't want a lining. The lengthwise (least stretchy) grain of the lining is parallel to the pocket opening.

2. Chalk a straight line between notches *a* and *b* on the wrong side of the patch. Place the edge tape along the chalk line on the facing side of the line and machine-stitch. I very slightly stretch the pocket while sewing the tape so I don't inadvertently ease the pocket onto the tape.

3. Machine-stitch one piece of lining (for the pocket) to the top edge of the patch, right sides together and using a ¼ in. seam. Press the seams toward the lining (drawing 1, p. 38). Fold the patch on the opening edge (line *a-b*), right side out, and hand-

Patch-pocket patterns

These patterns are average shapes for men's sport coats and are completely adjustable to other styles and proportions. They include ¼-in. seam allowances, except at the top, where they have cut-on facings, as indicated. If you're using a commercial pattern, trim seam allowances and adjust facings to match these patterns; bagging on requires ¼-in. seams. Linings don't need to be trimmed to shape, just roughed out the same size.

Plain patch

- 5½ in.
- 7¼ in.
- 1¼ in.
- Facing
- 1⅛ in.
- Facing
- *b*
- *a*
- *b*
- Notches
- Notches
- *a*
- Front
- Front
- 6 in.
- Straight
- Straight
- Bottom
- Breast pocket
- 8¼ in.
- Bottom
- Hip pocket

Cord, tuck, and pleated patch

- 1½ in.
- Seamline
- ⅜ in.
- *a*
- 3 in.
- Cord
- Pleat
- Tuck
- Straight
- Straight
- 7¼ in.
- *b*
- 1 in.
- Grid square = 1 in.

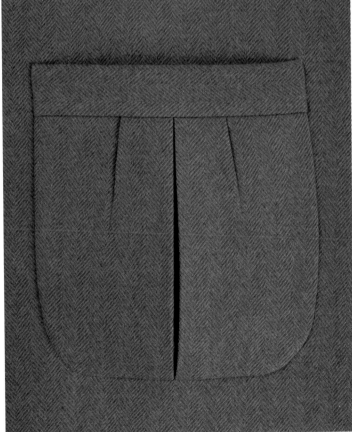

The plain patch pocket (top) is finished with hand topstitching that not only strengthens the pocket but also conceals the raw edges of the patch and its lining. The corded, tucked, and pleated pocket (above) was cut so the pleat would close without disturbing the woven pattern. The lining within isn't pleated, so the pleat won't spread completely open, but it does expand slightly when used. Either pocket could be false without any change in appearance.

baste along the fold. If the pocket is unlined, cross-stitch the facing to the pocket, keeping the stitches loose and invisible from the front.

4. Take the second piece of lining (for the garment), fold it back ½ in. to the wrong side, and place the fold against the patch/lining seam, right sides together (drawing 2 below). Hand-baste it to the patch, along the fold, and through all layers.

5. Turn the patch over (right side up) and hand-baste around the raw edges, about ½ in. inside the edge, catching the fabric to the linings. Keep all layers smooth. Then you'll be better able to machine-baste (with long stitches) about ⅛ in. inside the raw edges of the patch through all layers, which will hold everything firmly together within the seam allowance as you attach the patch. Trim the linings even with the fabric (drawing 2). Press the patch lightly and remove the hand-basting.

6. Place the patch in position on the garment. Use clay chalk to lightly outline the raw edge of the patch. The opening should be marked at the notches only. Chalk the position or balance marks (drawing 3). These balance marks will be partly on the patch and partly on the garment.

7. Remove the patch and copy the balance marks from the outside onto the inside of the patch. Use wax chalk for these inside marks so they'll stay nice and sharp. Extend the balance marks on the garment front inward. Chalk another patch outline

exactly ½ in. inside the original, using a ruler both to measure with and then to reinforce the line. See drawing 4, which shows an unlined patch. You'd mark the lined patch, one side or both sides, the same.

8. If you want a ticket pocket and you're not double-lining, make it now. If you plan to double-line the patch, you'll do it later (step 10). Fold in the raw edges of silesia about ⅜ in., miter the turn-in at each opening, and machine-stitch to the right garment front, as shown (drawing 4).

9. To bag the patch to the garment front, first position the reinforcing stays under the garment front as shown (drawing 4) so they'll be caught in the bagging-on stitches. Place the patch wrong side up on the garment front with the raw edge of the patch against the inside patch outline with the top even with the top balance mark and the two side balance marks matching. Machine-stitch, using just under a ¼-in. seam all around. The "just-under" amount is an allowance for the turn of the cloth and will vary with the cloth's thickness. For this technique to be successful, you must keep the raw edge of the patch lined up with the inside of the patch outline, maintain a uniform seam all around, and make sure all the balance marks match at the point of stitching.

10. Machine-stitch the remaining loose edge of the second piece of lining to the garment front, close to the edge of the fold,

Patch pockets

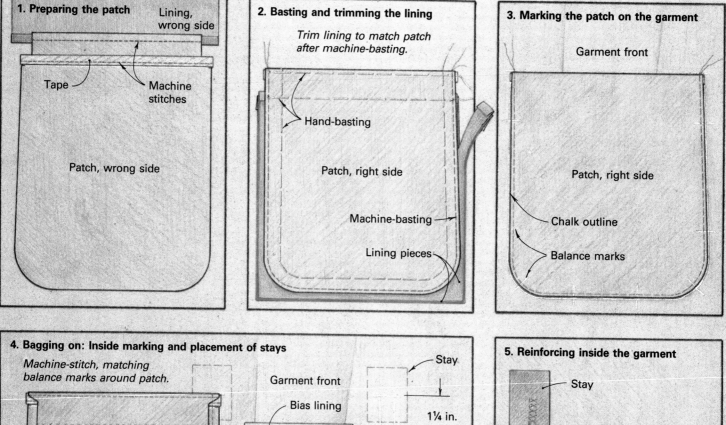

1. Preparing the patch

Lining, wrong side

Tape — Machine stitches

Patch, wrong side

2. Basting and trimming the lining

Trim lining to match patch after machine-basting.

Hand-basting

Patch, right side

Machine-basting

Lining pieces

3. Marking the patch on the garment

Garment front

Patch, right side

Chalk outline

Balance marks

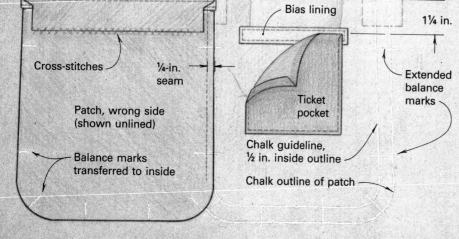

4. Bagging on: Inside marking and placement of stays

Machine-stitch, matching balance marks around patch.

Cross-stitches

¼-in. seam

Patch, wrong side (shown unlined)

Balance marks transferred to inside

Stay

Garment front

Bias lining

1¼ in.

Extended balance marks

Ticket pocket

Chalk guideline, ½ in. inside outline

Chalk outline of patch

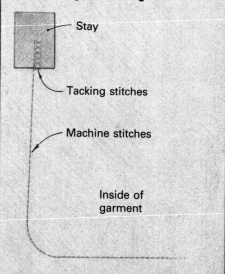

5. Reinforcing inside the garment

Stay

Tacking stitches

Machine stitches

Inside of garment

shifting the pocket so you can sew just inside, and sew right to the edges of the lining. Install the ticket pocket inside the lower-right pocket, as described in step 8. Again you'll need to shift the pocket around so you can get at the ticket-pocket seams.

11. Fold out of sight the seam allowance at each side of the pocket openings and reinforce by hand from the inside with a tacking stitch (drawing 5, facing page). Use hand silk to match, and go through all layers except the pocket front. Press the pocket edges to open the machine-stitched seam so the pocket stands away from the garment front. If desired, hand-stitch around the pocket to match the hand-stitching elsewhere on the garment.

Patch pocket with cord, tucks, and pleat

This pocket provides procedures that may be adapted to any fancy patch pocket. Variations might include patch with cord (separate band on top of patch), cord and tucks (little knife pleats), and cord and pleat(s) (box, inverted box, or knife). To make a pattern for any variation, start with a paper pattern of a plain patch pocket, but fold the desired pleats into another, larger piece of paper. Center the plain-patch pattern on top of the folds, trace around it, and cut the patch shape from the folded paper. Smooth out the folds, and that's your pattern. For a cord, you need to allow for seams (to attach cord to patch), for the width of the cord, and for a facing to turn in.

The pattern at the bottom of p. 37 is a common treatment for this style patch. To match stripes or plaids, adjust the size of the central pleat, if possible, so the plaid or stripe appears uninterrupted when the pleat is closed.

1. Machine-baste the pleat and tucks with long stitches from the wrong side. Press the tucks and pleat; the tucks should be pressed toward the pleat, and the pleat should be pressed so the inside fabric falls equally each side of the seam. This will form an inverted box pleat.

2. Machine-stitch the cord to the top of the patch, using a ¼-in. seam. Press the seam allowances toward the cord.

3. From this point on, the procedures are the same as for the plain patch pocket, starting with step 1. I recommend a double lining and no edge stitches for this pocket.

False patch pocket

The false patch pocket looks just like a patch pocket because it is. The only difference is that just inside the patch the garment front is cut through to allow access into a regular coat pocket. This is to lessen the bulge created by any content. It's adaptable to any style patch. You'll need all the parts of the double-lined plain patch pocket, except that you'll substitute pocketing fabric for lining. The patch is bagged on just the same as any other patch.

1. Tape the patch between the notches, and stitch one piece of the pocketing, instead of lining, to the top edge of the patch, as in steps 1, 2, and 3 of the plain patch pocket.

2. Without folding the patch over the tape, arrange the patch on the garment, and chalk guidelines around it. Then make balance marks and the inside guideline as usual. Also chalk a guideline for the pocket opening 1¼ in. down (the width of the pocket facing) from the patch opening (drawing 1 at right).

3. Machine-stitch the second pocketing piece to the garment by placing the edge of the pocketing against the opening guideline and stitching a ¼-in. seam. The seam should extend ⅛ in. beyond the inside pocket outline.

4. Bag on the pocket as usual. Fold the pocketing pieces out of the way, as they shouldn't be included, and be sure to include the reinforcing pieces in the seams at the patch mouth (drawing 2).

5. Cut through the garment on the pocket-opening guideline to within ¼ in. of the seam ends and angle out to the seam stitches. Push the second pocketing piece through the opening. Fold the patch facing (and attached pocketing) down over the taped edge and baste along the fold; then push that pocket piece through.

6. From the back, lift the pocketing pieces; the edges of the seam allowance from the pocketing/facing seam from step 1 should butt the lower edge of the slash through the garment. Join them with a baseball stitch (drawing 3), which closes the slash.

7. Reinforce each opening from the inside with a tacking stitch, using hand silk. Fold the raw edges of the pocket and pocket facing so they'll be inside the tacking stitches. Stitch the two pocketing layers together, forming a pocket (drawing 4). Finallly, press the patch and finish it with hand topstitching if desired. —S.H.

False patch

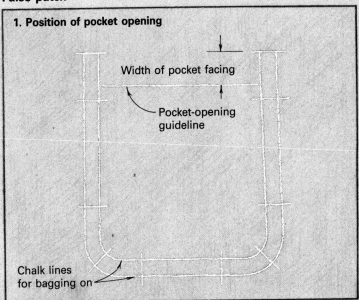

1. Position of pocket opening

Width of pocket facing

Pocket-opening guideline

Chalk lines for bagging on

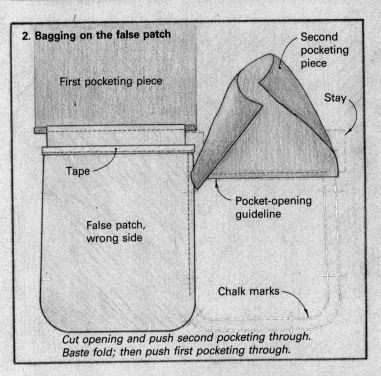

2. Bagging on the false patch

First pocketing piece

Second pocketing piece

Stay

Tape

Pocket-opening guideline

False patch, wrong side

Chalk marks

Cut opening and push second pocketing through. Baste fold; then push first pocketing through.

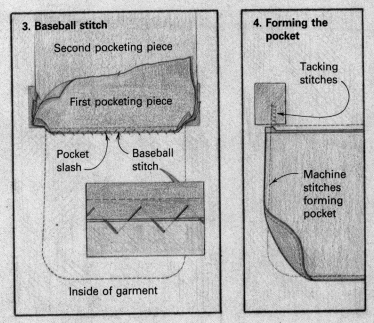

3. Baseball stitch

Second pocketing piece

First pocketing piece

Pocket slash

Baseball stitch

Inside of garment

4. Forming the pocket

Tacking stitches

Machine stitches forming pocket

Perfecting the Lapel

How to succeed with the trickiest part of a tailored jacket

by Margaret Komives

if you're an experienced seamstress who can't turn out a perfect collar and lapel on the jackets you sew, you're not alone. This is one of those areas in which pattern instructions, or even a shelf full of good tailoring books, can't provide the information you need to get good results: How much do you need to ease *your* fabric, using *your* pattern, to get a smooth roll, to conceal the undercollar and edge seam, and to keep the lapel points from curling up, all at once? Whether you're speed-tailoring with fusibles or custom-tailoring by hand, conventional methods all require considerable judgment or plain guesswork.

I've come up with a method that works equally well with speed- and custom-tailoring. It allows you to establish the exact relationship of the collar and lapel facing to the jacket and undercollar, right side out, as you'll wear them, before you sew the units together. At the same time, you'll be able to hand-shape the lapel points and the notch between them. The method is just as good, and easier, if you're making a shawl collar.

Cutting the collars—The first step, cutting out the upper collar, is an opportunity to refine the pattern shape. I've often noticed, after making up commercial jacket patterns, that excess fullness appears inside the collar at the back of the neck. This can be eliminated with a minor correction. I lay the upper-collar pattern on the fabric with the neckline seam angled ⅛ in. off the fold at the neckline edge (drawing at right). When I join this seam to the unchanged back-neck facing (or to the jacket's back neckline when there's no facing), I just stretch it. The fullness is eliminated, and the inner neckline of the upper collar lies smooth, regardless of the fabric or my tailoring method.

I cut the undercollar (without the ⅛-in. offset) in two sections on the bias so I have

Margaret Komives (facing page) wears her latest creation, a blue velvet suit designed by Ralph Lauren for Vogue Patterns. The collar and lapels are by Komives.

the same grain line at both collar points. If there's no separate undercollar pattern, I cut one from half the unaltered upper collar but leave extra for a seam allowance at the centerline. I also check the roll line, and if the fall isn't wider than the stand by at least ¼ in. (as shown below), I lower the line with a marking pen, then transfer the new line to the appropriate fabric sections. This helps ensure that the collar will cover the seam at the back of the neck when the jacket is completed.

Shaping the upper collar—I prepare the collar by doing some shaping. My method is similar to the one used by a tailor, but it's simplified so that anyone can manage it. First I put in a running stitch on the roll line, anchoring it at the cross seam on one end and leaving enough thread at the other end to use as a drawstring. Using a dark marker, I mark the thread where it leaves the fabric so that I can see, and measure, precisely how much I'm drawing it up (photo at top left, p. 42). The amount I need to draw up depends on the posture of the wearer. For a more rounded back or a head-thrust-forward posture, I draw it up almost 2¼ in. For the average figure, 1½ in.

is sufficient. I then fasten the thread so that it can't slip.

I place the collar wrong side up on the ironing board, spray it with a mist of water, and press it from the neckline edge up to the ease thread, thus shrinking out the fullness. I repeat the procedure from the outer-collar edge until the fullness is completely shrunk away. Then I remove the gathering thread. Of course, this is easier to do with a good wool or a fabric that's not too firmly woven, but even after reinforcing the red twill in the photos by fusing a weft-insertion interfacing (Stacy's Suit-Shape) onto it, I could still shape the collar easily. I usually use this method on the upper collar and don't bother to shape the undercollar if I'm speed-tailoring. Because it's bias-cut, and reinforced only in the stand, I've never had a problem with it.

Turn of the cloth—The rest of my method is based on respecting a basic sewing fact—the turn of the cloth. If you fold in half a double layer of fabric that's perfectly aligned at the edges, the outer layer will pull away from the under layer at the edges because it needs more length than the inner layer to go around the fold. How much more de-

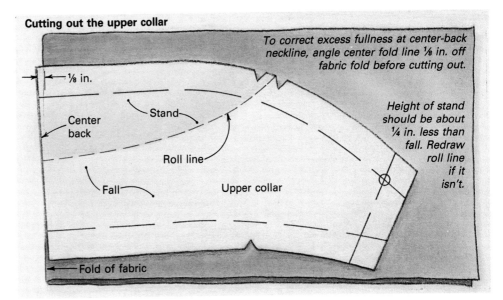

Cutting out the upper collar

To correct excess fullness at center-back neckline, angle center fold line ⅛ in. off fabric fold before cutting out.

⅛ in.

Center back

Stand

Roll line

Fall

Upper collar

Height of stand should be about ¼ in. less than fall. Redraw roll line if it isn't.

Fold of fabric

From *Threads* magazine (August 1989) 24:56-61

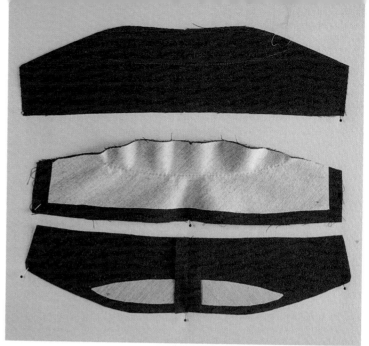

Komives presses out the fullness on each side of the thread she has used to gather and shape the upper collar's roll line (above). She marked the thread so she could measure exactly how much she drew it up. At right, from top to bottom: Upper collar with roll line stitched for shaping; shaped upper collar, flipped over to show the fusible interfacing Komives likes for speed-tailoring; and undercollar, assembled from two bias-cut pieces and interfaced in the stand area only.

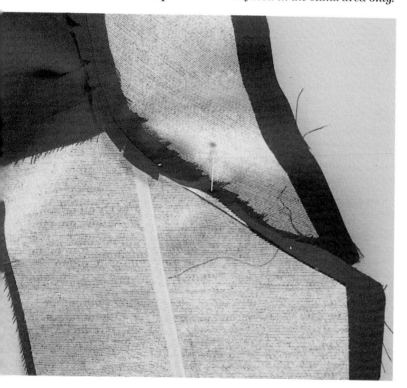

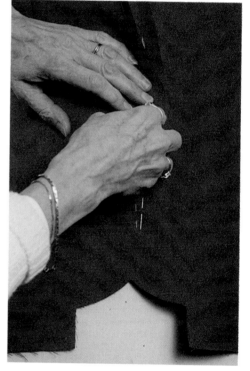

The completed upper collar and facing unit (left), show how the neckline seam ends at the inner corner of the collar notch. Komives has used a strip of iron-on hem tape to tape the lapel roll line.

After pinning the facing/collar unit to the jacket along the neckline seam only, Komives puts the jacket on a dress form (right) and aligns the raw edges below the roll line, pinning them together. Above the roll line, she arranges the facing to fall smoothly without trying to keep the edges matched.

pends on the fabric. A lighter-weight fabric needs less than a heavier or bulkier one. This is the cause of many tailoring problems, especially at the lapel-edge seam, where the roll line creates excess length in the jacket and undercollar. You can't accurately predict the amount of excess without years of experience. Some patterns allow an additional amount of fabric in the upper collar and facing, but the patternmakers have no idea what the bulk of your fabric will be, so their allowance is an estimate. The "tailor's blister" (ease created by pinning out a pinch of fabric at the lapel point) allows fullness in only one area, but it's a gradual, allover ease, which is most desirable.

To achieve this, in exactly the right amount for my fabric, I prepare all the parts of the collar and lapel and try them on, pinned together only. This way, I can establish the roll line and the fall of the upper collar before I commit myself to a seam at the edges.

Preparing the facings—With the exception of the collar parts described above, I cut all the pieces exactly from the adjusted pattern and transfer all the markings to the fabric, especially the actual stitching lines. I mark these with tiny dots (from carbon or chalk) about every 6 in. along straight lines, closer on curves, and at corners. I fit and sew the entire bodice, interfacing it according to the method I've chosen, either fused or pad-stitched. In the photos at top right and bottom left, above, I fused Stacy's Suit-Shape to the facing and upper collar with a reinforcement of Armo's Whisper Weft at the undercollar stand.

In this case, I taped the roll line on the facing with iron-on hem tape, cut in half lengthwise (to ¼ in. wide), then spot-fused first at a point ¼ in. behind the roll line of the facing and about 2 in. up from the base of the roll line. Positioning the tape like this makes for a softer roll than putting it

right on the line. I aligned the hem tape next to the marked roll line, marking where it crosses the collar seam, then stretched it as far as it would go (about ⅜ in.) beyond the seam so it was shorter than the roll line. Then I spot-fused the marked end to hold the easing in place, distributed the ease under the loose tape, tacked it at the center, and then held the iron down along the whole line in sections. The custom tailor's taping method offers a lot more control than this fused method, and I'd use it for fitting a lapel over a large bust, but fused tape works well for most figures.

Next, I stitch the upper collar to the facings and the undercollar to the jacket at the neckline seams, which I've staystitched and clipped. It's important to end these seams right at the inside corner mark of the lapel notch. I leave the threads unfastened for possible correction later on (photo at bottom left). I trim both seams to ⅜ in.

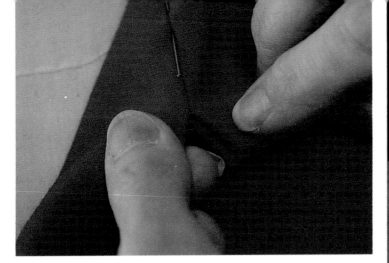

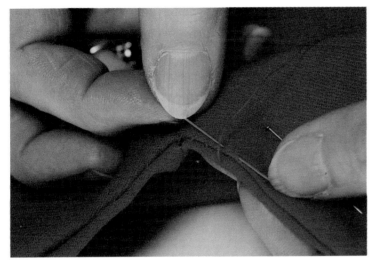

At the notch, Komives checks the neckline seams (top, left) to see that they end at the same point, top and bottom, correcting them from the inside if needed. Then she folds the seam allowances in place (above) so the left and right sides are the same and the seamline can't be seen. When satisfied, she slipstitches the seam from the outside (center, left).

After completing the notch shaping and pinning the remaining raw edges in position, Komives trims the edges (left) so they're exactly even, holding them together while stitching to preserve the folded-in ease.

or ½ in., depending on the strength of my fabric. I clip the seams and press them open, but I don't clip into the seam allowance at the corner mark unless the seam turns upward. In that case, I fuse a tiny square of reinforcement interfacing, like Pellon's Knit Shape, into the corner before clipping.

If the corners of the facing or collar are curved, I take time out at this point to make a cardboard template in the shape of the curve from the pattern. I trim the seam allowance of the upper collar or facing to about ⅜ in. and press it over the template exactly on the pattern markings to form a perfectly curved corner, on the top layer only, for the time being.

Aligning the parts—At this point, I pin the neckline seam of the facing unit to the corresponding seam of the jacket, wrong sides together, seam on top of seam, carefully matching shoulder seams and stopping just

short of the collar notches. Then I arrange the whole thing on a dress form; on a shaped, padded hanger; or on a friend so that it's smooth and hangs naturally. It's usually necessary to support the shoulders with pads to get the best drape. With one hand under the collar to keep the parts together, I roll the upper collar smoothly over the undercollar on the roll line. Next, I roll the facing over the jacket, also on the roll line, paying no attention to whether the raw edges line up. Then I pin the two layers of fabric together at the base of the roll line (bottom-right photo, facing page), but I make sure the edges are aligned. From here on down to the hem I pin the front seam allowances together smoothly, edges aligned. Around the curve, if there is one, and at the hem, the edges may not match, but that's all right.

Back to the lapel, I again roll it over my hand so it lies in what will be its finished

position, but this time I pin the seam allowances securely, wherever they fall. I also pin the seam allowances of the collar, keeping the roll snug over my fingers. I double-check that all is smooth, even though the seam allowances probably won't meet exactly. The differences should still be about the same on each side. If they're not, I suspect a problem. When all meets my approval, I check and adjust the thread ends of the collar seam at the notch and fasten them when they match (photo at top left, above). Then I'm ready to tackle the notches.

Creating the notches—I don't trim or clip the seam allowances at the notches. I fold and pin the edges of the upper unit inward on the stitching line and fold the lower seam allowance to almost meet it (photo at right, above). The upper layer should extend a bit over the underlayer and have just enough ease to create a slight roll. The

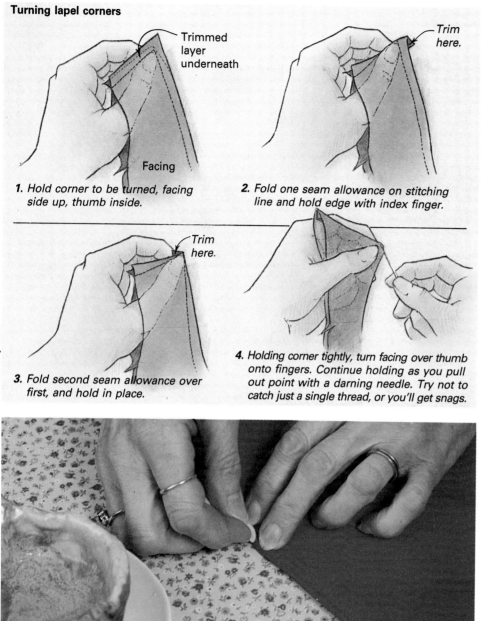

Turning lapel corners

1. Hold corner to be turned, facing side up, thumb inside.

Trimmed layer underneath

Facing

2. Fold one seam allowance on stitching line and hold edge with index finger.

Trim here.

3. Fold second seam allowance over first, and hold in place.

Trim here.

4. Holding corner tightly, turn facing over thumb onto fingers. Continue holding as you pull out point with a darning needle. Try not to catch just a single thread, or you'll get snags.

Illustrations by Clarke

With a small piece of dampened fabric, Komives moistens just the seamline at the edge of the lapel so only this area gets steam when ironed, reducing imprinting on the garment face.

edges should look the way I'd like them to when the jacket is finished. I then slip-stitch these seams either to the end of the notch, as I'm doing in the photo at left center, p. 43, or just around the curve, if either part is curved.

When I'm satisfied with the way everything looks, and all the raw edges are pinned or basted securely to their mates, I take the jacket off the form and trim the seam allowances so all the cut edges are exactly even (photo at bottom left, p. 43), trimming the wider edge to meet the narrower one. This way, I keep the cut edges together when I'm ready to sew, but at this point I know that they have been adjusted for the turn of my cloth. For even more accuracy, I make marking snips about 4 in. apart all around the trimmed seam edges. There should be a snip about 2 in. above and below the base of the roll line. You can expect a bit more fullness in the facing between

these points, which you should ease in as you make the seam to help establish the roll. If the fabric is ravelly, I use a thread or chalk mark instead of snips. After I've trimmed and snipped everything, I remove pins and bastings, separate cut edges, and turn and pin right sides together.

With one exception, I'm careful when I pin to align the edges and the snips. From the base of the roll lines upward and around the collar, I pin the upper-collar and facing edges 1/16 in. inside the jacket and under-collar edges for pin-basting so there will be a tiny bit more ease to ensure that I can conceal the undercollar unit when I'm doing the final pressing. Tailors call this "favoring" the upper-collar unit.

At last I'm ready to stitch. I sew the collar first, with the undercollar on top and following the undercollar seam marks. The collar notch is finished by the slipstitching, but you can machine-stitch it again. Don't

stitch all the way into the corner—stay a stitch away. A slight space in the stitching is better than a pucker; and since the fabric hasn't been clipped at the corner, there should be no problem. It's a good idea to shorten the stitch length when you're machine-stitching around curves and corners.

Final steps—Before trimming any of the seams, I turn the collar and lapel corners to the right side to make sure they're symmetrical. When I'm satisfied, I turn them back out, press the seams, and then trim. The upper unit's seams should be trimmed all around to about 1/4 in., and to 1/8 in. around curves. The lower unit's seams should be narrower, trimmed to about 1/8 in. all around. Clipping shouldn't be necessary unless an inward (concave) curve calls for it. Stronger, more closely woven, less ravelly fabrics can take closer trimming.

For the final trimming and turning of the collar and lapel points, I trim the underside corners extremely narrow (less than 1/8 in.), but I leave the upper layer (the facing/upper collar) at 1/4 in. I fold the wider seam allowances to the underside (drawing at left), and holding them at the point with pinched fingers, thumb inside, I pull the upper layer over my fingers, to the right side. If any of the point remains to be turned, I pull it out very gently with a darning needle. I find that this method works well for turning all square, or nearly square, faced corners.

Proper pressing is critical. From the wrong side I press the seams together, then open them, as far as possible, before turning. After turning, I roll the edges in the corners with slightly dampened fingers so the stitching is as far out to the edge as possible. Then, with a small, damp cloth I moisten just the edge (photo at left). This helps prevent imprinting of the seam allowances. With most fabrics, I press from the underside directly on the fabric with a dry iron. The dampness on the edge creates a perfect press.

The final step is to permanently attach the neckline seams together. I pin them from the right side first, seam on top of seam. Then I attach them by hand, using an invisible prick stitch, in the seamline, from notch to notch; or from the inside, by joining the two seam allowances, between the roll lines. It's all right to leave the rest of the seam unattached in the latter case.

When I've finished the entire jacket and removed any bastings, I apply a final press to the right side of the collar notch with a swatch of the fashion fabric placed over the area as a press cloth. I spray a mist of water over the area and press.

Margaret Komives is a frequent contributor to Threads. *For information on her book,* Tailoring Techniques *(self-published), send a SASE to Margaret Komives, 11108 N. Lake Shore Dr., Mequon, WI 53092.*

Selecting fabric for tailored jackets

If the lapel and collar techniques that I've described on the preceding pages have inspired you to try making a tailored jacket—perhaps for the first time—I'd like to share with you my opinions about fabric selection.

The shell fabric—When the jacket is finished, the most obvious thing about it will be the fabric, and especially the color. Don't be tempted by a piece of fabric just because it's on sale or because it seems to be of exceptional quality, unless it's also a color that's flattering and will coordinate well with other items in your wardrobe. It's not a bargain if you have to buy a closetful of new clothes to wear with it. It's also not a bargain if you have to buy underlining because the fabric lacks weight or body, or if the fabric won't press crisply and hold it's shape, no matter how attractive it may appear on the bolt.

The best results come from high-quality fabric, which is firm enough not

A tailoring disaster, the result of unsuitable fabric—too much polyester, too soft, and won't hold a press well.

to droop at critical points, like lapels and pockets, yet supple enough to be shaped into elegant collars and sleeves. Admittedly, it takes experience to pick out fabrics that have these contradictory qualities, but you *can* get some advance warning if you're willing to do a little testing. It's certainly worth buying and playing with ⅛ yd. of a fabric that you like before plunging into an expensive and time-consuming project.

I use two simple tests. First I make a few plain seams and try to press them perfectly flat. Then I try to crease the fabric. I might test a dart-shaped seam to see whether I can press out the dimple at the point. I also make about an 8-in. line of gathering stitches, by hand or machine, similar to the gathering stitches I used to shape the collar in the photo at top left, p. 42, or a sleeve cap. I draw up the fabric about 1 in. and then see if I can steam out the gathers, just as I'll need to do in the garment. Fabric has to pass all these tests reasonably well before I'll put my time into tailoring it, but I've learned this the hard way, as you can see from the disaster shown at left.

Even before you buy a test scrap, look for a fabric that doesn't ravel excessively; it will make putting in pockets and making bound buttonholes a lot easier. Smooth-surface solid colors require the greatest skill because every imperfection will show up. Heathers, slight textures, and tiny checks, like salt-and-pepper tweeds, are the easiest to work with. If you think you need more experience to recognize quality fabric, spend a few hours in stores, comparing the fabrics used in better garments with those used in less expensive ones. You'll notice that the best-tailored garments tend to use fabric that's firm, springy, almost wiry—but that doesn't mean scratchy.

Although quality wools are most likely to tailor easily, all-wool fabric is not the only good choice, nor does it ensure that the garment will turn out successfully. Wool blends, like wool/polyester and wool/nylon, can be good choices for either custom- or speed-tailoring,

particularly if you want a very light colored jacket, which is going to require a lot of dry-cleaning, but don't go over 45% polyester content, or you'll be courting disaster. The least likely wool fabrics, in my experience, are the soft and thin ones; if you're attracted to a soft wool, make sure that it's on the thick side (like camel hair) before you buy it for a tailored jacket.

Polyester adds crush-resistance, crease retention, and firmness when combined with another fiber. Rayon adds drape, and when combined with other fibers, results in a softer, more fluid fabric. As a rule, the more a fabric drapes, the less well it will tailor, but if you really like the fabric, select a collarless pattern or one with a shawl collar. Cottons, linens, and silks are good choices—alone or in combination with each other or with polyester—if the structure is firm enough for your pattern. If your fabric is washable and you plan to launder the garment, throw your test swatches into the washing machine to see if you'll need to touch up the seams—not easy to do once the garment is lined.

Patterns, linings, and interfacings—A quality pattern (usually more expensive) with basic lines will frequently have the best shaping and fit. The more vertical seams it has, the easier your pattern will be to adapt to a figure that's not standard. A two-piece sleeve pattern is virtually required for an attractive sleeve.

Interfacing, too, should be of fine quality. Be sure it's needle-ready. Preshrink or steam-press it, depending on the type you're using. A woven (like traditional canvas) or a weft-insertion interfacing, like Stacy's Suit-Shape or Crown's Armo Weft, will lend itself best to shaping the collar. I've used these interfacings and Stacy's Veriform for collarless jackets. For shawl collars, I prefer soft, three-way-stretch fusibles, like Sof-Shape or Pel-Aire, both by Pellon.

Polyester linings are very durable, but rayon linings are more comfortable because they breathe, are absorbent, and press in well. Rayon linings should be used exclusively with dry-clean-only fabrics, since they wrinkle badly when they're washed, and linings can't be ironed. I line only the sleeves and the shoulder pads of linen jackets, which need constant touching up with an iron. A twill lining is the most suitable, as it is the most flexible. Acetate linings don't wear well, and they lack the absorbency of rayon. For washable blazers, I like Hang Loose by Logantex or a lightweight polyester crepe de chine.—M.K. ☐

Techniques of a Woman's Tailor

Why a woman's coat can't be more like a man's

by Katherine Davis

*t*ailors for men and tailors for women share many construction techniques, but seldom does one tailor build coats for both. Building a woman's coat is commonly referred to as "soft tailoring." A woman's tailor strives for a different look than a man's tailor, who achieves the standard triangular masculine image by building up the chest and shoulder area with several layers of canvas and wool. In a man's coat, the sleeve cap is basically flat, with only a small amount of ease; the collar and lapels must hug the neck and chest. The coat must have the crisp, sharp look of "hard-edge" tailoring.

Women have a wider choice of coat styles than men, and there's no set silhouette. Making a muslin test copy, unusual in men's tailoring, is the best way to ensure that the selected style will look good and fit well. The muslin shell accommodates weight fluctuations during the building process. Men are not immune to weight changes, but theirs aren't usually as immediately critical to the fit. Women tend to show weight changes in the midsection, bust, back, upper arms, hips, and thighs.

The softer fabrics that are frequently used in women's coats adapt readily to the wide selection of styles and shaping, but most of these fabrics need to be underlined in order to prevent stretching. Underlining is never used in a man's coat, because men's tailors prefer hard-finished outer cloth, like worsteds and some wool flannels. The weave is dense and compact, which creates a hard, smooth finish. I underline the classic coats that I make with preshrunk 100% cotton batiste or lawn; I cut the underlining, using the body pattern pieces, hand-baste them to each piece, and treat the coat fabric and underlining as one layer during the construction.

The shoulder area of a classic woman's coat is fitted to the shape of the shoulders and around the curve of the bust. The lapels, collar, and coat and sleeve hems are interfaced with hair canvas to maintain their shapes. Pad stitches anchor the hair canvas to the outer cloth and, together with steam pressing, help establish the roll of the lapel and the collar. The amount of roll is dictated by the coat's design. Cotton twill tape fell-stitched along the line of the lapel and up around the collar stand prevents the roll of a lapel from stretching. The sleeve cap of a woman's coat has a soft, rounded look.

And last, a woman's custom coat frequently displays the skill of its maker in bound buttonholes. This beautiful detail never appears on a man's garment.

Select the best materials—I prefer 100% wools because they tailor the best. For the warmer months, I use a tropical-weight wool fabric, generally 7 to 9 oz./yd. Weights of 11 to 13 oz./yd. are good for winter. Considering the time and labor involved in custom tailoring, it pays to buy the best fabric you can afford in order to give longevity to the garment. Among the best fabrics are British woolens and worsteds, Scottish and Irish tweeds, and English and Italian flannels (photo at right, below). Some of the famous tweeds are Connemara, Donegal, Gala (Galashiels), Glengarry, Harris, Hebridean, Irish, and Shetland. Harris is one of the more popular handwovens from Scotland. Donegal, a kind of speckled tweed, is another frequently used fabric in women's tailored outerwear. Connemara tweed is a brighter version of Donegal tweed.

Unless woolen cloth has been labeled with words such as "ready for the needle," it must be preshrunk. Otherwise, it may shrink about an inch per yard. I don't recommend dry-cleaning wool, except for spot-cleaning, as it strips the wool of it natural oils and dries it out. I use a process that

Gundel Bowen (above photo, left) wears a gray wool-flannel suit with a 12-gore skirt, while Mary Wooldridge (right) is dressed in 100% wool tweed. Both suits are by Katherine Davis.

Davis's custom coat (facing page) includes well-fitted, but not built-up, shoulders; softly rounded sleeve caps and perfectly set sleeves; gently rolled lapels and collars; and bound buttonholes.

At right, a Donegal-tweed jacket lined with China silk cradles swatches of wool, including a Glengarry plaid (in full view). Davis likes silk thread because of its strength. Fabric underneath jacket is a Harris tweed.

The custom-tailored coat

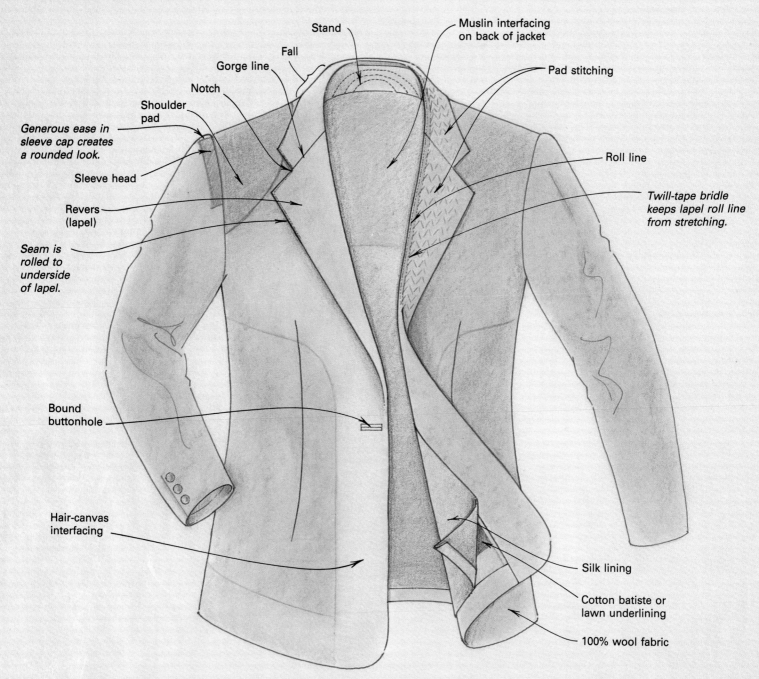

Stand

Muslin interfacing on back of jacket

Fall

Pad stitching

Gorge line

Notch

Shoulder pad

Generous ease in sleeve cap creates a rounded look.

Roll line

Sleeve head

Twill-tape bridle keeps lapel roll line from stretching.

Revers (lapel)

Seam is rolled to underside of lapel.

Bound buttonhole

Hair-canvas interfacing

Silk lining

Cotton batiste or lawn underlining

100% wool fabric

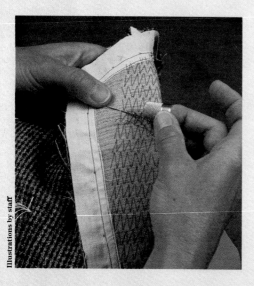

Davis shapes lapel over her fingers as she pad-stitches hair canvas to outer cloth.

An interfaced undercollar is already steamed into shape before upper collar is attached. Padding stitches anchor hair canvas to collar around stand, which is machine-stitched.

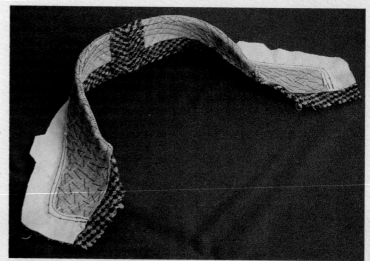

Illustrations by staff

British tailors have used for many years, commonly called "London shrinking." Originally, the cloth was brought to a large, open field; left overnight for the dew to settle on the fabric; and walked on the next morning to hasten the shrinking. The following procedure gives the same results.

Leave the wool folded as it comes off the bolt, right sides together, but pull threads and straighten the ends. Then baste the selvages together. Clip the selvages every few inches to allow the fabric to shrink without wrinkling.

Soak a flat sheet in water, wring out the excess, and lay it on a clean, flat area. Place the folded wool yardage on half of the wet sheet and cover it with the other half. Fold the sheet and wool in large, loose folds, making sure the folds are smooth and unwrinkled. Allow the wool to sit for four to nine hours, depending on its thickness. Don't let the sheet and wool dry out; otherwise, shrinkage will be uneven. After the allotted time, unfold the wool and remove it from the sheet. Leave the wool flat for another hour or two; then iron with steam, using a pressing cloth to avoid shine.

The softer look in a woman's coat challenges the tailor to figure out how to support the fabric. You may have noticed that, after only one year, the coat you bought off the rack has stretched across the upper back, and the lapel droops. Perhaps the skirt has stretched across the seat. Underlining prevents these effects in a custom coat but should not change the fabric's appearance. In addition to stabilizing the fabric, underlining allows the tailor to anchor small felling stitches and avoid unattractive ridges that often appear on softer fabrics at the hem and facing edges. Furthermore, when the outer cloth is a light color, the underlining prevents the tan tone of the hair canvas from distorting the true color of the coat.

Interfacing, the inner layer of fabric that forms the support structure of a garment, provides the shaping needed for the design characteristics of the coat. The type of interfacing is determined by the weight of the fabric and the amount of shaping desired. The most common interfacings are tailor's canvas, tailor's linen, wigan, muslin, and sateen. Tailor's linen is sometimes suitable for collar interfacing. Wigan, a lightweight, canvaslike cotton, and sateen, a firmly woven cotton, may be used as substitutes for muslin to interface the back of a coat and the sleeve hems and cuffs and to reinforce the pockets.

Tailor's canvas, in different degrees of firmness, is made of natural horsehair or goat hair, combined with cotton, linen, wool, or rayon. Armo P-1 hair canvas is one of the best woven interfacings for women's custom jackets and coats. I use it in the collar, lapels, coat front, and sleeve and coat hems. It has a softer hand than the hymo interfacing used in men's coats but, together with pad stitching and careful pressing, provides those qualities needed for shaping. Armo P-1 is generally stocked only by large fabric stores, but you can order it from tailoring suppliers.

Hair canvas sewn into seams creates bulk and resists creasing, so I sew it into only the armhole seams and a small portion of the underarm seams. I substitute a border of preshrunk muslin for the seam allowances of the canvas to make sure I achieve sharp edges for lapels, as explained below.

To stay the roll line of the lapel and to prevent stretching, I apply the "bridle," which is ¼- to ⅜-in.-wide cotton twill tape. The bridle begins at the top buttonhole and extends to the point where the collar meets the lapel and continues to the center back of the collar stand (drawing, facing page). I preshrink the tape and then apply it in two pieces with small felling stitches. The bridle keeps the lapel from stretching and from rolling beyond the roll line.

I prefer silk thread because of its strength and shaping qualities and because it doesn't permanently imprint on the fabric when it is used for basting. I use sizes 0, 00, and A for both hand and machine work. Sizes B through F are good for topstitching, hand-worked buttonholes, and hand-sewn zippers. My silk colors include four shades of gray, several browns and tans, black, white, and cream. When in doubt, I use gray because it blends with almost any color. Silk thread is expensive and is frequently difficult to find. My second choice is either a fine-quality, long-staple polyester or 100% mercerized cotton.

(continued on p. 50)

Muslin edges on canvas interfacing

Hair canvas interfacing sewn into the seams of collars and lapels makes the seamlines too stiff, and it resists pressing. There are several ways to reduce the bulk and stiffness; I like to replace the hair canvas at the seam allowances with muslin.

To make a pattern for the muslin strip, first mark the lapel-interfacing pattern 2 in. from all pattern edges of the front, neck, and shoulders (excluding the armhole). If the pattern has a shoulder dart, close the dart. Draw a line connecting the marks, and transfer all pattern markings (grain lines, buttonholes, lapel lines) to the 2-in.-wide area. Use a tracing wheel and paper to cut out the 2-in.-wide border from muslin, being careful to match the grain lines from the original pattern.

Before attaching the muslin to the hair canvas, prepare any darts that fall within the canvas. Slash one leg of the dart to the point and overlap the stitching lines. Stitch on the line; then stitch another line about ¼ in. away from the first for reinforcement. Next, trim the interfacing back to the stitching. The point of the dart tends to fray, so cut a small square of preshrunk muslin and machine-stitch the square over the point to reinforce it, going around all four edges and diagonally across.

Place the muslin on the same side of the hair-canvas interfacing as the muslin square; pin carefully. Cut away the canvas at the corner of the lapel, ⅛ in. inside the seamline. The canvas won't cause bulk in the corner when the lapel is turned. Machine-stitch the muslin strip to the canvas ¾ in. from the edge (assuming a ⅝-in.seam allowance) with regular-length stitches. For reinforcement, place a second row of stitching ¼ in. away from the first (1 in. from the pattern edge). Trim the muslin close to the second stitching line and the canvas in the front seam allowance close to the first stitching line. This method takes the place of taping the lapel and front coat edge. –K.D.

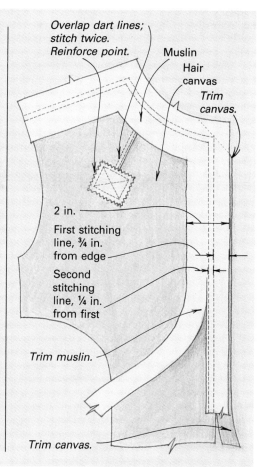

Overlap dart lines; stitch twice. Reinforce point.

Muslin
Hair canvas
Trim canvas.

2 in.

First stitching line, ¾ in. from edge

Second stitching line, ¼ in. from first

Trim muslin.

Trim canvas.

After pinning the ease in the sleeve cap by dividing the ease repeatedly in half (left), Davis stitches over pins that hold the cap in place (right).

Shoulders and sleeves—The area from the shoulder to the bust in a woman's coat gently follows the curve of the body; if the hollow of the shoulders is built up with padding, as is a man's, it tends to look stiff and awkward, a common problem when a man's tailor makes a woman's coat. For tailoring a classic coat, I recommend using the smallest shoulder pads that are needed to achieve the intended silhouette and not padding up the area in front of the shoulders. At the first fitting, when the major seams of the coat have been basted, I check the pitch of the sleeves for distortions. Checking the pitch of the sleeve means to rotate the sleeve either forward or backward in the armhole to eliminate any breaks or folds that occur in the sleeve when it hangs straight, or when the arm is flexed. The shoulder and neck seams may also need some adjustment at this time.

The sleeve cap, the area above the notches, has more ease than in a man's coat. Sometimes the ease is tricky to distribute without causing it to pucker around the cap. To set the sleeve smoothly, I use pins to hold it exactly in place, even when stitching. I find that basting, unlike pinning, still allows the two cloth layers to shift.

To set in the sleeve, first match the shoulder seam, underarm marking, notches, and small circles on both the coat and sleeves. Then pin at these points exactly on the seamline. Divide in half the fullness of one side of the cap from the notch to the circle, and again from the circle to the shoulder point, and pin. Do the same to the opposite side. Continue dividing the remaining ease in half, holding the sleeve cap face up with the edges curved outward over your fingers (photo at left, above). The pins should end up about ³⁄₁₆ in. apart around the cap.

To stitch the sleeve, I start at the underarm and work around, sewing over the pins (photo at right, above). You may occasionally hit pins, so discard the sewing-machine needle when you've finished the sleeves. Stitch the seam again ¼ in. from the first stitching line, between the notches at the underarm. Trim the seam allowance at the underarm between the notches, close to the second stitching line. I never press the sleeve area when using this pin method.

After the sleeve seam is finished, I prepare a sleeve head or cap lift from lamb's wool or wool flannel. I hand-baste it with a lengthwise fold at the armhole seamline, with the raw edges extending into the body of the sleeve. It supports and helps maintain the rounded shape of the sleeve cap.

Bound buttonholes—There are several ways to make bound buttonholes, but I've had the most success with the following method (drawing, facing page). I can make corrections and adjustments at any step of the process. The procedure described is for a buttonhole that's 1 in. long when finished.

Before you begin, be sure you've transferred all necessary alterations that affect buttonhole placement to the cloth. Buttonholes should be made before the front has been permanently stitched to the back.

Always make a trial bound buttonhole on a scrap of the coat's fabric. Each fabric is a bit different, and the results may surprise you. The button should glide easily through the sample. If it doesn't, extend the buttonhole length, or select another button. The thickness of the fabric affects the length of the buttonhole. A 1-in.-long buttonhole, for example, will be ⅞ in. or shorter when finished because of the thickness of the wool. To compensate for the loss in length, I extend the buttonhole to ⅛ in. beyond the center front.

Strive for as narrow a finished buttonhole as your fabric will allow; a narrow buttonhole looks sharp and neat. Make sure your guidelines are marked as accurately as possible. If a line is even slightly askew, remove it and start over again.

The buttonhole patch, which will form the folds of the buttonhole, can be cut on the straight or bias grain line. Use bias if the fabric ravels easily. For an interesting design detail, cord each fold with yarn to give it fullness.

A successful buttonhole is the result of accurate sewing and marking. I use graph paper to make patches because the grids help me to mark the stitching lines accurately. Cut rectangles that are 2 in. long by 2½ in. wide (¾ in. wider than the buttonhole on each side) from ¼-in.-grid graph paper; you need one rectangle for each buttonhole. Cut the fabric wrong side up, using the graph-paper pattern. Machine-baste two lines through the paper and fabric ½ in. apart in contrasting thread, each ¼ in. away from the patch center. Remove the paper and press the strip toward the wrong side on the basting lines.

Mark the buttonholes on the coat front with a "ladder": Using contrasting thread, run a line of machine or hand basting along the center front. For a 1-in. buttonhole, run a second line of machine basting 1 in. away from the center front, toward the inside of the front. To allow for the thickness of the fabric, establish a third line ⅛ in. away from the centerline, toward the coat's opening. Stitch crosswise lines extending beyond the vertical basting on the buttonhole center. Stitch another set of crosswise lines ¼ in. above the buttonhole lines.

Center one pressed fold of a patch on the top line and hand-baste it in place. Using matching thread and short stitches, stitch the patch through all layers ⅛ in. from the folded edge, beginning and ending exactly at the sides of the ladder. Leave the thread ends long; you'll use these later to pull at the corners of the buttonhole when machine-stitching the ends. Baste on the buttonhole line; then baste and stitch the other fold of the buttonhole patch in the same way.

Flip the front of the coat over and examine the interfacing side. The lines of machine stitching should be exactly ¼ in. apart and end exactly on the outside vertical basting lines. This is your chance to perfect the buttonhole. If the lines aren't straight and even, remove the stitches and begin the process again. When the two lines are perfect, pull threads to the interfacing side and tie them, but leave them long. If you want to cord the folds, use a blunt needle to pass the cord or yarn through each fold. Trim the ends even with the patch.

On the wrong side of the coat front, remove the interfacing from the area of the buttonhole, using small, sharp-pointed scissors. The cleared area should be a rectangle. Be careful to trim to the corner without clipping the thread ends.

On the right side, remove the basting and cut *only* the buttonhole patch lengthwise through the center. On the wrong side, cut the cloth between the parallel rows of stitching and diagonally to corners. You'll have to work quickly before the triangles at the corners fray and unravel.

Push the patch halves through the slash to the wrong side of the coat, tugging at the knotted long threads to make neat corners. Using your fingers, press and position the lips of the buttonhole into place and catch-stitch the lips closed on the right side. On the wrong side, place a treated press cloth over the buttonhole area and steam-press it.

With the coat interfacing side down, lift the coat until you can see the triangles at the ends of the slash. Use short machine stitches or hand stitching to stitch the triangles to the patch, again pulling on the long threads to line up the triangles and to make sure you catch the edges. Trim the edges of the patch even; then fell-stitch it to the interfacing. After you've finished all the buttonholes, remove the basting. Turn the coat to the right side and, using matching thread, stitch all four sides of the finished buttonhole rectangles with small blind stitches to stabilize them.

On the facing, mark the ends of the buttonholes with pins. Slash the facing between the pins, turn under the cut edges, and hand-stitch in place behind the buttonholes.□

Katherine Davis studied custom-tailoring methods with a British master tailor. She tailors only for women and gives courses in tailoring techniques and patternmaking at 802 Janice Dr., Annapolis, MD 21403.

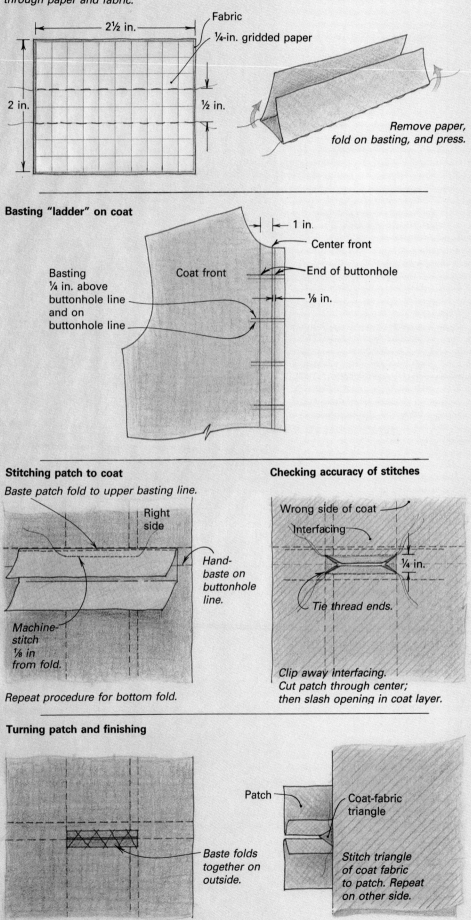

Making a bound buttonhole
(Procedures are for a 1-in.-long buttonhole.)

Cut buttonhole patches from grid paper.

Baste in contrasting thread through paper and fabric.

Fabric
¼-in. gridded paper
2½ in.
2 in.
½ in.

Remove paper, fold on basting, and press.

Basting "ladder" on coat

1 in.
Center front
Coat front
End of buttonhole
Basting ¼ in. above buttonhole line and on buttonhole line
⅛ in.

Stitching patch to coat

Baste patch fold to upper basting line.
Right side
Hand-baste on buttonhole line.
Machine-stitch ⅛ in from fold.

Repeat procedure for bottom fold.

Checking accuracy of stitches

Wrong side of coat
Interfacing
¼ in.
Tie thread ends.

Clip away interfacing. Cut patch through center; then slash opening in coat layer.

Turning patch and finishing

Baste folds together on outside.

Patch
Coat-fabric triangle
Stitch triangle of coat fabric to patch. Repeat on other side.

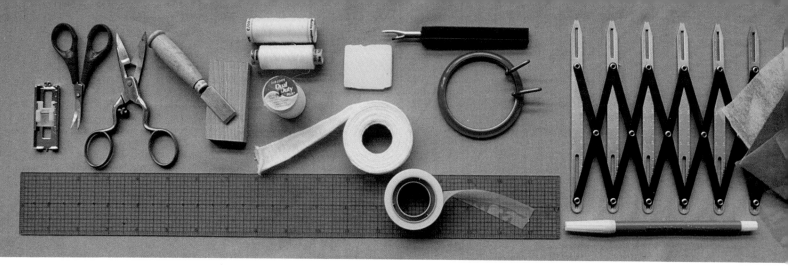

Beating the Buttonhole Blues

How to get the best from your machine

by Robbie Fanning

Some send their almost-finished garments home to Mom; others take them to an alterations shop; still others choose only zippered, snapped, or pullover patterns. Fear of making lousy buttonholes is widespread. Is a poor buttonhole the machine or the operator's fault? The answer depends on the machine, the thread, and the fabric. Once you understand how these elements interact, you should make better buttonholes or have reason to blame poor ones on your machine.

The machine—Aware of the home sewer's buttonhole phobia, manufacturers of sewing machines have been perfecting buttonhole automation for the last 30 years. First came a one-step buttonhole that didn't require the garment to be turned. Then came simplicity of stitch selection. Instead of moving a stitch-width dial back and forth four times, the operator punched a button once or twice. Next, a slot for the button was added to the buttonhole foot so the length of the opening didn't have to be measured.

Today, the ultimate buttonhole automation is found on top-of-the-line computer machines. Punch one button, tell the machine how long to make the buttonhole, and put it in memory. The machine will make the same buttonhole over and over.

You can still make a poor buttonhole on a computer machine—the bead length may be uneven, the thread may be too fat for the needle or fabric, the grain may be off, the fabric may pucker, or the distance be-

tween the beads may be so close that when you cut open the buttonhole, you slice the threads of the bead.

Start to make better buttonholes by using the correct foot—a buttonhole foot with two parallel grooves on its underside. Your machine makes a buttonhole by zigzagging down one side and then the other, in a forward direction for one bead, in reverse for the other. The parallel grooves enable the machine to move smoothly over the first bead of zigzag stitches without jamming.

A machine is more likely to make uneven stitches zigzagging backward than forward. If you tug on the fabric, or if the foot must climb over part of a seam allowance, the stitches may wobble. A sliding buttonhole foot (see photo above), which clamps onto the fabric and remains stationary while a foot within the foot slides up and down the buttonhole, solves this problem. If your dealer doesn't have one for your machine, determine if you have a high- or low-shank machine (distance from center of screw that holds on presser foot to bottom of foot when it's in down position is about ½ in. for a low-shank and 1 in. for a high-shank machine). Machines with similar shanks can sometimes use the same accessories.

In most cases, you'll have a better buttonhole if you loosen the top-thread tension a bit (not all machines allow this adjustment). This causes the satin stitch to form a nice mound on top and prevents the bobbin thread from drawing in the fabric underneath to form an unsightly tun-

nel. If the neck of shirts, blouses, or lapels will lie open, however, the underside of the buttonhole will show. Tighten the top tension so the loops don't show on the bottom, or stitch that buttonhole underside up.

One factor over which you often have no control is the distance between the two beads. If the beads are too close on your machine, you can use the correct foot and needle, choose the correct thread and interfacing, stitch the perfect buttonhole, and still slice the threads of the beads when you cut open the buttonhole. On computer machines, you can adjust the bead width, but the distance between the beads, which is programmed into a chip, can't be changed. On some mechanical machines, the dealer may be able to make a calibration adjustment to increase the distance slightly.

When you're buying a new machine, don't be distracted by a smooth, satiny bead—most good machines can be fine-tuned to produce one. Look, instead, at the distance between the beads, and ask the demonstrator to cut open the buttonhole.

The closeness of the stitches is a personal choice. The stitches in ready-to-wear buttonholes look more like loose zigzags than satin stitches. Consider how your garment will be used and how its fibers will hold up. For a closely woven shirt that will be washed and worn often, for example, you may want to put a fusible interfacing in the buttonhole area and use a close zigzag.

After the foot, the most important part of your machine is the needle. By the time

From *Threads* magazine (December 1989) 26:60-63

Buttonhole-making tools: sliding buttonhole foot, raised-tip scissors, buttonhole scissors, buttonhole chisel, machine-embroidery threads, Clo-Chalk, Surgitube, removable tape, seam ripper, machine-embroidery hoop, Simplex gauge, tear-away, water-soluble stabilizer, test samples, C-Thru ruler, water-soluble marker. (Photo by Mary Galpin Barnes)

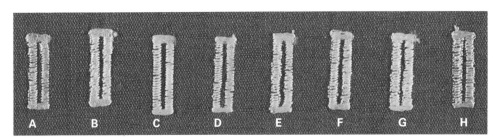

For comparison, Robbie Fanning made the same buttonhole with different threads. From left: (A) Mettler, 50/3, cotton; (B) DMC, size 50, cotton; (C) Metrosene Plus, 100/3, polyester; (D) Dual Duty, extra-fine machine-embroidery, cotton-wrapped polyester; (E) Gutermann, polyester; (F) Dual Duty, regular, cotton-wrapped polyester; (G) Molnlycke, polyester; (H) Belding Corticelli, size A, silk. Shown 1½ times enlarged.

you're ready for buttonholes, you've probably sewn for hours with the same needle. It may have become dull or gotten nicks from sewing over pins. To prevent dropped stitches or glitches in the bead, use a new, sharp needle, preferably a size 70 (10/11) or 80 (12), depending on the base fabric.

The thread—A fine thread is the secret to attractive buttonholes. Imagine hand-embroidering a satin stitch with all six strands of floss; it would look lumpy. On a miniature scale, the machine-made buttonhole is similar. You can lay in more strands of a fine machine-embroidery thread than of, say, regular cotton-covered polyester. (Most dealers load demonstration machines with machine-embroidery threads like Zwicky, DMC, and Mettler, because they handle a zigzag, a satin stitch, and decorative stitches well.) To make a keyhole buttonhole look handmade, however, use a topstitching thread or silk twist, with a sharp size 90 (14) needle. The photo above shows buttonholes stitched with eight different threads.

If your machine doesn't allow you to loosen top tension, try a heavier thread, like Dual Duty, in the bobbin and a fine thread on top. This will produce the same result—pulling the top thread slightly to the underside.

Some people recommend rayon machine-embroidery thread for buttonholes, but I don't like it. If you don't have a horizontal spindle, it tends to slip off the spool and twist around the spindle, causing jerks in the satin stitch or thread breakage. Its shine draws the eye to the buttonhole, it isn't strong, and it's slippery, so threads break or come unlocked. If you want to use it, however, buy a box of Surgitube, a tubular gauze bandage, from the drugstore. Slice off 1-in. tubes and place them on the rayon-thread spool. The thread will be released evenly without falling to the bottom. (This also works on serger thread.)

The fabric—When you delve into the mysteries of buttonholes, you learn to respect fabric grain. Buttonholes stitched parallel to the lengthwise grain of the fabric and the interfacing grain will nestle around the button. Those stitched cross grain, however, may stretch, sag, and ripple, allowing button to escape at stress points.

Women often automatically change vertical buttonholes on blouse patterns to horizontal so the buttons will have less propensity to pop out. Yet, this change can cause the very problem it was intended to solve, unless the buttonhole is stabilized.

The easiest way to avoid stretching the buttonhole, regardless of grain direction, is to put a stabilizer under it during stitching. You can use typing-weight paper, wax paper, or water-soluble or tear-away nonwoven stabilizer. Tear-away pulls away easily from the garment, provided you work slowly. It will leave a white cast to the buttonhole until the garment is washed, and sometimes even after washing. For neckline buttonholes that may be turned back, use two layers of water-soluble stabilizer instead.

A stabilizer also prevents tunneling—the bunching together of the fibers—on lightweight fabrics. The fibers tend to pull together, creating a small tunnel under the zigzag stitches that is released in a pucker at either end of the buttonhole. Adding a nonwoven stabilizer temporarily fools the fabric into being medium-weight to heavyweight; yet there's no stiffness after the tear-away is removed. Alternatively, if there's room at the garment edge, you can use a small machine-embroidery hoop to hold the fabric absolutely taut for each buttonhole.

The base fabric generally determines the buttonhole style. Lightweight wovens usually call for a standard buttonhole with a bar tack at each end and a narrow bead and short length (because the buttons are usually small and delicate). However, machine buttonholes are generally calibrated for medium-weight wovens and thus have a wider bead than you might want. If your machine offers it, try a rounded-end buttonhole for horizontal placement on medium-weight fabrics, putting the rounded end closest to center front or back.

The problem with knit fabrics is that the buttonholes may stretch and ripple. Since knits don't ravel, you can use a more open zigzag. Better yet, use a stretch overlock buttonhole (for extra security on single knits you can add a cord to the buttonhole).

When making buttonhole placement or alignment changes, consider both fabric grain direction and garment design; vertical buttonholes create a more pronounced

vertical element. Don't automaticallly change the placement of buttonholes on bodices so that one buttonhole falls at the bustline stress point. This may backfire because the next button up may be too high to be comfortable or attractive when buttoned. The remedy is to learn to alter patterns so that you have enough ease in the bustline. Then you can put the buttons where the designer intended, avoiding popping buttons and gaping center fronts.

If you foresee trouble with the buttonholes, change your pattern. I've never had luck making buttonholes in cotton ribbing, so I change the closure to snaps or to fake buttoning (I sew on buttons but don't make buttonholes and never close the garment). Or, if the garment will fit over my head, I close it at the waist, sew it together invisibly, and put fake buttoning on top.

Measuring, marking, and cutting—I usually follow buttonhole-placement guidelines on the pattern, but not length markings. Buttonhole length is determined by the diameter and thickness of your button. Following Claire Shaeffer's method, I measure the button, using a buttonhole measuring strip, as shown in the drawing on p. 54.

While the Simplex tool for measuring buttonhole spacing is useful, I am habit-bound. I lay the pattern tissue over my garment on the ironing board and push pins through the centerline of each buttonhole marking. Then I lift off the tissue and secure the pins in the garment perpendicular to the buttonhole line. I find the midpoint on my buttonhole measuring strip by bringing the fold to the pin and creasing. I align this crease line to the pin on the garment and mark the two ends of each buttonhole.

I always use a C-Thru ruler so I can mark precise distances from the front edge, parallel or perpendicular to the edge. I draw the ends of the buttonhole wide enough so I can see them on either side of my buttonhole sliding foot when it reaches them.

The marking tool you use depends on the smoothness and color of the fabric and the way your machine makes buttonholes: You must be able to see the marks when you're stitching. for example, in the Viking sample (photo, p. 54), I drew a line of disappearing chalk, but since the Viking starts

Machine buttonholes compared

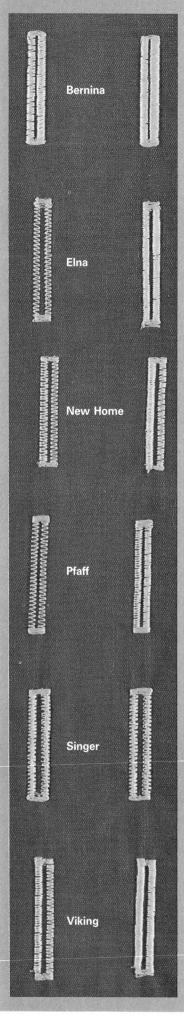

You'd think all machines would make buttonholes the same way, but they don't—some stitch down the left side and up the right; some do the reverse; some never stitch backward. Here's a rundown of the ordinary bar-tack buttonhole from six top-of-the-line computer machines. I used Metrosene Plus in the top and in the bobbin and a size 80 (12) needle on each. The fabric is backed with Stacy's iron-on Shirt-Fuse, plus a layer of tear-away stabilizer.

I made the first column of buttonholes in the photo at left at the automatic setting. To make those in the second column, I adjusted the stitch length to achieve a denser bead, which I prefer. The setting numbers for stitch width (W) and length (L) on computer machines are in millimeters. (On mechanical machines, the settings aren't measurements; the number 1 on one machine could be a very different setting from the number 1 on another.)

All machines except the Bernina 1130 can make other types of automatic buttonholes (keyhole, rounded-end, etc.) and other sizes of bar tacks. All but the Singer 6268 can adjust the widths of bar-tacked ones.

Bernina 1130. The stitch pattern is straightforward, and the stitch length and width are infinitely adjustable. I shortened the stitch length for the left bead. On the right bead, I pushed the "+" button once (push it after the first bar tack; otherwise, the stitches will pile up). The distance between beads seems close. The instructions and graphics are clear.

Elna 7000. The automatic setting is W 4.4, L .4, but I used L .1. Elna recommends that you reduce the speed setting. Making both beads even takes practice because the first stitch is backward; the machine has a fine-tuner to help. Practice with lines drawn on your sample so you can gauge where to start and how to line up the second bead. The computer graphics are clear and easy.

New Home Memorycraft 7000. The automatic setting is W 4, L .45, but I used L .3. The 7000 has two buttonhole feet, a sliding foot with a photosensor laser that allows for the thickness of the button and a foot that memorizes a length and repeats it. The stitch pattern requires stitching backward, so it's easy to misalign the buttonholes. Practice with lines drawn on your sample. The other buttonhole foot allows you to fine-tune the right bead with a "+/-" dial. The bead in the sample needs to be tightened, but I couldn't move the dial on the machine that I borrowed. An automatic tension regulator precludes loosening the top tension. There's one clearly marked button to push.

Pfaff 1473 CD. The automatic setting is W 4.5, L .5, but I used L .3. The sliding foot grasps the fabric, and the stitch pattern is straightforward. The manual suggests stitching slowly and reducing the top tension; the machine automatically slows at the bar tack. Without looking at the manual, you'd never figure out how to manually set the stitch width and length the first time. After that, it's easy. One subtlety: The centerline of the foot isn't the centerline of the stitched buttonhole.

Singer 6268. The stitch pattern is strange. The fabric is clamped securely between two long plates. The length is set behind the foot, where a button sits (markings on your fabric wouldn't help). You can't override the width or density of the bead. The guide in the lower plate prevents stitching a buttonhole more than 1¼ in. from the right side unless you fold the fabric. The instructions are easy.

Viking 990. The automatic setting is W 5, L .4; I used L.3, the only other option. Because of the stitch pattern, the buttonhole's centerline is obscured by the foot, so it's easy to make a crooked buttonhole. It ties off with three small stitches at the left side. The instructions are very clear. –R.F.

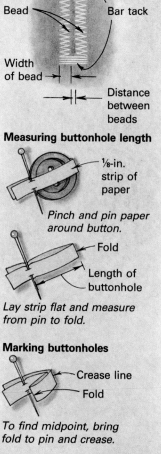

Machine buttonhole

Bead — Bar tack

Width of bead —

Distance between beads

Measuring buttonhole length

⅛-in. strip of paper

Pinch and pin paper around button.

Fold

Length of buttonhole

Lay strip flat and measure from pin to fold.

Marking buttonholes

Crease line

Fold

To find midpoint, bring fold to pin and crease.

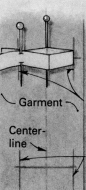

Align crease line with pin in garment, marking centerline of buttonhole.

Garment

Mark ends of buttonhole.

Center-line

Buttonhole length marked on garment

Mail-order sources

(The first three offer a free catalog.)

Clotilde
1909 S.W. First Ave.
Ft. Lauderdale, FL 33315
(305) 761-8655
Schmetz needles, Clo-Chalk.

Nancy's Notions
Box 683, Beaver Dam, WI 53916
(414) 887-0391
Buttonhole foot, chisel.

Sewing Emporium
1079 Third Ave.
Chula Vista, CA 92010
(619) 420-3490
Automatic buttonholer, sliding foot.

Treadleart
25834-I Narbonne Ave.
Lomita, CA 90717; (213) 534-5122
Janome automatic buttonholer; catalog, $1.50 (refundable).

at the front end and stitches backward, I couldn't see where I was going and stitched a crooked buttonhole. A better marking method for this machine would be a line of removable tape to guide the foot along.

On smooth, mid- to dark-value fabrics I use Clo-Chalk, a disappearing white chalk with a sharp edge. On light fabrics I use a water-soluble marking pen. People who have more time than I baste their guidelines.

Stitch your buttonhole slowly, with a light hand on the fabric. Arrange the garment so it will move smoothly over the needle plate, with nothing dragging the fabric away from the needle. Let the machine do its job without your pulling on the fabric. On the best machines, you don't have to touch the fabric once you've positioned the foot.

Before cutting the stitched buttonhole, stroke the area several times with the back of a seam ripper. Then insert it from the bar tack to the center of the buttonhole and rip. Repeat for the other end. You can also fold the buttonhole in half and make a snip between the beads with scissors; then cut to each bar tack. Place a pin perpendicular to the inner side of the bar tacks so you don't cut too far. You can also use buttonhole scissors. A section cut away from the blades lets you position the scissors at the garment edge and cut only in the buttonhole (works best on horizontal buttonholes), and a screw adjusts the length of the cut. The best cutting device is a buttonhole chisel. Place the wooden block under the buttonhole and push the chisel through the buttonhole for a clean cut. If the buttonhole is shorter than the chisel, position the fabric over the edge of the wooden block and cut one half at a time.

Test, test, test—Now you're ready to plunge in, but first set up a test situation identical to the garment—same grain direction as on garment and interfacing, same thread in top and bobbin that you'll use, same stabilizer underneath, and same seam situation. If your buttonholes are ⅝ in. from, and parallel to, the center front, will half the buttonhole foot ride on the trimmed seam allowance as you stitch one side of the buttonhole? If so, it may affect the quality of the stitches, especially on computer machines. Some computer machines count the number of stitches per buttonhole, not the desired buttonhole length. If stitches pile up because of a hidden seam allowance or bulk at a garment edge, that side of the buttonhole may be shorter than the other. Sometimes you can rig a shim out of folded fabric or a thin note pad so the two sides of the foot are evenly raised. Once you think that you've set your computer machine to the correct length, test twice more before tackling the garment.

After stitching the buttonhole, clip the top threads; then yank a little on the bobbin threads to pull the top threads to the back. Use sharp- or curved-pointed scissors to trim close to the stitching. Tweezers help hold the thread taut. Cut open the test buttonhole and slip the button through. This will reveal any problems with length, width, stitch density, or fraying fabric in the hole area. Here's how to correct or disguise fraying:

1. If the area is accessible on the garment, slip a rectangle of fusible web between fabric and facing at each buttonhole; stitch the buttonhole and place it right side down on a towel. Using a wet press cloth over each buttonhole, lock the threads of the beads and fuse the fabric fibers.
2. Put No-Fray on the buttonhole back.
3. Darken the white edges of the interfacing peeking out in the buttonhole area with a permanent marking pen in the color of the garment.

Write on your test samples in pen what you've tried so you'll learn the quirks of your machine. Sew an extra button onto the sample and put it in your sewing notebook with a notation on fiber content, interfacing, thread, and pattern number.

If you make a buttonhole that's too short, too long, or unattractive, cut the stitches on the back side with sharp scissors or your ripper. The thread on the top side should lift off easily. Then use removable tape to lift off the small thread ends and fuzz. Put fresh stabilizer under the buttonhole and stitch a narrow zigzag around the hole. Slowly stitch a second, wider satin stitch around, letting the needle swing off the fabric into the hole with each stitch.

If you conclude that your poor buttonholes are your machine's fault, here's what you can do: Have your buttonholes made; they'll cost about $.75 to $1 each. Join the American Sewing Guild and make friends with better machines than yours. Make a concealed buttonhole flap to hide your buttonholes. Sew buttons on top, but don't make buttonholes; put snaps behind the buttons. Change the buttons to heavy-duty gripper snaps. Use your intended pattern, but add a seam at center front; leave areas unstitched for buttons to come through. Hand-stitch corded piping to the front edge, leaving unstitched areas for the buttons to slip through. Learn to make bound or faced buttonholes. Let Mom make your buttonholes with her good old template buttonholer.

Two last bits of advice: Your buttonhole can't properly close around a button sewn without a shank. If you machine-sew buttons on, tape a toothpick to the top of the button and finish the shank by winding the thread tails around it. Finally, be easy on yourself. Except on jackets that you remove, few people notice your buttonholes, unless threads are hanging off. Trim them. ☐

Robbie Fanning is a contributing editor of Threads. *She thanks Copp's Sew Smart and Douglas Fabrics, both in Palo Alto, CA; New York Fabrics in Cupertino and Menlo Park, CA; and The Quilting Bee in Los Angeles, CA, for the use of their machines.*

An alternative to automatic buttonholes
by David Page Coffin

After watching my machine (a mechanical Pfaff 1229) make buttonholes for me a few hundred times, I realized that it wasn't doing anything much—just picking two different zigzag widths and three needle positions and cranking them out in the right order. I'd always wanted the buttonholes narrower, with less space in the middle (fewer threads to clip and snag), so I decided to try improving on the built-in buttonhole by adjusting the preset parameters and running through the steps manually. I was delighted by the results (see photo above).

The key to my success is that on my machine I can adjust the needle position exactly where I want it; I'm not restricted to a few settings, or to ½ mm clicks. If you can't make precise needle-position adjustments on your machine, it will be harder to fine-tune your buttonholes.

I mark the ends of the buttonhole and start with a centered bar tack about half the width of the preset one on my machine and narrower than the finished buttonhole. I adjust the stitch length to satin stitch and make two stitches forward and two backward. This creates a sort of rounded bar tack when the thread is machine-embroidery cotton, which I always use for buttonholes. Then I switch to my narrowest zigzag and to a right-of-center needle position. Determining exactly how far right is the critical part; once I established the position on either side of center that would give me the narrowest cuttable gap, I marked the settings on the needle-position dial with tiny dots of white-out.

After I've finished the right side, I make the rounded, centered bar tack again, then switch into reverse and to my left-hand needle position. At the top, I tie off by making a few very short straight stitches, but I do them in the center, on top of the bar tack, so they're invisible, and they hold the starting stitches too.

With all my machine settings marked, I can make a buttonhole as fast now as the machine used to do on its own, and it's a much nicer one.

David Page Coffin is an associate editor of Threads.

How Madame Grès Sculpts with Fabric

Her simple shapes, bias-draped and pleated, have made her the grande dame of elegance

by Arlene Cooper

the couture salon of Alix Grès is located in a lovely old Parisian building on the rue de la Paix, overlooking the Place Vendôme. I enter Maison Grès from an elevator off a courtyard. All is white, serene, austere, elegant, with high ceilings and large windows. The elevator is flanked by niches into which life-sized classical sculptures of women have been set. I wait on a white leather sofa for Madame Grès to descend from the atelier. She has the walk and carriage of a middle-aged woman, and while she is inches shorter than my own 5 ft. 2½ in., she conveys none of the frailty one reads about. Her face is lively, her eyes really wonderful. She is wearing her usual turban and an angora-jersey skirt and sweater over a cashmere turtleneck. Her voice is full, rather low. As she enters the room, she issues a reminder: She has only 15 minutes to spare before meeting a client. She doesn't make herself comfortable when she sits down to my right, on the edge of the sofa. In 19 minutes, she'll be gone, murmuring regrets.

I have traveled to wintry Paris in April, having submitted in advance the questions I intend to ask Madame Grès. A shy and fiercely private person, her aversion to interviews is well known. Forewarned of the brevity of the interview, I dare ask only about her design process and how she works with fabric. Her desire to accommodate me is evident in her answers.

Madame Grès's fame rests mainly on the draped and pleated silk-jersey or chiffon evening gowns in the classical mode that she has been creating for over 50 years. Her work is known for its prodigious use of luxury fabrics in a personal method that is both time- and labor-intensive and virtually impossible to copy, but her work provides inspiration for anyone who makes clothes and loves fabric.

Her career—Madame Grès was born to a bourgeois Parisian family. Her father was an industrialist named Barton. (Both *Alix* and *Grès* are assumed names; *Alix* was invented to replace a detested first name and years later *Grès* was borrowed from her husband—an anagram for his given name, which he used for his work as a sculptor.) She was brought up strictly and as a child was taught dance, music, and art, especially sculpture. She dreamed of becoming a sculptress, but that was not considered proper for a girl at that time, so she turned to making what she called "living sculptures" and thus started dressmaking, she says, "without knowing it." The improvisational nature that characterizes so much of Madame Grès's work thus had early roots.

She began watching and emulating the work of a family friend who was employed at a fashion house. After sketching and studying cutting for three months, Madame Grès began making toiles (draped and sewn fabric patterns) to earn her living. Because of her original, sculptural approach, her designs sold very well. Encouraged by a well-connected friend of the family, she showed the toiles to the Commissionaires of the Chambre Syndicale, and although she burst into tears of nervousness before them, they were impressed enough to permit her to establish herself as a couturière.

In 1934, with the same family friend as a business partner, she opened Alix Barton Couture at 83, rue de Faubourg St. Honoré. Her work was greeted with enthusiasm. The March 1934 issue of *Paris Vogue* carried an advertisement announcing the opening, and in May *L'Art et la Mode* featured an Alix gown and evening coat on its cover. The first collections consisted of daywear and satin or brocade evening gowns. It was not until her third collection, when Madame Grès had been inspired by the beauty of a silk-jersey fabric she had ordered, that the draped and pleated evening gowns for which she is best known first appeared.

Her unique approach to dressmaking led to meteoric success. Her innovations produced clothes of exceptional beauty, prized for their sumptuous fabrics, their good taste and originality, their great simplicity, and their enhancement of the wearer. "No woman is physically perfect," she says, "nor is she perfectly hopeless. Each has her own share of beauty. . . . I like to make a body look beautiful, to enhance its qualities, to make a waist look thinner, a bust higher; I want people to guess about the shape underneath." Small wonder that her designs were sought by wealthy, fashionable women.

In 1941 she left Maison Alix and fled wartime Paris with her infant daughter. When she returned in 1942, she was persuaded by Lucien Lelong, then president of the Chambre Syndicale, to open her own couture house. Maison Grès opened at 1, rue de la Paix, and Madame Grès's 1942 collection was in the French national colors: red, white, and blue. It was closed by the Germans for a time during World War II, but Maison Grès is still at the rue de la Paix address (although her July 1986 collection was shown at the Jacques Esterel showroom on rue de Faubourg St. Honoré).

Today, as 50 years ago, Alix Grès herself produces her couture collections. It is she who works with the fabric manufacturers. At the beginning of each season they bring samples of their new collections to her and she selects what she likes. She is then presented with books of samples, from which she narrows down her choices, and the fabrics are delivered to the workroom. It is she who decides what the collection will include—a process of inspiration rather than of planning; she who drapes the fabric on live models, makes the toiles, and supervises the workroom staff and fittings. And it is she who travels with the collection to New York and Tokyo to ensure that her devoted clients have access to her clothes.

Madame Grès's contribution to *haute couture* is a legacy of timeless clothes. What every sewer can learn from her is an awareness of the special qualities of each fabric, plus a willingness to experiment and use fabric in unconventional ways that enhance its essence. One need not be an expert dressmaker; a beginner may improvise too, as Madame Grès herself suggests. "What I was doing was new," she told Ingrid Bleich-

From *Threads* magazine (April 1987) 10:50-55

roeder in an interview. "I didn't know the *métier*—sewing, cutting. Ignorance is a very important thing—it has purity and innocence. It leads you to try things that others wouldn't dare attempt. In the beginning there were minor inconveniences: The dress would look *magnifique,* but I wouldn't know if the poor lady would be able to lift an arm or sit down all evening."

Her approach—Alix Grès's passion for fabric and her aversion to cutting it are as central to her work as is her background as a sculptress. In an interview with Ben Brantley (*Women's Wear Daily,* November 7, 1979), she said, "From the beginning I didn't want to do what others were doing in any way; I wasn't able to because I didn't have the knowledge. That was one reason I took the material and worked directly on it. I used the knowledge I had, which was sculpture." Although she considers essential the presence of a live model on whom to drape, while in the mountains during the war, she made her own dummies with hay, some wood, and a tin. She bought fabric from the market and continued to drape clothes.

She told Bleichroeder: "By touching a piece of fabric..., it is possible to know its soul, its character. While I drape a mannequin with silk, it reacts between my hands, and I try to understand and judge its reactions. Thus, I give a dress I create the line and form the fabric itself wishes to take. ...By touching it [the fabric], I know what I am doing, but I can't make it do what it doesn't want to do. There is a complicity, like a perfect marriage."

Madame Grès speaks with great pleasure of the extraordinary fabrics that used to be made in Europe. In 1938, for instance, Bianchini produced a gold-and-silver silk lamé with Persian miniatures at the rate of a few inches per day. When *haute couture* was very important, she says, the fabrics were exclusive to each house, but now only the manufacturers of ready-to-wear clothes command enough yardage to justify the production of exclusives.

An extra-wide silk jersey became known as "Alix jersey" in honor of Madame Grès because she was the first to use it for dresses rather than underwear and because she was instrumental in its development. Madame Grès told me that both Monsieur Calcombet and Monsieur Rodier, jersey manufacturers, used to tease her during the height of her popularity by asserting that she used enough jersey to surround the world. Later she would be equally innovative in her use of faille, taffeta (which she draped and puffed), and djersakasha, a cashmere jersey, which was the predecessor of angora

Here, in one of her more formal, close-fitting garments, which she made in the '50s, Madame Grès has draped and puffed taffeta to create a cocktail dress that she calls "paper-taffeta." Photo courtesy of L'Officiel de la Couture et de la Mode.

jersey. Djersakasha was woven as a tube, so Madame Grès could use it without seams.

Before it becomes a Grès design, fabric is draped into pleats, folds, or smooth areas and then stitched into place, usually with X-like tacking stitches. Only then is it cut. "The cutting process is all-important," Madame Grès says. "When preparing a collection, I always use up three pairs of scissors." Ordinarily, the entire process is executed first on a toile Madame Grès makes herself, which is then fitted and pinned on a mannequin. Madame Grès is unique in her limiting of the number of seams. "I have always respected the body structure and the natural movement of a given material. I limit the number of seams in order to give a better impression of freedom, of suppleness of the silhouette."

The next step is fitting the garment fabric itself on a live model. Then the piece is sent to the appropriate workshop for assembly and finish sewing: one for tailored clothes like coats and suits, two others called the "soft" workshops for dresses, evening gowns, and so forth.

Her designs and constructions—The technique of constructing clothes with pieces cut on the bias was devised by Madeleine Vionnet in 1926. It led to simplified forms of dress that conformed to the curves of the body. By the early 1930s, when Alix Grès began her couture career, it was the prevailing mode in both *haute couture* and *prêt-à-porter* (ready-to-wear). Madame Grès

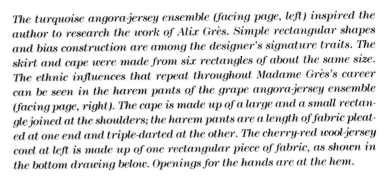

The turquoise angora-jersey ensemble (facing page, left) inspired the author to research the work of Alix Grès. Simple rectangular shapes and bias construction are among the designer's signature traits. The skirt and cape were made from six rectangles of about the same size. The ethnic influences that repeat throughout Madame Grès's career can be seen in the harem pants of the grape angora-jersey ensemble (facing page, right). The cape is made up of a large and a small rectangle joined at the shoulders; the harem pants are a length of fabric pleated at one end and triple-darted at the other. The cherry-red wool-jersey cowl at left is made up of one rectangular piece of fabric, as shown in the bottom drawing below. Openings for the hands are at the hem.

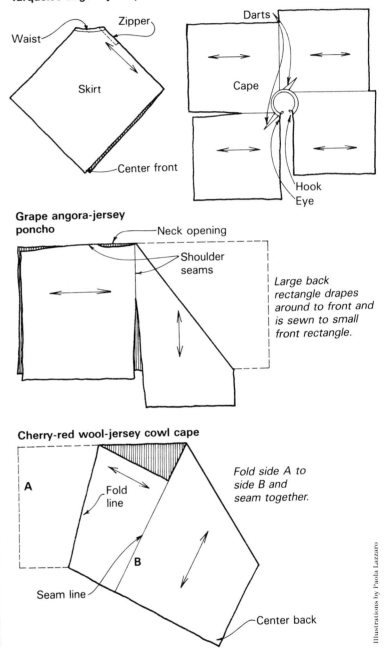

Turquoise angora-jersey ensemble

Waist — Zipper
Skirt
Center front

Darts
Cape
Hook
Eye

Grape angora-jersey poncho

Neck opening
Shoulder seams

Large back rectangle drapes around to front and is sewn to small front rectangle.

Cherry-red wool-jersey cowl cape

A
Fold line
B

Fold side A to side B and seam together.

Seam line
Center back

Illustrations by Paola Lazzaro

made the technique her own and became one of its greatest advocates. Even through the 1960s and 1970s, when very structured and highly constructed boxy clothes were prevalent, she continued to work with the bias technique, modifying and reworking earlier experiments. Her pieces were cut on the bias or on the straight grain and used on the bias. The bias-cut dresses of the 1930s followed the lines of the figure, but Madame Grès also found ways to use bias to skim the body rather than cling to it.

Many of the designs of Madame Grès are based on simple concepts. Those familiar with Dorothy Burnham's book *Cut My Cote* and the work of Max Tilke will recognize the relationship of Grès's pieces to regional costume. Both have a high regard for fabric and a desire to use a loom width with the least possible amount of desecration.

The turquoise angora-jersey ensemble shown in the left photo on the facing page and in the top drawing above is different in every respect from the labor-intensive

gowns that were for me synonymous with the name Alix Grès. The gowns are formal, body-hugging, and of very light, smooth silk jersey; this simple ensemble is informal, body-skimming, and of a heavier, textured jersey. I love it for both its tactile appeal and its economy of design.

The skirt and cape were constructed from six almost-square rectangles of nearly equal size. The skirt consists of two rectangles, and a corner of each rectangle has been cut away in a curve to form the waist. The

Alix Grès. Photo by her daughter.

A panel of cartridge pleating is attached to the top of the lined bodice of this gray-blue dress and is left open at the sides. The overlap conceals the hook-and-eye closure at the V of the neckline. More pleating is attached with twill tape at the hipline and stitched to the skirt a few inches below the hipline. The pleats then open to give the skirt its fullness.

two rectangles are then seamed on each side of the waist with a zipper inset into the left side seam, and the waistline is finished with self-binding. The rectangles are cut on the straight grain so that the bias points fall at the center front and center back. The cape is constructed of four rectangles and is fashioned on the same principle as the skirt: cut on the straight grain with curved cutouts at the corners for the neck. Since the cutouts are attached to a self-fabric neckband, they are given darts or eased so that they conform to the roundness of the shoulders. The hook-and-eye closure is at the left side of the neck, and the four bias points fall at the center front, the center back, and the sides. The pieces are hemmed all around, except where they are seamed for 8 in. on the right shoulder and 14 in. on the left shoulder and at center back. Madame Grès's seams are usually pressed open and hand-finished with overcast stitching, while hems are frequently narrow and machine-stitched.

In addition to its use of straight-grain pieces on the bias, the ensemble, dating back to the '70s, illustrates another important Grès trait: the creative reworking throughout her career of a single theme—in this instance, capes. In October of 1934, the publication *Femmina* heralded, "We will have capes. . . ." It featured an Alix ensemble of a gray cape over a gray jersey blouse and black satin skirt from the second Alix collection. The same issue also featured cape-and-skirt ensembles by other designers; Alix Grès was not unique in designing them. She was, however, unique in continuing to design them throughout her career without regard to whether they were in fashion at any given moment. Indeed, Madame Grès's best work to this day has remained apart from fashion trends.

In the grape-colored angora-jersey ensemble shown in the right photo on page 58, the large rectangle at the back drapes around and is sewn to a small rectangle at the front in two places to form shoulders and a neck opening. Ethnic influences appear often in the work of Madame Grès. A 1935 *Harper's Bazaar* featured an Alix "Arabian" gown "with an oriental trouser skirt through which you thrust your burnished toes." This trouser skirt bears a striking resemblance to the wrap harem pants from the grape-colored angora-jersey ensemble. The pants are a slightly shaped length of fabric pleated at one end and triple-darted at each side of the other, drawn through the legs and fastened at the waist with narrow cloth bands.

The cherry-red wool-jersey cowl shown in the photo on page 59 is another of those simple-once-you-know-what's-happening designs, but in fact, its construction is most difficult to analyze. The garment is made up of one very slightly shaped rectangular length of fabric. Its front, which has openings for the hands at the hem, can be draped high or cowled low. The one seam is on a diagonal in the back, and the resulting bias point falls low at the center back (see bottom drawing, page 59).

It's impossible to discuss the designs of Madame Grès without also discussing one of her signature details: pleating. The bodice of the gray-blue dress shown at left is on the bias in front, with a draped asymmetrical V-neckline and narrow dolman sleeves. Attached to the lined bodice is a panel of cartridge pleating that begins above the bustline, forming the top of a heart shape, and extends to below the bust. The pleated bust panel is stitched to the bodice at its top and is open at both sides. The overlap of the applied panel conceals the hook-and-eye front closure that begins at the V of the neckline and continues on the left to the hipline. From the bottom of the bust, a V-shaped inset extends to the hipline, where the cartridge pleating repeats. The V-shaped inset is stitched at the right and open at the left side. The pleating, which is on the straight grain, is attached with twill tape a few inches below the hipline, stitched to the skirt 3 in. to 4 in. below the attachment, and then released, giving the skirt its fullness in front. The back neckline has a characteristic Grès V-shape.

In the right-hand photo on the facing page and in the drawing is a garment that is gathered at the shoulder, created for Diana Vreeland, and made of a variegated black-and-white-striped lightweight silk. The drama of the dress is enhanced by the way in which the striped fabric emphasizes the straight grain and bias. In the usual Grès manner, the gathers at the shoulder are stitched to a ribbon attached inside the shoulder seam.

Sometimes, for special clients like Diana Vreeland, Madame Grès deviates from her practice of making a toile first and works directly in the garment fabric. A bolt of cloth is brought in and unrolled, a corner of the cloth is tucked into the client's bra and pinned in place, and the draping process begins. With inimitable enthusiasm, Vreeland speaks about a Grès fitting. She adores being fitted, is in "another world" during a fitting, and always learns from the process. According to her, being fitted by Madame Grès is so extraordinary because an original garment is actually created on the body. □

Arlene Cooper, costume and textile historian, was assistant for the "Dance" exhibition, which was on view at the Metropolitan Museum of Art in September 1987. The garment at right on the facing page is from the collection of the Fashion Institute of Technology (FIT); all other garments are from the Costume Institute of the Metropolitan Museum. All photos by Brian Gulick, unless otherwise noted. Anyone who is interested in more of the work of Alix Grès should see L'Art de Madame Grès (Tokyo: Bunka Publishing Bureau, 1980. Edited by Sahoko Hata).

Above, this striped dress of natural-and-brown fleece has one major seam up the back on the left side, incorporating the closure. Auxiliary seams at the shoulders and across the back yoke allow for ease. The garment at right was made for Diana Vreeland. The striped silk fabric is gathered at the shoulder. The graphic visual impact is enhanced by the strategic use of straight-grain and bias-cut fabric.

Diana Vreeland's striped silk dress

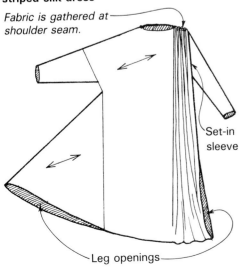

Fabric is gathered at shoulder seam.

Set-in sleeve

Leg openings

A Dressmaker Extraordinaire

Discovering the secrets of Madeleine Vionnet's creativity

by Betty Kirke

i remember when I first saw a dress by Madeleine Vionnet. I was walking through the galleries at the Costume Institute of The Metropolitan Museum of Art, having returned to work after vacation. I found a few mannequins dressed for the upcoming 1973-74 exhibition, *Inventive Clothing, 1909-1939.*

An evening gown with a skirt hem high in the front and low in the back caught my eye. "Oh," I said to my boss, the late Elizabeth Lawrence, who was dressing the mannequins, "that is copied from Balenciaga!" "Afraid not," she said, "Vionnet did it first." Examining the dress further, I found little self-roses around the neckline, a halter neck, a wrapped-waist—the dress could have been worn out that very evening. It was dated 1917.

I had to know more about this designer. In the library I read that she was born in 1876 and by age 13 was apprenticed to a dressmaker in a suburb of Paris. She advanced quickly and by her mid-teens had found a job in a Parisian house. In her late teens, she went to work in London for a dressmaker, Kate Reilly, who bought models each season from the French couture. Vionnet copied patterns from these garments and supervised making dresses in the current styles for individual clients.

When Vionnet returned home to Paris, she chose to work for the Callot Soeurs. She was assigned to work under one of the sisters, Mme. Gerber, who was responsible for the new models of the house. She stayed

Madeleine Vionnet (left) drapes a dress concept on her wooden doll in 1923. (Photo by Theresa Bonney.) The comfort and elegance of a halter neck, the functional ease of body-skimming bias cuts, and the precise details, such as the 153-seam velvet patchwork or the satin appliqué at right, were hallmarks of Vionnet's sensibilities. In her 20-year career, she created over 12,000 garments. (Photo by Maria Cosindas; collection of Union Française des Arts du Costume.)

From *Threads* magazine (February 1989) 21:66-73

Vionnet's midriff bodice twist (above) and her shoulder twist (left) control fullness, eliminate darts, and add a decorative touch. The dress, cut and seamed on the straight grain, hangs on the bias. (Midriff: Photo by Hideoki, courtesy of Kazuko Koike; collection of the Costume Institute of The Metropolitan Museum of Art. Dress: Photo by Cliff Ames; collection of UFAC.)

Rather than turn back the hem and risk ruining the eyelet pattern (right), Vionnet used a chain stitch to join the picot motifs. While most circular-cut skirt hems today hang out unevenly, this one hasn't, in 50 years. (Collection of The Edward C. Blum Design Laboratory.)

here for five years, refining her craftsmanship in cutting, fitting, and sewing dresses, until she was engaged by the head of the House of Doucet to create new models for his clients. She left Doucet in 1912 to open her own house. Possibly due to the onset of World War I, the house closed in 1914.

After the war, Vionnet reopened in the same place. Acceptance was there. By the early '20s, American clients were as numerous as the Europeans. She soon moved to larger quarters on Avenue Montaigne, where her work force grew to 1,200. She retired in 1939. Her most notable contributions were her bias cuts, halter necks, and dresses that slipped over the head. She worked out these ideas on a wooden doll.

That is what the history books have to say about Madeleine Vionnet. Upon examining more of her work, I saw clothing construction completely different from that of the other designers in the exhibition, all members of the French haute couture, and different from anything I had experienced as a garment designer and manufacturer. In each piece I discovered another way in which a garment could be put together, whether it was the shape of the pattern parts, the manipulation of the fabric for decoration and shaping, or the complete adherence to the principles of dressmaking. Everything was thought through to the smallest detail. Everything was precise.

Creating original models: Background—The literal translation of *haute couture* is "high-class sewing." What was sewn were dresses, copies of the original seasonal models that each house presented, made to order and to fit the individual client. Producing an original model is accomplished in three steps: conception and planning (sketching and draping), interpretation (patternmaking), and execution (cutting, fitting, seaming, and finishing).

At the Callot Soeurs and other couture houses in 1907 a new model was conceived improvisationally—the final fabric or a muslin was draped on a live mannequin. Draping was extemporaneous, not the formulaic system that the fashion industry thinks of as draping today. Patternmaking,

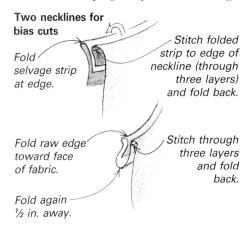

Two necklines for bias cuts

Fold selvage strip at edge.

Stitch folded strip to edge of neckline (through three layers) and fold back.

Fold raw edge toward face of fabric.

Stitch through three layers and fold back.

Fold again ½ in. away.

the next step, was most often accomplished by the head dressmaker, the premiere.

At the Callot Soeurs, after Mme. Gerber draped her ideas on a live mannequin, Vionnet, as premiere, would have in turn been responsible for making the first pattern. It is logical that Vionnet used both drafting and draping methods in interpreting Mme. Gerber's designs.

Drafting a pattern is often referred to as flat patternmaking because a pattern is constructed on paper, using the measurements of the body. Flat patternmaking has been the main method of making patterns for centuries. Basically, the body is divided into four parts, and a shape is made to correspond to each part: front and back bodices and front and back skirts, plus a fitted sleeve. Darts are used under the bust and above the hips to fit the bodice into the waist, and above the shoulder blade in the back to fit the cloth into the neck or shoulders. Once put into muslin, the fit can be checked against a dress form or body. From this sloper, various cuts can be produced.

Draping suggests manipulation of the cloth, placing muslin (or toile) on a dress form, pinning in or cutting away excess cloth to acquire fit, and adding cloth to embellish some part of the body. Draping probably originated so that cloth could be manipulated into configurations that couldn't be achieved through drafting.

Today, the planning of an original model is almost exclusively done by sketching, and the interpretation by drafting or draping recipes. That is somewhat how I was trained and how most of us at the Costume Institute viewed the construction of clothing. Vionnet didn't work like this when she draped on her wooden doll, and therein lay the mysteries we were encountering.

Construction: A preliminary look – Vionnet's halter necks, wrapped waists, and circular skirts are easily recognizable cuts. Vionnet also manipulated fabric. The twist often replaces a dart, especially in the bust area. It functions both structurally and aesthetically, holding in excess material that would otherwise have to be stitched and cut away.

A feature of the twist is that there will be fullness at both sides of the turn. In the midriff bodice (facing page, center), after sufficient fabric was draped over one breast, the fabric was twisted once spirally, which held it in and released it where it was needed to cover the other breast. For the dress at left on the facing page, Vionnet used a twist at the shoulder. Normally, a dart would have been used from the shoulder down both the front and back. Vionnet manipulated the fabric to remove the excess for fit and decoration at the same time.

With a little examination, it was easy to identify those of Vionnet's dresses that were on the bias. Of course, Vionnet never invented the bias cut. If you look at dresses from the 19th century, you find pattern parts laid on the textile at an oblique angle, to be cut, sewn, and hung on the body on the bias. Vionnet was very upset at being designated the inventor of that cut. She never claimed for herself that place in history, only the expansion of its use.

I remember bias cuts being worn in the late '30s, when I was very young. It was not a cut I admired – the garment hugging the body to the point of distraction so every imperfection was emphasized, bubbly seams that never laid flat. I suspect now that that was due mostly to Vionnet's poor imitators. Vionnet's bias cuts were different.

I wanted to know how Vionnet had mastered the cut and hang of the bias, but that would have to wait. With the deadline of the approaching opening, all attention was on preparing, dressing, and placing the mannequins. The sole luxury allowed was to note the choice of seams, facings, hems, and stitches, and to admire Vionnet's work.

The seams Vionnet chose could be the usual overcast seams seen in most dresses of the haute couture. The green dress of velvet patchwork on p. 63 demonstrated that to the extreme. Seams for all 153 parts were opened and overcast, as were all neck and hem edges, and a flat gold thread was couched over the seams on the right side. The same treatment was given to the edges.

Vionnet stated in a postopening interview that one reason she started to use bias was that it possessed an inherent stretchability. By making dresses that could be put on over the head, she created garments that were both easy to get into and out of and comfortable to wear. This anticipated the functional quality we find in knits today.

Once into the use of bias as a stretchable medium, there would be problems to solve on both sides of the spectrum. When she didn't want the stretching to occur, what should she do? When she wanted it to occur, what solutions would she devise?

Generally, when curved seams are opened, the seam allowance won't lie flat when pressed back. If the allowance is convex, the outer edge is longer than the seamline and will tend to ripple and be bulky. If the allowance is concave, the shorter edge prevents the allowance from lying flat by holding it in. If the edge of the allowance is stitched, whether by machine or hand, that, too, will hold in the edge of the seam.

There are solutions to this problem. A narrow seam lessens the difference in the lengths of the edge and the seamline. Slashing the allowance sufficiently, as close to the seamline as possible, permits the edge to open, thus correcting the difference in lengths. A third choice is to eliminate stitching at the edge.

Vionnet used all these methods. Because she worked so many parts and seams on the bias, she had additional problems of allowing the stretch to be at its optimum. On one coat, intended to hug the hip area, the seams were heavily slashed, and there was no overcasting stitch at the edges of the allowance – not a finish one would ordinarily attribute to a haute couture garment.

There were other considerations when hanging the cloth against the body on the bias. Because each fabric, by its fiber and weave, is going to react a little differently, Vionnet's dresses were not lined. If they were sheer, a separate lining or slip was supplied, and each part was allowed to go its own way. Coat linings were attached only to the neckline and the front facing of the opening. Often jackets had no lining.

Necklines cut on the bias presented another problem. On a dress with slightly dropped shoulders, to prevent bias stretch at the finished edge, which was on the true bias, folded on-grain strips were stitched to each neck edge and turned back, as shown in the drawing on the facing page. The selvage was intact, so there was no need for clean seaming, making the edge thin and flat, while controlling the neckline stretch.

Another neckline, the concave edge of a circular cut, was slightly scooped in front and back. It was not necessary to add a part; the solution was inherent in the cut. It works on the same principle as the concave seam allowances. The edge will be shorter than any seamline placed within the part and will thus prevent any stretching of the finished neckline. Vionnet simply folded the raw edge twice, as shown in the drawing, hiding it inside the second fold, on the reverse. Only a narrow edge shows to finish the neckline.

Vionnet overcast and turned up edges for many hems, even if the cut was bias. For circular cuts and sheer fabrics, she usually resorted to picoted or rolled hems. The hem on the dress at right on the facing page, a circular cut made in eyelet, demonstrates Vionnet's care for finding solutions that considered problems of both structure and aesthetics. Rather than turn back the hem, which would have caused an uneven intrusion into the pattern of the eyelet because of the circular cut, Vionnet cut the eyelet at the hemline. Now she had one layer of uneven eyelet pattern. The resolve for this was again both functional and aesthetic. A buttonhole chain stitch secured each loose end of the eyelet motifs, simultaneously creating an even finish line for the hem.

Learning design principles: Taking patterns – When the exhibition opened, none of the clothes on view could be touched. My intention to research beyond seams, facings, hems, and stitching commenced nonetheless. After researching published material, I started to take patterns from other pieces. The following year I went to England and France for more research. I subsequently made several trips to France, gathering information and taking patterns.

I was fortunate to have met Vionnet on my first trip, as she died in early 1975. I visited her twice. She wasn't in good health; we arrived two days after her 98th birthday. I had to promise not to ask her any technical questions, as she couldn't always think of the answers. This she found upsetting.

She had just received photos from the exhibition. The second condition of my visit, that I'd limit it to 20 minutes, was soon forgotten in discussion and explanations.

I told her of my intention to study her techniques and possibly publish them in book form. She was pleased, as she had always wanted to do this herself, but of course, it was now too late. Vionnet had her housekeeper, Solange Lerond, bring me some of her personal clothing.

Solange brought some evening gowns and a box of pieces from the early '20s. Vionnet then decided that I should try on each piece. I was hesitant, as the one time she stood, Vionnet fit well under my chin. Then, too, there were my broad shoulders. I had completely forgotten about the bias cut. The clothes stretched to fit around my body, although they were too short. Vionnet told me I could take whatever I wanted to copy. I selected two evening gowns from which to make patterns. One is the pajama skirt in the sketch on p. 67.

By taking patterns, I hoped that I would be able to understand and dispel some of the mysteries that Vionnet's cuts posed. As Elizabeth Lawrence often said, "To understand a designer, you have to get into his

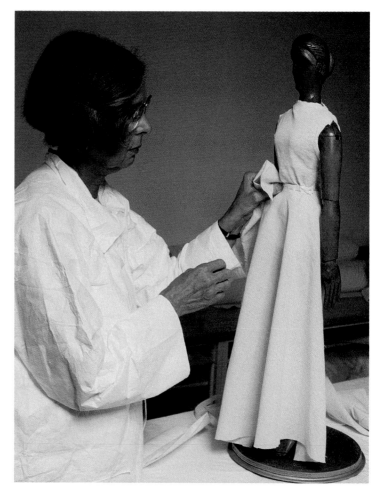

To take a pattern from a garment, author Betty Kirke chooses one warp or weft yarn as home base, measures the length of perpendicular yarns, and plots the measurements on dotted marking paper. If the fabric has distorted due to bias stretching, her method corrects this.

At right, Kirke demonstrates why the circular skirts created by Vionnet never hung unevenly. In draping their patterns, rather than drafting them, Kirke was able to compensate for the variations in the stretchability of the fabric. She allows less fabric to fall at center back, where it is on the true bias.

mind; to understand a dress, you must allow it to tell you what it is all about."

The easiest way to take a pattern from an existing garment is to take it apart, lay the pieces flat, and draw around them. The next easiest way, when a garment can't be taken apart, is to do a rub-off. In this method, another fabric, generally unbleached muslin, is laid over and pinned to each part, one at a time, with the grain of the overlay fabric carefully aligned to that of the part being copied. With tailor's chalk, the seams and darts are then rubbed every inch with horizontal strokes. The chalk marks register the difference in the texture of the seam and the weave of the fabric beneath, making the seamline clearly discernible. Neither of these methods could be applied to a museum object, especially by one who is a conservator of textiles and costumes. There was another consideration.

Since there would be so many pieces cut on the bias, and since there would likely be deformations of the weft and warp grid because of the bias stretching, I chose a system that would address that problem as well. The theory behind the method is that all textiles start as a width of rectangular fabric. Within this shape, warp yarns of equal length lie in one direction, and perpendicular to them lie weft yarns of equal length. In making pattern parts, some of these yarns are cut away. If a part has had a great deal of shaping, there are many curves to be determined. Therefore, if one

yarn is selected as home base, yarns perpendicular to it can be measured, and the lengths from home base to the edge can be recorded. Not every yarn has to be measured—only enough so that a fairly accurate cutting line is established.

Luckily, the first patterns I took were of Vionnet's earlier designs. They were sometimes unorthodox, although simple in construction: a rectangular shape, cut and sewn on the grain, but hung, when assembled, on the bias. Her adherence to cutting and sewing on the grain of the fabric as much as possible helped keep her bias cuts out of the category of unattractive memories.

For these pieces, graph paper is sufficient for drawing the pattern. Measurements taken off the parts of the dress must be scaled to some predetermined ratio that will relate to the grid of the graph paper. It's easiest to equate one square to 1 in. or 1 cm.

Weighting the bias before cutting

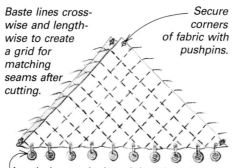

Baste lines crosswise and lengthwise to create a grid for matching seams after cutting.

Secure corners of fabric with pushpins.

Attach dressmaker's weights along bottom.

For the most part, however, I transferred the pattern parts from the dresses to dotted marking paper. Marking paper is used by garment manufacturers in laying out pattern parts of different sizes so they can fit the width of a particular fabric as a preliminary step before cutting in mass production. It is dotted so that all three directions of the fabric—warp, weft, and true bias—are marked, the former two, every inch. It eliminates the need for scaling. Being able to transfer the pattern parts full size was particularly useful in recording those cuts that were still an enigma to me.

In taking a pattern of Vionnet's circular-cut skirts, where fabric has been cut away at the hem and waistline, the lengths of the yarns in both directions must be measured. Because the skirts were generally much wider than the fabric in which they were made, the fabric was pieced on grain. I found taking measurements off the piecing seamline a good place to start. I drew a line corresponding to the seam length on the dotted paper. Then, about every 2 in. along the pieced line, I measured the length of a particular perpendicular yarn to the hem edge or waistline seam and marked the dotted paper accordingly until there were sufficient marks so a hemline and a waistline could be drawn with the aid of a curved ruler, as shown at left, above.

If the piecing won't allow perpendicular measurements to give the entire hemline or waistline, then one of the perpendicular lines must be selected to strike off again, in a direction parallel to the first seamline. This method can be applied to the most complicated pattern parts, if one works slowly and figures out what yarn as home base will best lead to the edge.

By the time I had taken a few dozen patterns from Vionnet's dresses, I had included, besides circular and simple geometrical shapes, bias and traditional shapes, along with such manipulations of the cloth as twists. There were also slashes and parts like gussets and godets. The slash was often, but not always, found with insets, such as the gussets and godets. It was clear what purpose the slash served with godets: to add more cloth, more fullness, at a specific area of the body. It was not yet clear what use Vionnet intended for the gussets.

The details make the difference: The nature of fabric—At this point I had to admit that not all my questions about the construction of Vionnet's dresses had been answered. Mysteries remained, particularly concerning circular cuts, which I had first-hand experience in manufacturing.

We would cut and seam circular skirts, then put them on a dress form so the bias skirt could do its stretching before the hemline was determined. This "hang-out" period was at least 48 hours. After completing the dresses and shipping them to the stores, we advised buyers that they were best stored flat for a long period. I knew that in time there would be more stretching, resulting in a skirt with an uneven hem.

Vionnet's circular-cut skirts hadn't hung out unevenly, some not in 50 years. Perhaps this was due to some of the anomalies I'd found in taking patterns of these cuts. Some weren't on true bias center front and center back. The pieces weren't always cut symmetrically, and one side might be slashed with a gusset added, while nothing was done to the other side. I didn't know why, but I had a clue. I had read in one of the periodicals how beautiful Vionnet's circular skirts were with their ripples always equal in size and fullness at the hemline.

At this point, we were packing the exhibition for Kyoto, Japan. I was to be part of the installation crew. Of course, I needed clothes, especially for the opening night and final party. I decided to make a circular-cut skirt of two quarter circles, for front and back. Rather than draft the pattern, I draped it, keeping in mind that the final garment should have even ripples at the hem.

I placed the lengthwise grain, the selvage side, down the right side, pinning a point at the waist. I then cut away and dropped, stretched, or eased along the waist until a waistline was established, making sure each ripple I created at the hem appeared even with the preceding one (right photo, facing page). When I got to the left side, I found I had not yet reached the weft grain. Since I had what I wanted in even hem ripples, I

cut away the excess fabric. I repeated the procedure when I draped the back. This time, there was much less left over, confirming what I had found—that pattern parts weren't always on the true bias, nor were they always symmetrical. It also helped explain why, in some dresses with a waist seam and two-piece bias-cut skirt, one side of the waistline was cut a little deeper.

To fit a quarter circle to the waist, the apex has to be cut away, not straight across, but in a concave curve. In drafting this pattern, the curve would be drawn equidistant from the apex. The response of the fabric when hung along this curved edge, however, is not equal. On one side, the fabric will hang from warp yarns, which won't stretch at all. On the opposite side, it will hang from weft yarns, which will stretch little or much, depending on the weave and yarn structure. The central area will hang on the bias and stretch a lot. The very center, on the true bias, will stretch the most.

To control the ripples at the hemline, one must control the amount of fabric stretching into and collapsing under each point of the waistline above. The fabric must be cut and placed along the waistline according to its stretchability at each point. The warp grain side will be cut deeper than the weft side, and the bias, with the most ability to stretch, must be restrained from doing too much. At the true bias, I stretch the fabric horizontally and force some of the fabric into the area of less stretchability.

Theoretically, each ripple will then have the same number of yarns, the same weight, and the same degree of stretching. The even hemline should persist.

I made this skirt in 1975. I've had it on a hanger ever since, just to see if it will develop an uneven hemline. It has not yet hung out. My conclusion is that in draping this way, evenly distributing weft and warp yarns in each ripple, if there is hang-out, each ripple is going to hang out equally.

I was to learn much later, from one of Vionnet's employees, that Vionnet had also devised methods of controlling the bias before it was cut and sewn. She weighted the bias with lead dressmaking weights, hanging the fabric on the wall, as shown in the drawing on the facing page. A corner of the fabric was secured to the wall; then the remainder was spread in a flat triangle, with heavy dressmaking weights attached along the bottom. Longer fabric was looped and folded back up so two layers could be weighted at the same time. In her designs that were cut on the bias, and many were derived from traditional pattern parts, Vionnet prepared all the fabric with the weighting treatment. In addition, to have more control of the hang and fit, she basted crosswise and lengthwise lines on the cloth at equal intervals to create a grid. The grid was used to match sides of symmetrically cut bias parts to one another for assembly.

My second garment for the Kyoto trip was to be a modified version of Vionnet's

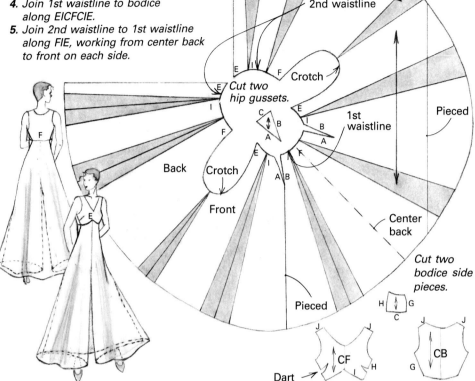

Sketch and pattern of pajamas from Vionnet's personal wardrobe, 1937

Construction sequence

1. Assemble bodice.
2. Insert hip gussets.
3. Join crotch seams.
4. Join 1st waistline to bodice along EICFCIE.
5. Join 2nd waistline to 1st waistline along FIE, working from center back to front on each side.

For Kirke's modifications to half-circle skirt, fold out excess.

2nd waistline

Crotch

Cut two hip gussets.

1st waistline

Pieced

Back

Crotch

Front

Center back

Cut two bodice side pieces.

Pieced

CF

CB

Dart

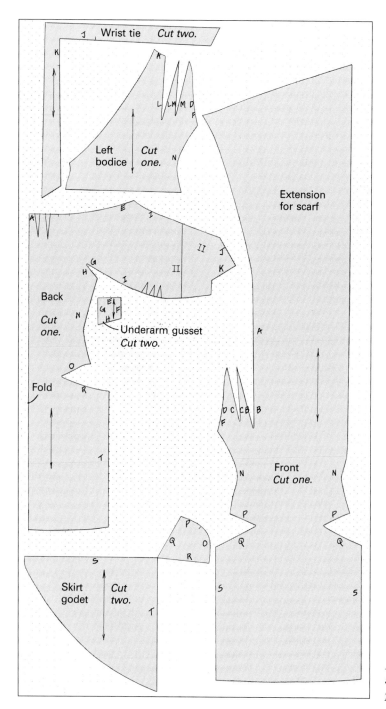

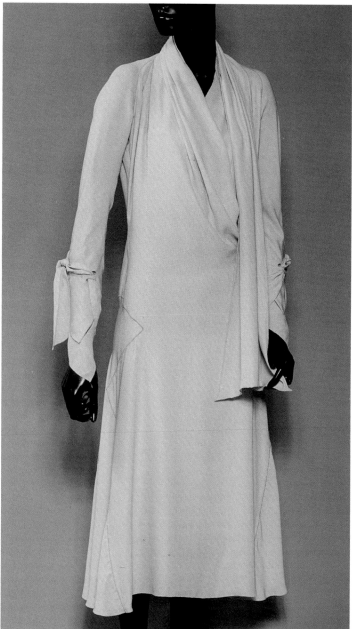

Bias for stretch combined with gussets and godets for shaping spheres create anatomical cuts that match the body's curves. Kirke's pattern for the dress is at left. (Collection of Judith Bocker Grunberg.)

personal pajama dress. The pattern called for a three-quarter circle. I had a piece of black silk shantung that was left over from the shirt I was planning to wear with the pajamas. One modification would be to cut the pants at the natural waist. And, since the shantung would be of a stiffer hand than the crepe that Vionnet used, the other modification was to reduce the fullness at the hem. I decided to remove this fullness by converting the three-quarter circle into a half-circle by folding equally sized and placed darts out the paper pattern from hemline to waist and crotch (shaded areas in the drawing on p. 67).

Since I was in a rush, I skipped what a good dressmaker would have done—try out the new shape in muslin before cutting the shantung. When I tried the pants on after having sewn the crotch seams, I was heartbroken. All the ripples were in the back.

The hemline at the front was flat. It wasn't at all what I had visualized.

I don't know why I did what I did next, whether it was out of anger, frustration, or divine inspiration. I took the scissors and slashed from the waist down about 3 in. on the grain at the center of each side in front. When I pulled open the slashed area, I had ripples at the hemline. I then filled in each area with a triangular gusset. I love these pants and wear them often. More important, one of the uses of the gusset was at last known to me, and this in itself was a clue to other, still unsolved mysteries of Vionnet's cuts.

Sometime after returning from Japan, I found a doll almost exactly like the one used by Vionnet. With a good, healthy doubling of the measurements, the patterns draped on this doll fit me fine. Now I could have first-hand experience in draping the

styles that most interested me. Having an articulated form made achieving graceful-fitting sleeves possible; having one this size allowed me to see instantly the whole of each concept. When draping on a full-size dress form, I always have to step back to see the entire toile that I'm draping.

In draping the Vionnet dresses on the doll, another theory for the use of the gussets had surfaced. The doll was made to the exaggerated female shape fashionable in Vionnet's time. Vionnet's garments of the '30s fit close to the body. The theory was that when cloth has been slashed and spread and a gusset has been inserted, it changes from two- to three-dimensional, becoming a virtual sphere. If you think of the upper and lower hip areas, and the bust, you'll see that this is so.

When I started to drape, intending to verify my theory, it didn't quite work. After

Vionnet cut the white crepe pajama at right to simulate an evening dress. It was worn with a wrapped-waist bodice and velvet circular cape in 1931. (Photo by George Hoyningen-Huene; courtesy of Harvard Costume Library.)

much frustration, I realized that I'd been thinking of the body only as convex spheres. There's one huge concavity to be dealt with: the waist. I don't know why it took me so long to see that. Vionnet had many gussets at the waist. They're the easiest to drape.

Back when I was doing research through the periodicals, I ran into an expression that mystified me. The journalist referred to Vionnet's dresses as "anatomical cuts." Could anything be more anatomical than directly dealing with the convex and concave parts of a woman's body? Add to it the use of bias for stretch, the advantages of circular cuts, the twist, and all the dressmaking considerations. I've worn all the clothes that I duplicated and modified. They move better and fit better than anything else I wear. They are, in addition, timeless and elegant.

From this research and my experience in copying, adapting, and draping the work of Vionnet, I've come to realize how simple and logical her choices are, from the shapes of the pattern parts to the manipulations of the fabric and the precise execution. Certainly these are marks of an excellent dressmaker. I understand now, especially after draping on my wooden doll, that Vionnet couldn't have planned any of the concepts other than by draping. The pattern parts could never have been drafted. The way the fabric was laid against the doll and later hung away from the body dictated many of the choices that Vionnet made in her use of the bias and the slash with its gussets and gores. As she had said, "You have to know the obedience of the fabric." Certainly this was a mark of an excellent technician.

Vionnet insisted on referring to herself as a dressmaker. That is how she described herself when I visited her. The former employees I met always cringed when I would refer to her as a designer. "No," they would say, "she was a technician."

Obviously, Vionnet was more. As a dressmaker and technician, she brought into being something that had never existed before, a way of dividing the surface of the body. Then, through her imagination of how dresses could be made, she devised new pattern parts. This is being an artist. Madeleine Vionnet was unquestionably a dressmaker extraordinaire. □

Betty Kirke, costume conservator at the Design Laboratory of The Fashion Institute of Technology (FIT) in New York City, is currently completing a book on Madeleine Vionnet. Photos by Irving Soleri, courtesy of the Edward C. Blum Design Laboratory, FIT, except where noted.

Improving the Bottom Line

How to choose hand- and machine-sewn hem finishes

by Alice Allen

ashion news nearly always concerns itself with hemlines, but generally the newsworthy item is length, and not technique. Fortunately, after many years of dictating hemlines, today's fashion houses have conceded to the demands of modern life: Different lengths for different lifestyles.

Regardless of the length, a hemline calls for a finished edge at the bottom of the garment. Except in the case of fabrics such as tulle, net, and felt, or with borders that are embroidered, which merely need to be cut to length, hems usually require turning under and stitching to the garment. Simple as this may sound, there are countless hemming techniques. These techniques are dependent upon style, fabric texture, and the available tools.

Planning

Planning for hems should begin at the fabric store. The yardage you purchase must allow you enough length to turn up an appropriate hem. Bulky fabrics, knits, and full, flared skirts will have narrow hems. Lightweight fabrics will often have deep hems, and sheer fabrics traditionally have rolled edges if cut on the bias, and very wide hems if cut on the straight grain. Plaids, border designs, and horizontal stripes need careful planning for the best effect in final hemming, so allow extra of these fabrics for maximum flexibility.

Here are some general guidelines for hem depth as it relates to fashion style:
Skirts/Dresses
• Flared or gore: 2 to 3 in.
• Straight: 3 in.
• Circular: up to 1 in.
• Children's: 3 to 5 in.

The bias-cut flounce at the hem of Giorgio Armani's linen skirt was serger-overcast, then carefully seamed and beautifully pressed around its graceful bottom line. (Photo by Donato Sardella for W)

Blouses/Shirts
• Overblouse: 1 to 1½ in.
• Shirttail: up to 1 in.
Jackets: 1½ to 2 in.
Straight-leg pants: 1½ to 2 in.

Even if you need no extra length for a turned-up hem, for fitting flexibility it's a good idea to allow an inch or two when you're cutting out your garment.

Before hemming the otherwise completed garment, let it hang unhemmed for a day or two (allow maximum time for a bias-cut or stretchy garment). This will relax the garment, ensuring that its lines will drape properly and that the hem won't grow.

Final measurement

Mark the turnup location you want with a chalk or pin line. On most styles you'll want the hem parallel to the floor. For utmost accuracy, have someone mark your hem while you stand naturally, in one position, with your body weight distributed evenly, and wearing the garment with suitable undergarments, shoes, and a belt, if the garment requires one. As your hemming assistant walks around you, he or she should measure the skirt hem from the floor upward with a yardstick or hem marker.

If an assistant is not available, the next best choice is to place your unhemmed garment on a dress form that conforms to your body size, shape, and height. If you don't have a dress form, use a hem marker, like the one in the photo at right, that will permit you to mark your garment as you wear it, standing naturally. The absolute last choice is to hem the garment by measuring it flat on an ironing board. If this is your only option, try the garment on several times during the pinning process so you can adjust your measurements for the varying contours of your figure.

Mark the hem length at the outer sweep of the skirt, every 2 or 3 in. Then check for evenness, correcting any marks that are obviously out of line.

Raw-edge finishing

The next step is to trim the garment to the hem depth you've decided on and finish the raw edge. For an edge cut on the straight or near-straight of grain, turn the hem to the inside of the garment on the marked line, and trim the side seam allowances in the hem turnup area so the seams are graded. Then baste ½ in. from the fold, establish the cutting line with chalk and a hem gauge (the familiar 6-in. metal sewing ruler with a sliding marker is ideal), and trim away the excess fabric.

Unlike an edge cut on the straight grain, a curved hem inevitably has excess fabric in the turnup area. This excess must be eliminated before the edge is finished to prevent bulk and show-through where hem meets garment. To keep the excess fabric to a minimum, cut the curved-edge hem less deep than the straight-cut hem. To shrink the fullness from the outer edges,

sew short lines of ease stitches (10 stitches to the inch) at intervals ¼ in. from the raw edge of the hem. Put the garment on the ironing board, wrong side out, and pull up the ease thread at each interval, fitting the hem to the garment. Place a piece of heavy paper (a grocery bag is perfect) between the hem and the garment. Press lightly with steam to shrink out the fullness, keeping the iron perpendicular to the horizontal hem so you won't stretch it sideways. This technique works beautifully with all natural fibers, and to some extent with synthetics. Tie off the ease threads on the inside of the hem.

Now you need to select a finish for the raw edge. Fabric texture—whether bulky, slick, raveled, or tightly or loosely woven—usually determines the choice, but sometimes more than one finish is appropriate.

Seam binding—Seam binding is attached to the unfinished, turned-up edge by sewing machine and is suited to fabrics that ravel easily or have a coarse edge. It is designed to be stiff enough to lie flat without drooping over to expose the hem edge, even though it is attached at its bottom edge only, as shown in the drawing at right. Whichever technique you eventually use to attach the hem to the garment, the stitches will be concealed by the binding.

Polyester seam binding needn't be preshrunk. With fiber other than polyester, steam-shrink the binding, shaping it to match any curve in the hem. Beginning at a side seam, place the wrong side of the tape to the right side of the hem, with the top edge of the tape ¼ in. above the hem edge. This overlap provides better protection for the raw edge than flush placement would, and it allows the edge thickness to taper off for less bulk.

Machine-stitch the binding to the hem along the lower tape edge, using a medium-length straight stitch. Turn under the cut edge of the seam binding for a neat finish when you get back to the starting point.

Machine overcasting—Machine overcasting, by serger or zigzag sewing machine, can effectively cover ravelly edges. Machine zigzag stitches control raveling with minimum bulk, while serging can simultaneously cover and trim the raw edge to size.

If you are serging the outer edge, run the overlock stitch around the outer hem edge. If you prefer to zigzag, stitch a medium-width, medium-length zigzag along the outer edge, with the outer stitch falling on the edge of the cloth (wide zigzags tend to bunch up the fabric). Either finish is appropriate for medium-heavyweight washable fabrics with coarse or ravelly edges.

I use the machine blind hemstitch (four straight stitches followed by a zigzag stitch) as an edge finish. It is frequently just the right amount of protection against seam raveling, yet it is even less bulky than overcasting.

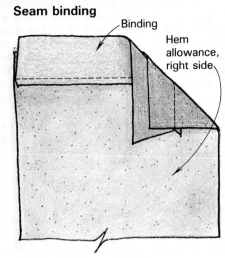

Machine-stitch seam binding to hem edge so binding overlaps hem ¼ in.

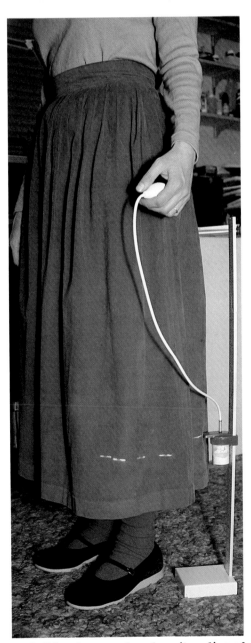

A chalking hem marker deposits a line of chalk on your hemline when you squeeze the bulb. As long as you stand naturally, it's ideal when you have to make hems by yourself.

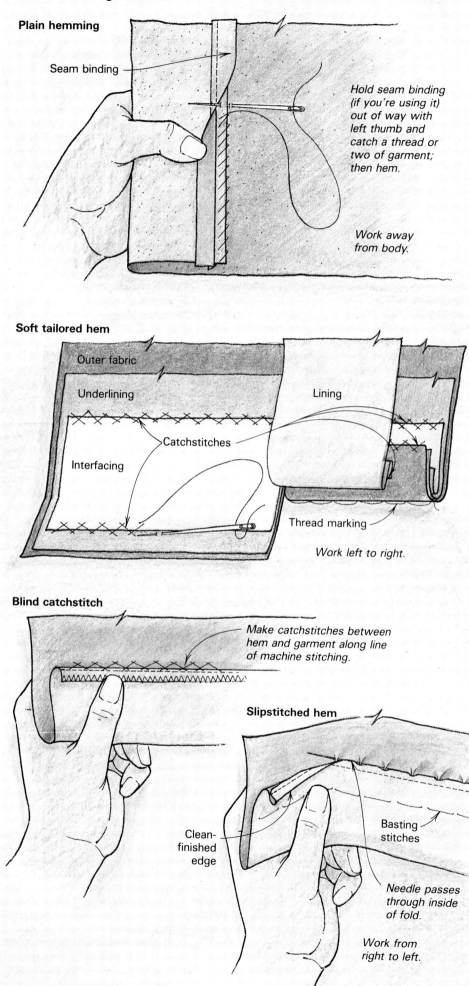

Hand hemming stitches

Plain hemming

Seam binding

Hold seam binding
(if you're using it)
out of way with
left thumb and
catch a thread or
two of garment;
then hem.

Work away
from body.

Soft tailored hem

Outer fabric

Underlining

Lining

Catchstitches

Interfacing

Thread marking

Work left to right.

Blind catchstitch

Make catchstitches between
hem and garment along line
of machine stitching.

Slipstitched hem

Clean-
finished
edge

Basting
stitches

Needle passes
through inside
of fold.

Work from
right to left.

Clean-finishing—This is a machine-stitched finish in which the outer edge of the hem is turned under approximately ¼ in. and stitched close to the fold. It is suitable on washable, tightly woven fabrics that are lightweight to medium weight. I like it on full, straight-cut, lightweight cotton skirts.

Pinked-and-straight-stitched finishing—A minimal edge treatment, this is appropriate for nonraveling fabric and garments you plan to line. However, unless your pinking shears are very sharp, pinking often chews the fabric, creating raveling where none had been, so it isn't my favorite. Sew a medium-length machine stitch around the outer edge of the hem, ¼ to ⅜ in. from the raw edge; then pink the hem's outer edge.

Attaching hem to garment

The final step in making a hem is attaching the turned-up edge to the garment with either hand or machine stitches. You should base your choice on the fabric type, the garment style, your tools, and your skill.

Hand hemming stitches—When done with the proper thread, tension, and stitch size, hand stitches creates a high-quality hem. On the face of the garment, they should be almost invisible, catching only a thread or two, and if it's thick enough, just on the inside of the fabric. Hand-stitched hems should be made with one strand of matching thread cut the length of hand to elbow and with a thin, flexible needle. Begin with a backstitch in the side-seam allowance, and start new threads in the same way.

Plain hemming, also known as slant stitch or whipstitch (shown at top left), is often used with seam binding or clean-finished edges. It appears as even, slanted stitches along the outer hem edge. Right-handers should work with the basted lower garment edge in their left hand and sew away from the body, with the needle moving right to left, and at right angles to the hem, pricking the garment, then going through the hem edge. Whipstitching frays or breaks easily unless it is protected by seam binding.

The *catchstitch* is a hand zigzag stitch worked from left to right, with the needle held parallel to the hem edge, making the zigzags about ½ in. apart. Be careful to let the thread relax between stitches. Also prone to fraying if not protected, the catchstitch is more flexible and provides more even support than plain hemming. With a little practice, you can do it very quickly.

A common hem treatment that calls for the catchstitch is the *soft tailored finish,* shown at center left. For the well-defined but soft hem of underlined jackets or skirts in wool or linen, a bias-cut interfacing is placed between hem and garment. Cut bias strips of medium-weight woven interfacing 1 in. wider than the depth of the hem and long enough to fit the circumference of the hem. You can piece the strips to fit the garment circumference. Mark the finished gar-

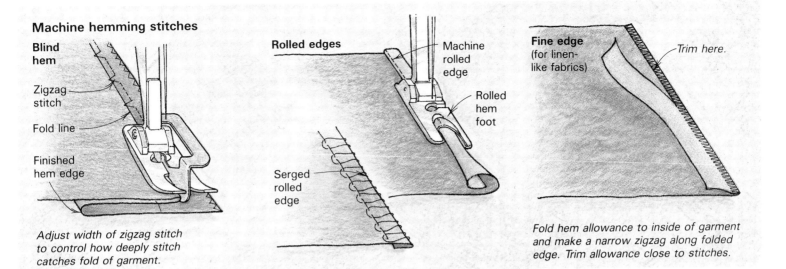

Machine hemming stitches

Blind hem

Zigzag stitch

Fold line

Finished hem edge

Adjust width of zigzag stitch to control how deeply stitch catches fold of garment.

Rolled edges

Machine rolled edge

Rolled hem foot

Serged rolled edge

Fine edge (for linen-like fabrics)

Trim here.

Fold hem allowance to inside of garment and make a narrow zigzag along folded edge. Trim allowance close to stitches.

---

ment edge with a thread line. Pin the interfacing on the wrong side of the garment, on top of the underlining, with its lower edge ⅝ in. below the thread-marked hemline. Attach both edges of the interfacing to the garment underlining with catchstitches. Turn the hem to the inside and catchstitch it to the underfacing. Then catchstitch the lining to the turned-up hem. Steam-press only to preserve the soft edge.

The *blind catchstitch* conceals the catchstitch between garment and hem. Machine-stitch around the hem ¼ in. from the finished edge. Fold the hem at the turnup; then fold it back against the garment at the machine-stitch line, and make a catchstitch along the line of machine stitches, working from hem to garment. This invisible technique is appropriate on thick or heavy fabrics because the stitch doesn't travel over a bulky edge and will be less likely to dimple the face of the garment.

The *slipstitch*, sometimes called the blindstitch, is also almost invisible on both sides of the garment. To make the slipstitch, clean-finish the raw edge, creating a fold, and then baste the hem to the garment ½ in. from the just-finished edge. Conceal the slipstitch inside the fold by passing the needle through the underside of the fold about ¼ in. Next, prick through the fold to the garment fabric, moving the needle from right to left enough to catch a thread or two of the garment. Then slip the tip of the needle back into the fold, as shown at bottom left on the facing page. With practice, you won't have to entirely remove the needle from the fold until you run out of thread.

Machine hemming stitches—These stitches include the blind hem, straight stitches that go through the garment, and zigzagged and rolled hems that finish raw edges and complete the hem at the same time.

The *blind hem* requires a special machine foot, normally supplied with a zigzag machine that can produce the stitch, shown in the left drawing above. It is particularly suited to woolens and medium-weight fabrics, and with careful adjustment can pro-

duce excellent results, giving the illusion of handwork, yet with the strength and evenness of machine work. To make a blind hem, finish the raw edge; then baste the hem to the garment ½ in. below the raw edge. Turn the hem back against the garment, put the raw edge under the foot, and arrange the blade of the foot to touch the fold. The stitch will catch the folded hem every three or four stitches as it zigzags to the left. On most machines it's possible to fine-tune the stitch width to ensure that the needle barely catches the fold so it won't show too large a stitch on the right side when it's unfolded and pressed.

The *machine-stitched, or topstitched, edge* is the hem we've all seen on blue jeans. It can be used on a wide range of fabrics, from silkies to firm knits, and has found its way onto many styles of garments. For wovens, clean-finish the raw edge, or merely fold the edge under and hold by pressing, pinning, basting, or glue-sticking. Then stitch the edge to the garment, making sure the stitching is parallel to the hem. On bulky, more casual attire, and on knits, machine-stitched hems vary from ½ in. to the more common 1 in. Shirts and silky dresses often use ¼-in. to ½-in. machine-stitched hems. I keep an eye on fashion ready-to-wear to watch the trends in machine hems, which, like silhouettes, vary from season to season and subtly dictate the current fashion feeling.

For knits, you can omit clean-finishing. Just turn the hem depth to the inside of the garment and machine-stitch the hem, catching the hem edge to the garment and finishing the edge at the same time. I get the most attractive results with a straight stretch stitch and a ballpoint needle. You can also use a double needle and two threads on top, keeping the raw edge underneath between the needles. The bobbin thread will zigzag over the edge, finishing it securely, and will form a slight ridge as it draws together the two rows of topstitching.

You can emphasize topstitched hems by using more rows of thread, usually ¼ to ⅛ in. apart. Each additional row of topstitching will also make the hem a bit stiffer, which

adds emphasis. Experiment with the spacing of the rows, and with heavier, shinier, or contrasting threads for more impact.

The *rolled edge* is traditional, and appropriate, for the curved edges of chiffon or lightweight silks. Don't hesitate to consider machine-rolled hems for these and many other lightweight fabrics and on straight or curved edges. The serger technique, for two- and three-thread machines, covers the roll with thread and usually creates the roll with carefully adjusted thread tension, as described in each serger manual. The sewing-machine version closes the roll with a line of straight stitches. It requires a special foot (available for all machines), shown in the center drawing above, to create the roll and keep it even as it is stitched. With matching threads, these are very subtle, high-quality finishes, and they are much easier to make than hand-rolled edges.

The *fine-edge finish* is appropriate for straight hems on lightweight linens and crisp, linen-textured fabrics. Turn back the hem allowance to the inside and press along the hem edge. Then sew a short, narrow stitch, and zigzag along the folded edge, with the right-hand zig falling just off the fabric, as shown in the right drawing above. Trim the excess fabric away on the back, as close as possible to the stitching.

* * *

When you've finished the last hemming stitch, critique the effect you've achieved by asking yourself the following questions: Is the hem inconspicuous, flat, smooth, and uniform in depth? Is the hem parallel to the floor? Is the hand-stitch tension even, uniformily spaced, and not too tight? Is the turned-up edge wide enough to provide the weight necessary for the garment to hang well?

Proper hemming is important. The hem should be the final touch to an attractive garment—a suitable finished edge. The hem speaks volumes; it is the silent voice of a garment beautifully constructed. □

Alice Allen is a sewing specialist for Bernina.

Clothing Connections
Variations on a seam

by Claire Shaeffer

Seams are literally the threads that hold a garment together. Most are plain and inconspicuous, but they can become unusual, eye-catching details that transform ordinary garments into extraordinary designs.

Decorative seams are probably the easiest, quickest means to creating original designs. They work best on simple garments made of few pattern pieces. Tailored garments and casual styles support decorative seams better than soft, feminine designs.

Beyond the common topstitched and welt seams are a wealth of decorative seams. Wrong-side-out seams let you play with seam allowances. They may be folded and stitched to the garment, cut into shapes like points or scallops, fringed, or trimmed and covered with a strap of a second fabric. Inserting piping, ribbon, or lace in seams is another decorating technique. Binding one or both seam allowances with bias in either a matching or contrasting color is a third way to enliven seams. A design can have one decorative seam as a focal point, many seams for trim, or more than one type of seam.

Decorative seams often eliminate the need to finish seam edges, which makes them good for unlined jackets and coats and reversible garments. Look for other design ideas in ready-made garments, catalogs, etc.

When planning how to use decorative seams, consider the fabric's hand, color, and texture, and its structure or surface design. Most decorative seams are better suited to crisp or firm fabrics than to very soft materials. Fabric added for piping and additional stitching lines stiffen seamlines, which may interfere with the natural movement of soft fabric. Also consider the fabric's transparency, weight and thickness, fray quality, and care requirements. Some decorative seams were invented because

From *Threads* magazine (April 1989) 22:24-29

the garment fabric was too thick to have a regular seam or too transparent to be left uncovered. Fringed seams are ideal for hand-woven fabrics and those that ravel easily.

Although few decorative seams require extra yardage, I often buy an additional ⅛ yd. to ¼ yd. so I can experiment with different materials, seam widths, and construction techniques before I select a seam. Some seams require more than ⅝-in.-wide seam allowances; others require less. To save time and avoid limiting my choices, I select a seam before I cut the fabric. If the seam requires complementary fabrics or trims, I assemble them before cutting.

Decorative seams take more time to make than plain seams and are harder to alter. Before cutting out your garment, adjust the pattern so it will fit properly. Then redraw the seam allowances for the chosen seam.

Wrong-side-out seams — Wrong-side-out seams (photo, p. 76) start with a plain seam stitched with the wrong sides of the fabric together. They differ in the way the seam allowances are treated.

The *edgestitched wrong-side-out seam* can be used on straight and almost-straight seams and in widths from ¾ in. to 2 in. They are attractive on casual designs and particularly practical for unlined and reversible garments.

Nonravel or nonwoven fabrics, such as synthetic suedes and leathers or fabrics that you can finish with serging, may be cut with the exact finished seam-allowance width; add ¼ in. to allowances of fabrics that ravel so you can finish the edges.

Stitch on the seamline with wrong sides together. Press the seam flat with seam allowances together; then press the seam open. For nonwoven fabrics, zigzag or straight-stitch the raw seam edges to the garment, basting the seam allowances in

Stitch seams wrong sides out; then play with seam allowances. The edges of a seam in reversible fabric are turned under and edgestitched in place (above, left). Seam allowances of nonwoven or non-ravel fabric can be cut to resemble the ridges of a dinosaur's back (second from left). Straps for covering trimmed seams can be contrasting fabric (second from right) or self-fabric (right).

place prior to stitching, as needed. For fabrics that fray, fold the edge under ¼ in., baste, edgestitch the seam allowances to the garment, and press.

The Zandra Rhodes *dinosaur seam* is a wrong-side-out seam with shaped seam allowances that aren't stitched to the garment. In the original version, 1-in.-wide seams of a felt coat were stitched wrong sides together and clipped in triangular shapes so they look like the ridge on a dinosaur's back.

The *strap seam*, especially attractive on reversible and unlined garments and some transparent fabrics, is a wrong-side-out seam with trimmed seam allowances covered by a separate strap. The strap can be made from ribbon, decorative braid, lace, bias tape, leather, suede, felt, self-fabric, or contrasting fabric. Although strap seams are usually straight, they can be shaped.

Cut out the garment with ⅝-in. seam allowances. If the strap material has edges that don't ravel, cut it the desired width and length. If the edges will be turned under, cut it the finished width plus ½ in. so each edge can be turned under ¼ in. With the garment's wrong sides together, stitch the seams, press them open, and trim to ¼ in. With right sides up, center the strap over the seam. Pin and glue-baste or thread-baste the strap in place. Edgestitch both sides of the strap to the garment. I use a zipper foot to edgestitch easily.

The *fringed seam* (top photo and drawing, facing page), designed by handweaver Gail Nehrig, is a wrong-side-out seam strengthened by two lines of zigzag on each side of the seamline. It emphasizes the quality of handwovens, loosely woven fabrics, and fabrics woven with heavy yarns. It's stronger than a seam that's just stitched and unraveled, and it looks great on casual designs.

Determine the finished fringe width, and cut the seam allowances of the garment to that width. With the garment's wrong sides together, stitch on the seamline. Press the seam open. With the garment right side up, lay a yarn or thread pulled from extra cloth next to the seamline; zigzag over the yarn to hold it in place, with a stitch length of 3mm (9 sts./in.) and the stitch width as wide as needed so the needle won't split the yarn. Repeat on the other side of the seamline.

Fringe the seam by clipping the seam allowance every 4 in. to 8 in. so the short yarns can be easily removed. If threads from the fringe are caught in the seamline, trim them close to the seamline.

The *fringed French seam* (bottom photo and drawing, facing page) is made like a regular French seam, but the seam allowance shows. Suitable for lightweight to medium-weight fabrics that ravel, it's stitched with wrong sides together, then again with right sides together, leaving most of the seam allowance exposed on the garment's right side.

Decide on the finished width of the fringe and add ⅝ in. to allow for the second seam. For a ½-in.-wide fringe, for example, cut the seam allowances ⅞ in. wide. With wrong sides together, stitch the first seam the fringe width plus ¼ in. (¾ in. for a ½-in. fringe) from the raw edges. Clip the seam allowances to the seamline every 6 in. to 10 in. Clipping the allowances will enable you to flatten a curved seam. Press the seam open, then again with right sides together, pressing the seamline at the edge. When stitching a curve, be sure the seam allowances are spaced evenly so that there will be no gaps in the fringe. With right sides together, stitch ¼ in. from the edge (⅛ in. will be lost in the turn). Press the stitched line. Unravel the raw edges to fringe the seam.

Piped seams—Piping for a seam can be made with or without cording, from bias or straight-grain fabric strips, or it can be a length of ribbon, lace, braid, fringe, rickrack, leather, a selvage strip, synthetic suede, or even a zipper or ruffle. Most piping is a contrasting or complementary color, or it is cut from self-fabric on a different grain. When applied to fabrics that must be matched, such as plaids and stripes, piping can interrupt the flow of color bars so the seamlines don't have to match perfectly. When you're piping fabric that has a diagonal design, you have several possibilities: You can cut the strips on the bias, parallel to the selvage, or on the crossgrain.

When designing piped seams, balance the piping's weight, size, and color and the location and number of seams with the garment's appearance. Piped seams should make a statement but not overpower the fabric physically or overwhelm the garment visually.

Decide how the piping material will be cut. *Plain* or *uncorded piping* is a strip of fabric folded in half lengthwise, wrong sides together. Piping cut on the bias is easier to place on curved and angled seams. Some materials, such as leathers, synthetic suedes, and knits, have more stretch on the crossgrain than on the bias. If the seams are straight or almost straight, and the piping doesn't have to be shaped around curves and angles, it can be cut on the grain that will most enhance the design. This is an important consideration when you're sewing fabrics with stripes and diagonals.

Piping can be as narrow as ⅛ in. and as wide as 2 in. To determine how wide to make the strips, add the seam-allowance width to the finished width of the piping and multiply by 2. For a ¼-in.-wide piping with ⅝-in.-wide seam allowances, for example, cut the strips at least 1¾ in. wide. When I use piping, I'd rather trim the piping seam allowances to match those of the garment than end up with allowances that are too narrow. I find that bias strips in particular tend to narrow, so I add an extra ½ in. to 1 in. to the strip width.

To make piping, you can join the strips as needed to make one long strip or cut individual strips for each seamline. When you're stitching lengths of bias together for piping, be sure the seams are on the lengthwise grain, except for fabric with horizontal ribs or stripes. When you're stitching fabric with a horizontal pattern, sew the seams parallel to the fabric design. Fold the strip in half lengthwise, wrong sides together; if you want a sharp crease, press the fold line. Stitch the piping at the finished width from the fold line.

With a garment section right side up, match the seamlines of the piping and garment. Pin and stitch the piping in place on the seamline, as shown in the drawings at left, p. 78). Complete the seam by stitching the garment with right sides together. Press.

Corded piping can be very tiny for trimming evening gowns and little girls' dresses, or it can be large for trimming casual designs and bedspreads. The width of the piping strip varies with the size of the cord. To determine the width, wrap and pin a fabric strip around the cord. Add seam allowances, remove the cord, and unpin. To cord the piping, place the preshrunk cord on the wrong side of the strip. Wrap the strip around the cord and match the raw edges. Use a zipper or cording foot to enclose the cord. Don't stitch so close to the cord that the stitching will show on the finished gar-

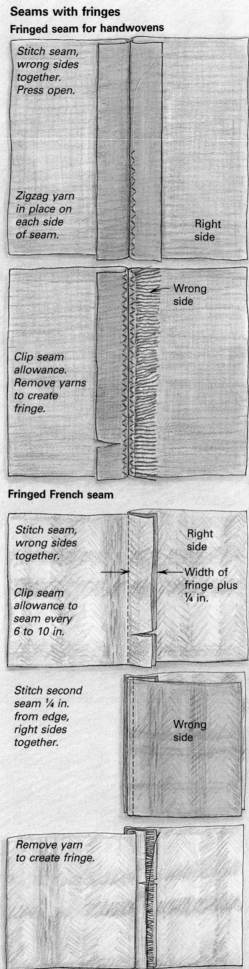

Seams with fringes

Fringed seam for handwovens

Stitch seam, wrong sides together. Press open.

Zigzag yarn in place on each side of seam.

Right side

Clip seam allowance. Remove yarns to create fringe.

Wrong side

Fringed French seam

Stitch seam, wrong sides together.

Clip seam allowance to seam every 6 to 10 in.

Right side

Width of fringe plus ¼ in.

Stitch second seam ¼ in. from edge, right sides together.

Wrong side

Remove yarn to create fringe.

The fringed seam is held open and flat by yarn zigzagged in place along each side of the seamline.

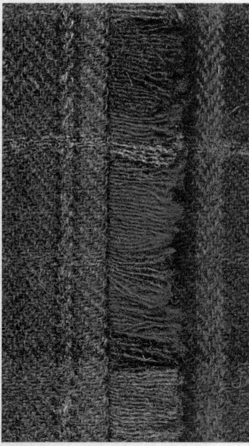

A French seam with a fringed seam allowance is reinforced by a second seam on the wrong side.

Thin or thick cords and piping strips cut on the bias create different piping effects.

Piping types and applications

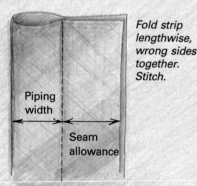

Uncorded piping

Fold strip lengthwise, wrong sides together. Stitch.

Piping width

Seam allowance

Corded piping

To determine width needed for piping, wrap fabric around cord and add seam allowances.

Use a zipper foot to stitch cording in piping.

Piping measurement

seam allowance

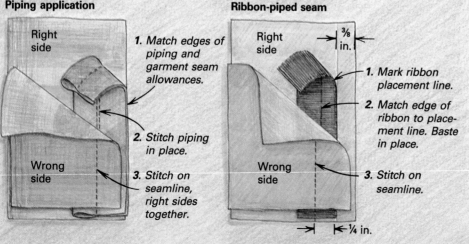

Piping application

Right side

Wrong side

1. Match edges of piping and garment seam allowances.

2. Stitch piping in place.

3. Stitch on seamline, right sides together.

Ribbon-piped seam

Right side

Wrong side

3/8 in.

1. Mark ribbon placement line.

2. Match edge of ribbon to placement line. Baste in place.

3. Stitch on seamline.

1/4 in.

ment. Apply corded piping the same as for flat piping, but use a zipper foot.

Piping for a ribbon-piped seam is one layer of fabric with two attractive faces. Select piping material that's the desired finished width plus 1/4 in. When using the selvage as a piping, cut it with a 5/8-in. seam allowance when fabric permits. Using a temporary marking pen or machine stitching, mark the garment's seam allowances 3/8 in. from the edge (drawing at bottom right). Align the edge of the piping with the marked line (or for a selvage with a 5/8-in. seam allowance, align it with the garment's seam allowances). Pin the piping; then baste or stitch it in place. With the garment's right sides together, stitch on the seamline.

Bound seams—Besides being decorative, binding neatly finishes the edges of seam allowances and can reduce the bulk of the fabric at the seamline. If the garment fabric is lightweight to medium weight, you can bind both seam allowances together (left photo, facing page); I first saw this seam on a Jeanne Marc design. For medium-weight to heavyweight fabric, such as suit wool or corduroy, you can bind one seam allowance and lap it over the second (center photo). For very thick or heavyweight fabric, you can stitch only the binding together, which reduces the bulk at the seamline, then bind the garment edges separately (right photo). The binding can be store-bought double-fold bias tape, folded braid, or unfolded custom-made bias.

The seam allowances for a bound seam, in which both seam allowances are bound together, are usually the standard 5/8 in. With wrong sides of the garment together, stitch on the seamline. With the seam allowances together, press flat, and trim the seams to 1/4 in. Insert the raw edges of the seam allowances between the folds of purchased, prefolded bias-tape binding. Align the folds of the binding with the seamline; pin and edgestitch through all layers. To make sure you catch both tape edges, use a narrow zigzag stitch. For a different look, bind the folded edge of the binding with a second binding in a different shade, color, or width.

With *unfolded custom-made bias,* I get better results if I use a slightly different method. Stitch the seam and trim the seam allowance to 3/8 in. Cut the bias strips 2 in. wide. With the right side of the bias next to the right side of one garment section, match the raw edges; then pin them (drawing at left, facing page). With the garment on top, stitch on the seamline. Wrap the bias around the seam, turn the raw edge under, and match the fold to the seamline. Baste the fold in place and edgestitch. According to Jeanne Marc's fabric designer, Jeanne Allen, to successfully use custom bias, the bias strips must be wider than you think you need, and acute curves shouldn't be bound.

The *bound-and-lapped seam,* used by the Austrian manufacturer Geiger on boiled-wool jackets, is also suitable for reversible and unlined garments. Geiger uses fold-over braid; purchased and custom-made bindings are also attractive.

Select the binding and measure its finished width. Cut the seam allowances on the overlap ⅛ in. narrower than the binding's finished width to allow for the thickness of the fabric (center drawing, below). Before stitching the seamline, bind the raw edge of the overlap as for a regular bound seam, aligning the edge of the binding with the seamline. If the garment is reversible, bind the underlap as well. If it isn't reversible, use your favorite edge for the finish.

With right sides up, lap the edges, matching the seamlines; then baste them. Generally, the front laps the back or side panel, and the garment laps the sleeve. Topstitch on the seamline.

The *bound-and-stitched seam* is suitable for thick, bulky fabrics and reversible and unlined garments. The seam allowances of the thick garment fabric are trimmed away and replaced by thinner binding, which is stitched together at the seamline instead (photo and drawing at right, below).

The binding can be wool fold-over braid, bias binding, ribbon, twill tape, or synthetic suede or leather. Estimate the amount of binding required before beginning: this decorative seam requires more binding than you might initially guess. Measure the lengths of all seamlines and multiply by 2.

Trim away all seam allowances on the garment; if the fabric is very thick or bulky, trim away an extra ⅛ in. to ¼ in. When using fold-over braid, examine it to see if one side is wider than the other. Open the braid so it's wrong side up. With the gar-

ment section right side up, place the fabric on top of the wider side of the braid. If the fabric isn't bulky, match and pin the raw edge to the fold line of the braid; if it's bulky, allow for the turn of the cloth and position the raw edge ⅛ in. to ¼ in. from the fold line. Turn the garment section wrong side up and baste or glue in place. Repeat this step for all edges.

With garment sections wrong sides together, match and pin the edges of the braid together. Stitch the braids together on the fold lines. Press the seams open. Baste the braid; then edgestitch it to the garment so both edges of the braid are secure. □

Claire Shaeffer of Palm Springs, CA, has written seven books, including The Complete Book of Sewing Short Cuts *(1981) and* Claire Shaeffer's Sewing SOS *(1988).*

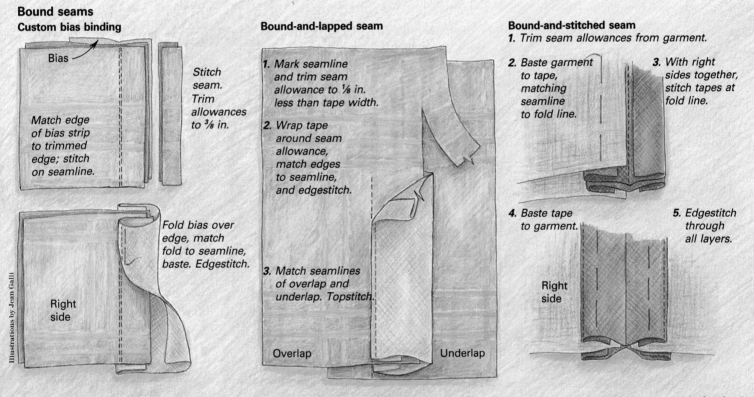

Bound seams
Custom bias binding

Bias

Match edge of bias strip to trimmed edge; stitch on seamline.

Stitch seam. Trim allowances to ⅜ in.

Fold bias over edge, match fold to seamline, baste. Edgestitch.

Right side

Illustrations by Jean Galli

Bound-and-lapped seam

1. Mark seamline and trim seam allowance to ⅛ in. less than tape width.

2. Wrap tape around seam allowance, match edges to seamline, and edgestitch.

3. Match seamlines of overlap and underlap. Topstitch.

Overlap

Underlap

Bound-and-stitched seam
1. Trim seam allowances from garment.

2. Baste garment to tape, matching seamline to fold line.

3. With right sides together, stitch tapes at fold line.

4. Baste tape to garment.

5. Edgestitch through all layers.

Right side

To bind seams in thin fabric with purchased folded bias tape, stitch the seam, trim the seam allowances, wrap with bias, and edgestitch.

For a bound-and-lapped seam in a nonreversible fabric, bind the overlap; then topstitch the overlap to the underlap on the seamline (blue).

In a bound-and-stitched seam, binding strips are sewn together to form the seam, then edgestitched to the garment fabric.

Balenciaga
The architect
of elegant clothing

by Harold Koda

The simple, precise notations on this working toile (left) reveal Balenciaga's understanding and use of grain in the structural engineering of this blue gazar evening dress (1967). The innovative and dramatic silhouette is the result of a careful manipulation of the bias.

from the opening of his Paris house in 1937 to its close in 1968, Cristobal Balenciaga, a Spaniard, was the acknowledged leader of the French couture. Christian Dior, perhaps Balenciaga's nearest rival, compared the rarefied world of *la mode* to an orchestra in which all the designers are musicians and Balenciaga is the conductor. "Where Balenciaga leads," he said, "we follow."

Although innovations by the master were radical, they were so carefully evolved that their influence endured. The boxy, semifitted suit; tunic dresses; flyaway peasant top; and chemise were all controversial when they first appeared *chez* Balenciaga, but each became, if only in variation, a style worn by every woman of the postwar period.

After the exotic cut-and-stitch improvisations of designer Poiret, the unshaped pattern pieces of the 1920s, and the radical elaborations of the bias in the 1930s, the impeccable tailoring techniques of the late 19th century were again the fashion. Women like Carmel Snow of *Harper's Bazaar,* Diana Vreeland of *Vogue,* Mrs. Loel Guinness, and the Baroness Pauline de Rothschild understood and expected nothing less than perfection in their dress. And, as the acerbic Coco Chanel stated flatly, "Balenciaga is the only one who can design, cut, put together, and sew a suit or gown entirely alone...."

Respect for tradition—This complete mastery of the techniques of tailoring distinguished Balenciaga from his rivals. The pure geometry of his designs suggests radical invention, but, in fact, it is the result of historic references to regional dress and traditional techniques. Perhaps it is the very novelty and aggressive simplicity of some of his forms that obscure the essential classicism of his training. His shapes are unprecedented, but each is obtained by long-established tailors' skills—the balanced grain line, the well-placed seam. The stark modernity of Balenciaga's evening dress of midnight-blue gazar (a firm silk fabric), effortless in effect, is possible only through the technical mastery evidenced in the notations covering his working toile (see photo, facing page). Cecil Beaton said succinctly, "[He] is fashion's Picasso, for like that painter, underneath all his experiments with the modern, Balenciaga has a deep respect for tradition and the pure classic line."

Even the most inventive of his cuts, the single-seamed coat from his 1961 collection (left photo, page 82), is an elaboration on ancient garment construction. One center-back seam joins two panels of fabric that constitute the coat's body and sleeves. But Balenciaga isn't a copyist. He omits the

The boxy, red semifitted suit at far right, which skims the body in front and falls loosely in back, was met with stunned silence by a 1952 audience accustomed to the New Look's sharply defined waist. It was, however, to become the silhouette of choice for women in the next decade.

The red and brown linen tunic dresses (1955) introduced a line and proportion since elaborated on by almost every major designer in the French couture. The green linen ensemble is an example of Balenciaga's 1964 refinement of the kimono-sleeve construction and bias cut.

underarm gussets typical of the prototypes and inserts small trapezoids at the shoulder instead. Additional shaping is accomplished by darts—over 20 in the collar alone—concealed in the patterning of the plaid. The simplicity of the regional garments that inspired it is maintained, but is enhanced by Balenciaga's brilliant tailoring.

A master of illusion—His clientele included the most elegant women: Princess Grace of Monaco, the Duchess of Windsor, Mrs. Paul Mellon—almost every woman with the refinement to understand him and the resources to afford him. These ladies of the best-dressed lists appreciated his carefully thrust-back collars, which, as Mrs. Guinness described, "let a woman and her pearls breathe," and also visually lengthened and straightened the curve of the neck. And though the mannequin-thin bodies of these clients didn't demand it, the skim-the-front, loose-in-back tailleurs suggested a willowy quality beneath that complemented the less svelte. Moreover, Balenciaga's manipulation of proportion through bracelet-length sleeves and bolerolike jackets also created the illusion of an elongated, lithe body.

Though he dressed the most refined beauties of his day, though he was considered the connoisseur's couturier, Balenciaga became most popular with fashion professionals for his ability to flatter the matronly figure. Because of his ingenious cuts, his coats and suits were staples of the American fashion industry. For example, his scarf-coat of duvetyn (a soft, napped fabric), shown on the facing page, which is open at the side seams, transforms the wasp-waisted, post-New Look silhouette through the resultant flying panels that drift over the figure rather than define it. With a technique typical of Balenciaga in its simplicity, the draped sleeves are formed by the tacking of each pleat through the fabric and lining onto a narrow inside tape.

Timeless designs—Perhaps Balenciaga's most effective illusion was his canting of the waistline—high in front, low in back (see right photo, below). Since the waist-

Above, Balenciaga's single-seamed coat (1961) recalls regional dress in the simplicity of its pattern. Its prototypes, found in many cultures, are the one-piece garments folded along the shoulder line. A pinned toile is shown at left; the opened pattern piece is in the background. Because of the double-breasted front overlap, there is a center-back seam; without the overlap, the coat might have been constructed of one piece. Tailoring devices, however, transfigure the rudimentary form. Over 20 darts in the collar alone are concealed in the carefully matched plaid fabric; trapezoidal gussets at the shoulders introduce the shaping and permit the proper hang of the coat. Unlike this garment, the regional prototypes are persistently two-dimensional.

The red-velvet lounging robe at right (1943) is derived from a Spanish coachman's coat. The flattering canted waistline begins at the lower rib cage and dips to the small of the back, encircling the body's narrowest ellipse and concealing its bulges.

line is an ellipse that hits the narrow lower rib cage and dips to the small of the back, touching only the beginning of the stomach and the flatness of the upper buttocks, inches seem to magically disappear. Balenciaga has eased fullness into the seam to obliterate the further burgeoning of the anatomy. The mind's eye continues the lines established by the fitted yoke, and the true body is obscured.

Manufacturers who paid an admittance fee, or "caution," were allowed to attend the couture showings. The caution was then applied toward the cost of any models, or designs, the manufacturer might wish to purchase. These models were, in every detail, identical to the original samples worn in the live presentation. And, although the caution at Balenciaga was high and defrayed only a portion of any final design purchases, American manufacturers felt that the expense was well worth it.

The common knowledge on Seventh Avenue was that a Balenciaga model could be used for years after its introduction, with only slight modifications. This was so for several reasons. First, Balenciaga's styles tended to anticipate and create trends. Second, Balenciaga, unlike many of the other designers of the couture, did not make radical seasonal shifts of silhouette and hem lengths that outmoded the previous year's styles. As revolutionary as they might be upon introduction, Balenciaga's styles evolved slowly over many collections and effectively avoided a built-in obsolescence. And last, Balenciaga's inventive cuts were adaptable to variations in individual structure even in ready-to-wear interpretations. The fact that a Balenciaga could be worn by a woman a size larger or smaller than originally intended also meant that it would continue to fit over time, despite any weight gain or loss.

Austerity and extravagance—In contrast to the somewhat festive atmosphere of the house of Dior, where cheers and applause were anticipated delights, a sense of asceticism and a monastic dignity characterized the house of Balenciaga, as well as many of his designs. Referred to by everyone as *le maître*, or *le dieu*, Balenciaga demanded a seriousness of purpose in his workrooms. The metaphors for his salon, studio, and ateliers were invariably those of a church, of some secret place of a mystical order. Even his assistants were referred to by everyone as Balenciaga's "little monks." His mannequins, too, with their unimpeachable elegance, strode quickly down the runway, never smiling, with an intimidating sobriety. Conversation and clapping were tacitly discouraged at his shows. Still, from this hushed, reverential environment and from a man obsessed with the perfection of his calling, came not only the most exquisite simplicity, but amazingly, extraordinary luxury and opulence as well.

Balenciaga married the austere and reductive with the fantastically rich; strong

The draped sleeves of the tan wool scarf-coat (1950) have been "quoted" by designers as varied as Givenchy, Kawakubo of Comme des Garçons, and Ungaro. They are formed by a narrow taffeta ribbon that runs inside the sleeves, from neckline to cuff, with each pleat tacked at approximately 4-in. intervals. Despite its dramatic effect, the coat's armhole construction is actually a simple variation of the kimono.

Balenciaga created architectural effects by exploiting the inherent property of the fabric, as shown in this silk-taffeta evening gown (1960). The volume of the skirt is formed by a self-bustle of shirred fabric folded into the back waist seam. The gown appears to drop away from the body, but is supported by a tulle corselet. The front hem is cut away so that, as the wearer is walking, the movement of the air causes the skirt to billow and change shape.

Although Balenciaga was primarily concerned with form and structure, the designer often used extravagantly colored and textured embroideries inspired by the Spanish baroque. Shown below is a detail from the surface of a jet-encrusted and gilt-appliquéd 1952 reception gown.

architectural silhouettes with tissue-thin materials; quiet forms with aggressively extravagant surfaces. This dichotomy was evident even in his use of color: somber tones of the Spanish countryside or the ash black of Basque peasant costume on the one hand, and the brilliant reds, fuchsias, chrome yellows, and acid greens of the corrida and the flamenco stage on the other.

His extravagant embroideries were often inspired by the great Spanish baroque. Velvets and satins were encrusted with jet and heavy silk cording, leather appliqués leafed in gold, metal paillettes hammered to catch the light, and seed beads the size of sturgeon roe. But the strongest ornaments were those Balenciaga took from the bullring: hot pink pampiles (ball trim) that shimmered with silk floss, infinitesimal gilt sequins, and chunky rosettes of black silk grosgrain. Still, however richly decorated, the Balenciaga gown was above all a statement of form, an exercise in the maximization of shape with the most minimal seaming and understructure.

Unlike Charles James, a contemporary with whom he is frequently compared, Balenciaga sought to achieve architectural effects through the inherent properties of his materials. A James ball gown is supported by layers of buckram, boning, net, and crinoline. The volume of a Balenciaga is in the structure of the cloth, in the reinforcement of grain through judicious seaming, and with almost every gathered form, a seam allowance that doubles as a supporting self-ruffle. The final effect of this buttressing seam allowance is

The ivory silk gazar wedding gown (1967) is the ultimate example of Balenciaga's mastery over seaming and the bias. The shoulder and center-back seams are the only structural seams; there's a horizontal piecing seam at the waist to widen the fabric. If the fabric had been wide enough, this garment could have been made of one panel. In movement it billows into a pure cone, but at rest it falls into graceful bias undulations.

most impressive in Balenciaga's frosted silk-taffeta evening gown (facing page). The ballooning, wedge-shaped skirt is created by a wide, shirred extension of the outer fabric folded under at the back waist seam to form a self-bustle. The seductiveness of the gown is not in a sexy fit or daring décolleté, but in the sense of the gown's dropping away from the body. It is an effect created by the suspension of the dress on a lightly boned, tulle corselet.

Ultimately, however, the volume of a Balenciaga was generated by the motion of the wearer. Pauline de Rothschild compared the effect to a sail: "A woman walking would displace the air so that her skirt would billow out just so much; front, back, and sides would round out each in turn, imperceptibly, like a sea-swell." To facilitate the aspiration of each step, Balenciaga carved away a portion of the front hem. The back trailed lightly on the floor, and its drag would draw in the air to balloon the form. The apotheosis of this principle is the silk gazar wedding dress at left. Although the gown at rest is a graceful series of soft bias undulations, in procession it would form a pure cone. In effect, the gown's center-back and shoulder seams are the only structural shaping devices. There is no front seaming, only a long horizontal join at waist level, on lengthwise grain, which is a piecing device intended to widen the fabric. If Balenciaga had found a gazar of sufficient width, this final statement of his 1967 collection could have been accomplished in one continuous panel.

When Balenciaga abruptly closed his house in 1968, he told friends it was because his clients were gone and because he could no longer rely on the perfection of the materials he ordered. But, it may also be that by his last collections he had realized an absolute mastery over his craft. He had completely refined the possibilities of the pattern piece; his investigations had come to their logical and unsurpassable conclusion. □

Harold Koda is curator of the costume collection of the Edward C. Blum Design Laboratory at The Fashion Institute of Technology (FIT). The garments shown here were part of the "Balenciaga" exhibition held at FIT Sept. 8-Dec. 6, 1986. Photos by Brian Gulick.

Koos, the Master of Collage

Inspired solutions to machine-appliquéd edges unite art, fashion, and comfort

by David Page Coffin

Koos van den Akker hates it when people call his clothes art to wear. "Even when Cocteau and Picasso worked for Schiaparelli," he says, "that wasn't art–it's decoration. It's too easy." Fabric artists, makers of quilt wearables, and imaginative home sewers can be excused for seeing artistic elements in the rich surfaces and dazzling colors that fill this Dutch designer's Madison Avenue store. But Koos (pronounced like *coast* without the *t*) calls his trademark fabric-collaged garments "commercial clothes."

Koos maintains an exhilarating, playful inventiveness and a remarkable singleness of vision in the heart of that most fickle and pragmatic world–New York's Garment District. To find out how he does it, I spent several days with him and his assistant designer, Diane Hendry, at his Seventh Avenue workrooms.

"I have a background in classic clothes," says Koos, "and I can make clothes fit, so now I can be relaxed and make beautiful things without worrying about dressmaking. I love to make unusual combinations, and I enjoy clothes. They are absolute beauty–they were always on my path."

Beneath the swirling surfaces of a Koos creation is a basic garment: an oversized coat; a boxy raglan top; a straight, tailored Chanel-type jacket. These forms are ideal canvases, the frames for his fabric paintings, but they must also function as practical, modern clothing, and these unfussy geometries are perfect for action as well.

"People have no time for fashion. These days it's about Benetton and The Gap. My clothes must be perfect over a T-shirt and jeans. You should be able to throw them in the backseat of your car."

No matter what the fabrics in a Koos collage–from tissue to fur–the machine-stitched layers of color make a sturdy gar-

ment, a fantasy with pockets. When drape and flow are important, some garment parts may be "un-collaged," but Koos's multi-layered fabric is invariably soft and tactile. Almost incidental to his goal of making lovely things, Koos van den Akker has reinvented the quilted, appliquéd garment. Besides making it so beautiful that you must stop to admire it, he has developed such easy, design-sensitive construction methods that you know you just have to try making one for yourself.

The path to Madison Avenue–During World War II, when Koos was four years old, his neighborhood in Holland was bombed, and his family evacuated their house. "I was playing, and I ran outside in my costume–a crepe-paper skirt and wings on my back. When I was eleven, I made my first dress for my sister, and many more after that. My family would go to church three times every Sunday, and I'd make dresses for all my girlfriends. We'd sit in the front row so everyone could stare at us."

Koos left home when he was about 15 to attend the Royal Academy of Art in The Hague but soon gravitated to a fashion academy in Paris. Christian Dior's workers spotted him there, and he apprenticed with them for the next three years, making suits and dresses. He returned to Holland in 1965 to open a salon for custom clothes. "It was a beautiful shop...we had lovely windows. But it was not a success. My father helped me start it, but when he died, I left for New York." Koos took with him a portable sewing machine and $168.

"I arrived on a Saturday and went straight to the Empire State Building and loved everything I saw. On Sunday I went to the Guggenheim Museum, and on Monday to Macy's to buy fabric, and I was in business." He made a dress in his hotel room every night and soon was selling every-

The ability to combine the most unlikely of fabrics, layer them comfortably, and use their edges as design elements are the keys to Koos van den Akker's successful clothes.

Koos's fabric-collaged technique (facing page) begins with a layer of base fabric. Gauzes and laces can be combined with cotton flannel, and yards of bias tape create shapes within shapes.

Koos works on a sleeve for the resort collection. He begins with the on-grain green print sleeve shape, then cuts and pins new elements until he's satisfied. He'll then glue-baste and sew the collage elements flat and cover the raw edges with bias tape.

thing he could produce. "Thirty-five dollars a dress, custom-made, not adventurous. It was an easy period." Within two years, Koos opened his own tiny shop on Columbus Avenue, where he continued to personally make everything that he sold. This is where the Koos look evolved. Five years later, in 1975, he moved to 795 Madison Avenue, and he's been there ever since. "It's my joy, my kitchen, my lab."

Koos still spends most days at the sewing machine, but now 27 people help him produce his collaged garments: a wholesale line for a few department stores and his collection of one-of-a-kind creations, which has lured Barbara Walters, Glenn Close, Marilyn Horne, and Bill Cosby (Cosby wears Koos sweaters on his TV show) into his shop.

Where it all comes from—"I start with fabric. Silhouettes come later. Shapes are not really what I'm interested in. I love fabric, and I buy it in a very different way from other designers, who buy just what they need; they have it all figured out, have sketches—I don't sketch. I like to have a library of fabric." Koos's library is huge and staggeringly beautiful. Everything comes in bolts.

A typical Koos starts with the pattern pieces for a simple garment, cut carefully on-grain from a single base fabric. Depending on the fabric, and the season, the pieces may be stabilized with an underlayer and fused with a spray adhesive (3M #6065). Cotton jersey might support a gauzy madras, which also would permit a sleeve to be cut on the bias and still support multiple layers of random-grain collage.

With scissors and a practiced eye, Koos then carves through the heaps of contrast fabrics all around him on his worktable, finding shapes to fit within the pattern piece before him. I watched as Koos transformed the fabric in the photo above in less than 15 minutes, and with scarcely a backward glance, from a humble sleeve into an excerpt from his endless and ongoing abstract mental painting.

"My designs come from inside; it's impulsive. I have no control over it. I don't perfect it. I just do it. But I'll tell you an interesting story. A friend gave me a book a while ago about Dutch costume. I could care less what they wore then, and I never saw it when I was a child. When I grew up, my parents and our area, it was very plain. But there it all was in this book, the whole thing, the stripes against flowers, lace, leather, combinations—it gives me goose bumps to think about it. I'm still not interested in the old costumes, but they are exquisite. So this is where it comes from; I have nothing to do with it. There's no resemblance, yet it's all there. It has to do with heritage, whether you like it or not, but I'm not a folkloric designer. There's no label that fits. It's original. Not fashion, not art, just inspired clothes with a lot of details."

Inside the workroom—A sleeve as elaborate as the one I saw Koos making will become part of a one-of-a-kind garment. For his wholesale line, Koos's collage designs are simpler, and his staff will figure out how to reproduce multiples at their machines from his prototypes.

In another area, Diane Hendry works in much the same way, using a collage of fabrics to create one-of-a-kind Koos garments stamped with her more formal and symmetrical vision. She is largely responsible for the recent appearance of figurative shapes among the flurry of elements in the collages at 795 Madison Avenue. Diane won her job with a completely fabric-collaged fan letter to Koos. The letter demonstrated her mastery of his techniques and her capacity to make them her own. These days, Diane also hand-makes Koos's astounding born-again furs. Koos cuts up and machine-sews old fur coats as if they were fabric (photos on facing page, top and left), and adventurous customers bring in their furs for rehabilitation.

Says Koos, "Teaching someone young the tricks of fashion, of life, that's what inspires my life now. It's behind everything I do and directly inspires my work." Since 1985, Christian Francis Roth, the son of an acquaintance, who described Roth to Koos as determined to work in fashion, has been studying in Koos's workrooms. "I started when I was seventeen," Roth told me. "Koos taught me how to sew and cut and about fabric. I spent about nine months quilting coat linings so I'd know how to sew a straight line."

While studying nights at Parsons and FIT, Roth expressed an interest in designing. Koos lent him fabric, hired a patternmaker to work with him, and sent his seamstresses home with work for Roth's emerging line, which debuted as "Fall '88" with about 14 pieces. Roth's third collection, "Fall '89," which was shipped in July to Bergdorf Goodman, Bonwit Teller, and Saks Fifth Avenue, uses spare silhouettes, with an echo of Koos in the elaborate appliquéd cutouts. But these are witty images and figures—clothespins, puppets, and clocks, in black, and infrequently, on solid fabrics.

Drawing lines with fabric—As I pored over Koos's sumptuous originals, I was continually struck by how elegantly the basic problem of fabric collage—raw edges—had been solved. Koos's collages are actually a form of machine appliqué. Each appliquéd element is cut to shape and straight-stitched in place. Making a virtue out of necessity, Koos has evolved a couple of highly efficient strategies for covering edges. Their function is hardly ever obvious because they work primarily visually, adding a free linear element, and intricately shaped outlines, to the designs.

Rarely, Koos or Diane will decide to fold under the edges first. But usually they cover the edges with cut-to-shape thin leather or Ultrasuede patches, or with premade bias tape. Koos sends yards of appropriate fabric out to be formed into continuous rolls of tape, either ½ in. wide or, less often, ¼ in. wide (this is useful for both tight curves and small designs) when finished. The

Assistant designer Diane Hendry cuts old furs into new collaged coats (above and left). The collage techniques work easily for fur, leather, and imitations because the raw edges don't need finishing. Below, more formal designs—completed jacket backs.

top drawing at right shows how the bias tape is sewn around corners and curves to make a neat finish.

To easily make your own bias tape, use one of the tape-folding gadgets made by Clover. They come in several widths, starting with ½ in., they're inexpensive, and they work beautifully, especially combined with a rotary cutter and mat for efficient strip cutting. Follow Koos's example, and buy yardage just for making into bias tape. Make lots so you can cut long strips and won't have any seams to worry about.

Koos finds that very small stripes, checks, and calicoes work best graphically and that bias tapes of large prints take over, weakening the composition. When made in these simple textures, the tapes provide great control over the emphasis that he or Diane gives to the appliquéd shapes, softening or clarifying the boundaries. They make it easy to combine fabrics because the join between very similar fabrics needn't be lost, and wildly different fabrics can be unified by an allover network of the same-print bias.

The leather, of course, doesn't need edge finishing, and it adds instant contrast to almost any fabric. Leather patches can be cut to enclose very distinct shapes. Because of the wide variety of printed and textured real and synthetic leathers available, this technique has many possibilities for providing just the needed touch in a composition.

The upside-down Hong Kong finish—Koos takes the idea of decorative covered edges to it's logical conclusion by also finishing cuffs, collars, and openings with contrasting bias strips. If the garment is thin enough, the same bias tapes can do the job. If it's too thick, Koos will cut a wider strip. In either case, the method is the same, a variation on the standard Hong Kong finish, in which right and wrong sides are reversed.

The standard Hong Kong finish leaves one raw edge, usually on the wrong side. Granted, it's bias and won't ravel, but it's a good place for another decorative tape. Koos arranges the raw edge on the right side, where you'll see its covering. He starts on the garment's wrong side with a bias strip cut four times the width of the planned finish. He sews the tape wrong side up, turns it, and stitches in the ditch, then trims the raw edge with narrower tape (see center drawing). If he's using tape alone, he just unfolds one edge and sews in the crease, then topstitches on the right side of the garment.

If the bias strip is wide, it can't be eased simply around corners. It must be mitered (see bottom drawing). This takes some experience to do beautifully on very thick fabric because you have to allow for the thickness of the enclosed fabric, but it's worth the effort. ☐

David Page Coffin is an associate editor of Threads.

Illustration by Phoebe Gaughan

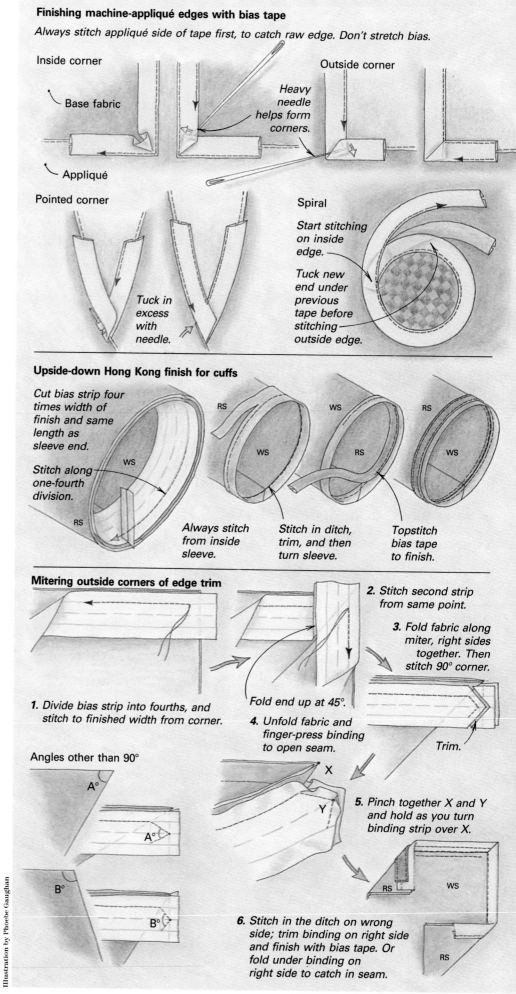

Finishing machine-appliqué edges with bias tape

Always stitch appliqué side of tape first, to catch raw edge. Don't stretch bias.

Inside corner

Base fabric

Appliqué

Outside corner

Heavy needle helps form corners.

Pointed corner

Tuck in excess with needle.

Spiral

Start stitching on inside edge.

Tuck new end under previous tape before stitching outside edge.

Upside-down Hong Kong finish for cuffs

Cut bias strip four times width of finish and same length as sleeve end.

Stitch along one-fourth division.

WS

RS

RS

WS

RS

WS

RS

WS

Always stitch from inside sleeve.

Stitch in ditch, trim, and then turn sleeve.

Topstitch bias tape to finish.

Mitering outside corners of edge trim

1. *Divide bias strip into fourths, and stitch to finished width from corner.*

Fold end up at 45°.

2. *Stitch second strip from same point.*

3. *Fold fabric along miter, right sides together. Then stitch 90° corner.*

4. *Unfold fabric and finger-press binding to open seam.*

Trim.

Angles other than 90°

A°

A°

B°

B°

X

Y

5. *Pinch together X and Y and hold as you turn binding strip over X.*

RS

WS

6. *Stitch in the ditch on wrong side; trim binding on right side and finish with bias tape. Or fold under binding on right side to catch in seam.*

RS

Handsewing Stitches

Which to use when and how to sew them

by Grace Callaway

despite the fully automatic and computerized sewing machines available today, none allows you to forgo handsewing entirely. There are certain processes that you just can't satisfactorily accomplish on a home sewing machine, and so you must know some basic hand-stitching techniques.

Sewing by hand is satisfying and relaxing, even though it can be time-consuming. But since it is portable, it is the perfect solution for what to do while you're sitting in the doctor's office, waiting for the kids to finish ball practice, or watching television. On a long trip you might even have time to make an elegant silk blouse.

Some guidelines—A few general guidelines can save you many a headache and ensure the success of your handsewing. For basic handsewing procedures, the needles you'll need are sharps and betweens. Sharps are about ⅜ in. longer than betweens in the same size, and both have small, round eyes. Thus, sharps are good for making long stitches, as for basting, and betweens are better for short stitches. Betweens are sometimes called quilting needles because they allow you to make small stitches through many layers of fabric.

Sharps and betweens both come in sizes 1 to 12—the larger the number, the shorter and finer the needle. For most sewing operations you'll need sizes 7 to 10.

Use high-quality, tempered-steel needles, which are flexible, yet not easily bent or broken. The needles should be perfectly smooth so that the points slide easily through the fabric without snagging and the eye doesn't fray or cut the thread.

Select your needle size according to the fabric, as well as the type of stitches—the lighter the weight of the fabric, the smaller the needle size. It's difficult to make short stitches with a long needle or inconspicuous ones with a thick needle.

Choose thread that is compatible with the type of fiber and the weight of the fabric, and be sure it fits the eye of the needle. If the thread is too large, you'll have difficulty getting it through the hole, and it may fray and break while you're sewing.

If it's too small, snarling and knotting will plague you. Size 50 thread is appropriate with a size 7 or 8 needle; a size 9 or 10 needle requires extra-fine thread. For all permanent stitching, the thread color should exactly match the fabric, or it should look one shade darker on the spool because the single strand in the fabric will be lighter.

The working thread should be approximately the length of your arm. This length is less likely to tangle than a longer one, and you won't tire as rapidly.

To reduce tangling, thread your needle with the end cut from the spool, and cut the thread on a slant for ease in passing through the eye. Never moisten thread before inserting it in the needle, as this makes some fibers spread apart. Moistening the back of the needle's eye, however, will help draw the thread end through.

To further minimize snarling, secure to the fabric the end of the thread that you passed through the needle. Do all handsewing with a single thread, unless the instructions specify a double one, as when you sew on fasteners.

Never tie a knot in the loose end of your thread, unless it's absolutely necessary, especially when you're sewing on fine fabrics, because the outline of the knot may show through. Secure the beginning and end of your stitching with two or three tiny backstitches, as shown in the top-left drawing on page 94. On the underside of the fabric, make a tiny stitch about 1⁄16 in. long, barely catching the top layer of fabric. Pull the thread through, leaving ½ in. dangling at the end. Make two more tiny stitches in the same spot to secure the thread. Get into the habit of doing this; instructions rarely explain it. The following instructions are written for right-handed people. If you are left-handed, substitute *right* for *left,* and *left* for *right.*

Basting stitches—Basting stitches, shown in the drawings on page 92, are some of the most familiar hand stitches because they often are used to mark construction details or hold several pieces of fabric together for accurate permanent stitching. Although machine basting is faster, it is best reserved for short distances or straight edges on sturdy fabrics. You have more control with hand basting, which is especially important when you're fitting a garment.

Basting thread should contrast with the fabric, but avoid using very dark threads on light fabrics, as they sometimes leave marks or stains. White or pastel thread will provide adequate contrast for your work. The type of basting stitch is determined by its location on the garment and the nature of the pieces being joined. Generally, make the stitch by weaving a needle in and out of the fabric. The ends of basted seams are usually not secured.

Uneven basting, in which the stitches can vary in length and spacing, can be used for most purposes. It is a quick method of marking grain lines and other construction symbols and of temporarily holding long, straight edges together.

Even basting, which is shorter and more evenly spaced than uneven basting and thus holds better, is used for basting curved edges, such as necklines, or for matching sections that need easing, such as set-in sleeves or the bustline seam on a princess-style garment. You may wish to backstitch once at the beginning and end of even basting on curved edges, since there is sometimes more stress on these edges.

The *running stitch* is even basting with about 8 to 10 stitches to the inch and usually is permanent. In French handsewing, this stitch is used for pin tucks, gathers, shirring, and fine seams on soft, delicate fabrics. Use a small needle and fine thread.

Slip basting, which is done from the right side of the fabric, holds seam lines in place for machine stitching. It is useful for making alterations while you're fitting a garment on the body or for matching plaids or intricate structural designs, such as deep V-shaped angles, sharp corners, or scallops and other curves.

Press under the seam allowance of one piece of fabric on the seam line. Then overlap and pin that piece in position on the right side of the other piece. Baste the sections from the right side of the garment so the pieces can be aligned.

Make a small stitch in the single layer of fabric and another stitch inside the fold of the seam allowance that you pressed un-

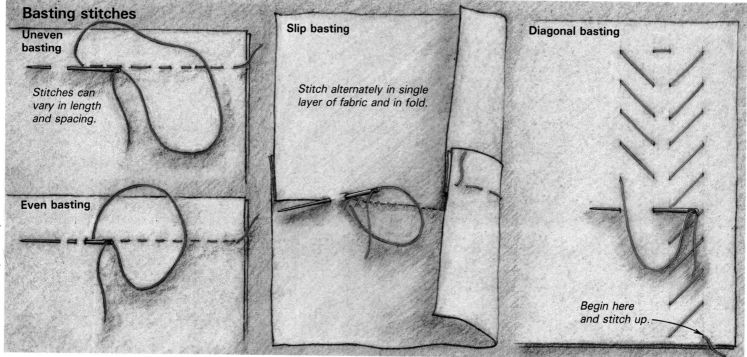

Basting stitches

Uneven basting

Stitches can vary in length and spacing.

Even basting

Slip basting

Stitch alternately in single layer of fabric and in fold.

Diagonal basting

Begin here and stitch up.

Illustrations by Vickie Joy Stansberry

der. Keep the stitch length ¼ in. or less to prevent the edges from slipping. Continue to alternate stitches between the single fabric layer and the fold.

Use *diagonal basting* whenever it's necessary to hold two or more layers of fabric together over a large area, as when you're basting an underlining to the outer fabric. The stitches can be long and far apart. Stitching the rows alternately from bottom to top and top to bottom is fast because you don't have to keep reversing the fabric with each new row. The diagonal floats will slant right as you go up the fabric and left as you come back down, producing a chevron pattern. You can also baste in only one direction, but you must cut the thread at the end of each row or keep rethreading the needle.

Whichever method of diagonal basting you use, keep the work flat on a firm surface to avoid fabric slippage or distortion of the grain lines. Small safety pins at 6-in. to 8-in. intervals help hold the layers in place as you work, and they won't catch the thread as straight pins would.

You can also use diagonal basting to hold seam lines flat for pressing or topstitching. In this case, make only a single row of stitches that are short and close together.

Hemstitches—Almost every garment has a hem edge that must be secured in an inconspicuous way (see drawings, facing page). Before beginning any hem, finish the cut edge of the fabric to prevent raveling by stitching on hemming tape or lace, pinking and stitching the edge, or turning and stitching it. Ease out fullness and turn the hem up to the wrong side of the garment. Baste it along the lower edge to keep the hem even. Pin the top of the hem in place.

The *slant stitch*, also called the whip stitch, is probably the most familiar and

fastest hemming stitch. It is not durable, however, because so much thread is exposed to snagging and fraying.

For slant hemming, hold the bottom of the hem in your left hand. Secure the thread on the underside of the hem, and working from bottom to top, make a stitch under only one thread of the garment and through the edge of the hem. Space the stitches evenly—not less than ¼ in. nor more than ½ in. apart. Make each stitch only about ⅛ in. into the hem edge. When the thread runs out, secure the end with two or three tiny backstitches.

The *vertical hemstitch* is similar to the slant stitch, but it's more durable because less thread is exposed. It is suitable for hems where the edge has been finished with tape.

After you've basted the lower edge of the hem, hold it toward you so you can work right to left. Secure the thread under the hem edge and bring it out on top of the hem about ⅛ in. below the edge. Make a stitch under one thread of the garment exactly above the point where the thread comes through the hem. Make another stitch through the hem to the left of the first one, coming out ⅛ in. below the edge. Continue around the hem, keeping the stitches evenly spaced, no less than ¼ in. nor more than ½ in. apart. Secure the end of your stitching under the hem edge.

The *slipstitch* is another familiar and even more durable hemstitch. Almost no thread shows, since it is enclosed in the hem edge. For this stitch there must be a fold at the top of the hem, either a turned-and-stitched fabric edge or a folded tape.

With the hem basted and pinned in position, hold the garment so that the hem's lower edge is away from you, and secure your working thread under the hem edge with a few backstitches. Bring the thread

through the fold at the top of the hem. Make a stitch under one thread of the garment and pull the thread through. Insert the needle in the fold of the hem edge and come out from ¼ in. to ½ in. to the left. Make another stitch in the garment. Then insert the needle in the fold again. Continue around the entire hem, keeping the stitches even in length. Secure the end of your stitching under the hem edge.

Use the *catchstitch* when you want a strong hemstitch with some give to it. The flexibility of this stitch, which has a zigzag appearance, makes it especially appropriate for knits. Because most of the thread is exposed, however, it is susceptible to snagging and abrasion.

Baste and pin the hem and hold the garment with the bottom of the hem toward yourself. Secure the thread under the hem edge and bring it through to the front. Make a stitch under one thread of the garment about ¼ in. to the right of where the thread is attached. Make a second stitch about ⅛ in. below the hem edge and ¼ in. to the right of the first. For each stitch, the needle is inserted in the fabric from right to left, and each stitch is made to the right of the previous one, so the thread crosses itself with each stitch. Continue alternating stitches between the garment and the hem ¼ in. apart, being careful not to catch the garment when you stitch into the hem. Secure your stitching under the hem edge.

Blind hemming, thus called because the stitches are made between the hem and garment layers and don't show, is not a specific stitch. The slant stitch, vertical hemstitch, slipstitch, or catchstitch can be used. Almost any edge finish can be used on the top of your hem, except a single-layer tape, which lets the stitches show through.

To prepare a garment for blind hemming, baste around the hem's lower edge and ¼ in.

below the top. This upper row of basting holds the hem in place better than pins and doesn't get in the way.

Fold back the hem's top edge with your left thumb and secure the working thread on the underside of the hem. Make a stitch under one thread of the garment and a second stitch in the back of the hem, using whichever hemstitch you've chosen. Keeping the hem's top edge folded back ¼ in., work around the hem, stitching alternately in the garment and in the back of the hem.

Backstitches—Backstitches (see drawings, page 94) simulate machine stitching when the stitches are of even length. They are strong enough for joining seams and were normally used for making garments before there were sewing machines. Many people still make fine garments, such as baby clothes or lingerie, entirely by hand, using the backstitch. Other uses include repairing seams, French handsewing, putting in zippers, understitching facings, topstitching, and securing the beginning and end of hand stitching.

The *even backstitch* is the most versatile and strongest of the backstitches. Secure the thread and bring it to the top side of the fabric about ⅛ in. from the right end of the seam. Insert the needle ⅛ in. to the right and bring it out ⅛ in. to the left of

where the thread came through. Pull the thread through. For each successive stitch, insert the needle just to the left of the last stitch made and come out one stitch length beyond where the thread emerged. On top, the stitches resemble machine stitching, and the underside looks somewhat like the outline stitch in embroidery.

When you're practicing, ⅛ in. is a good stitch length, though you may wish to shorten it when working on a garment. To become accustomed to various stitch lengths, machine-sew samples at settings of 8, 10, and 12 stitches per inch. Then practice handsewing rows of even backstitches beside the machine-stitched rows.

The *half backstitch* is made similarly to the even backstitch, except that the spaces between the stitches are the same length as the stitches. To make this stitch, bring the needle out two stitch lengths to the left of where the thread emerges. Then insert the needle only one stitch length back. The half backstitch uses less thread than the even backstitch because the stitches are farther apart, but it is also not as strong. It can be used for some repairs, however, when there isn't a lot of stress on the seam.

The *pickstitch* is a backstitch that catches only the upper layers of fabric and thus is invisible on the underside. The length and spacing of the stitches can vary a lot, de-

pending on the finished effect desired. You can use the even backstitch, half backstitch, or any other variation for pickstitching.

The pickstitch is primarily decorative and is often used for topstitching on fabrics that are too heavy to feed easily through the sewing machine. It also is useful for understitching facings, particularly on lightweight fabrics. It gives a softer finish than machine understitching because a single thickness of thread is used.

The *prickstitch* is another decorative variation of the backstitch. Its most frequent use is for handpicking a zipper in heavy fabrics that don't feed well through the sewing machine and in very soft ones that may suffer damage from the machine's feed dog. If you handpick a zipper, include other hand-stitched details on the garment, or it will look homemade.

The upper stitches are small and widely spaced. The technique is the same as for the half backstitch, except that the prickstitch goes through all layers of the fabric, as well as the zipper tape underneath. Thus, on heavy fabrics the stitches on top will be farther apart because the needle must pick up several layers underneath.

Overcasting—When you are sewing either sheer or lightweight fabrics, finish the seam edges by hand. The majority of machine

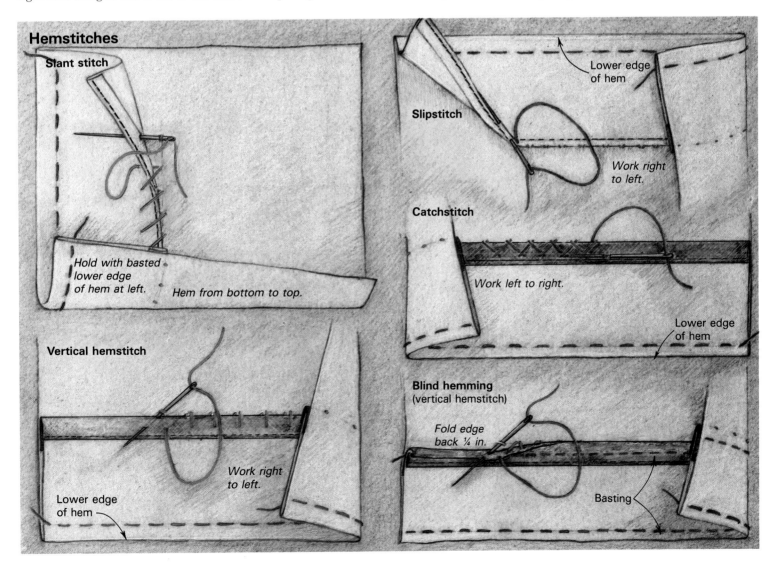

Hemstitches

Slant stitch

Hold with basted lower edge of hem at left.

Hem from bottom to top.

Vertical hemstitch

Work right to left.

Lower edge of hem

Slipstitch

Lower edge of hem

Work right to left.

Catchstitch

Work left to right.

Lower edge of hem

Blind hemming (vertical hemstitch)

Fold edge back ¼ in.

Basting

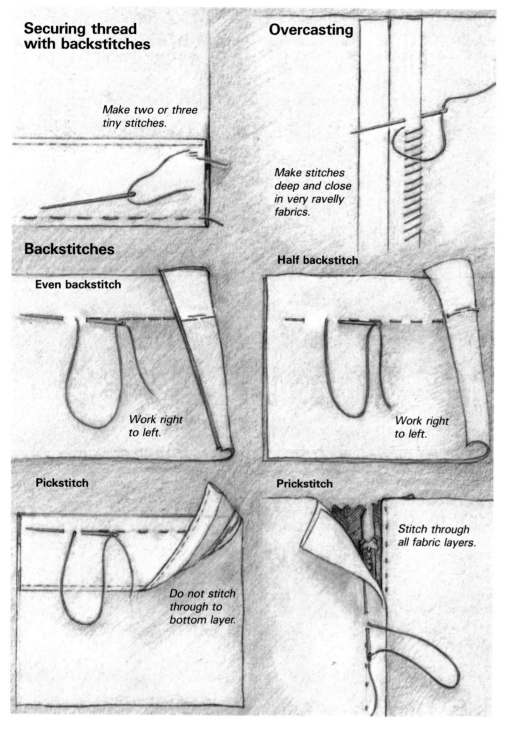

Securing thread with backstitches

Make two or three tiny stitches.

Overcasting

Make stitches deep and close in very ravelly fabrics.

Backstitches

Even backstitch

Work right to left.

Half backstitch

Work right to left.

Pickstitch

Do not stitch through to bottom layer.

Prickstitch

Stitch through all fabric layers.

seam finishes produce puckers or hard edges, which can damage the cut edges of fabrics such as lawn, organdy, crepe de chine, chiffon, and batiste. Hand overcasting, shown in the drawing at top right, is the softest and most appropriate seam finish for these types of fabrics. Adjust the stitch length and depth according to the amount of raveling that you encounter: The more the fabric ravels, the closer and deeper the stitches should be.

You work the overcast stitch like slant hemming, except that you don't stitch into the outer layer of the garment fabric. Whip over the edge of the seam allowance or other raw edge, forming diagonal stitches. Keep the stitches even and uniform in size. Work from whatever direction is most comfortable—bottom to top, top to bottom, right to left, or left to right.

Tacking stitches—During the construction of a garment, you sometimes need hand stitches to hold facings in place, anchor linings, reinforce stress points, or mark construction details. The stitches used are known collectively as tacks (see drawings, facing page), though they aren't all made the same way.

Tailor's tacks are used to mark construction symbols for the assembly of a garment. They take time, but are essential on fabrics that are delicate, thick, multicolored, or otherwise incapable of being marked by other means.

Traditional tailor's tacks are made with double sewing thread on double fabric. Make two stitches at each spot where you want a mark, leaving the second stitch as a loop on the fabric surface. Clip the thread between the tacks, and pull the layers of fab-

ric apart to the length of the loops. Cut the loops between the layers of fabric, and trim them close to the fabric.

Simplified tailor's tacks are made with double thread on double or single fabric. Make only one stitch at each spot where you want a tack. Clip and trim the thread between stitches.

Use contrasting thread for tailor's tacks. Trim the thread ends of the finished tacks very close to the fabric. This minimizes the chances of losing them before you stitch the garment together because they fall out only when the thread ends are too long. (You know how hard it is to remove the thread fragments where a seam has been ripped out.)

Cross-stitch tacks, which are decorative as well as functional, are among the various types of tacks used throughout garment construction and finishing. Single cross-stitches hold facings in place at seam intersections, while allowing the facing to move slightly without pulling, which whipping the edge in place does not. Multiple cross-stitches are often used to hold tucks, pleats, or folds in place on tailored garments.

To make the *single cross-stitch,* secure the thread end under the edge to be tacked down. Bring the thread out on the top side of the fabric. Insert the needle from right to left ¼ in. below and ⅛ in. to the right of where the thread is attached. The thread will slant down to the right. For the second stitch, insert the needle ⅛ in. to the right of where the first thread was attached, and bring it out where that thread exited. This will complete the cross-stitch. Make two or three more stitches in the same spot. Secure the thread under the seam or facing edge. When tacking through seam allowances, avoid stitching through to the right side of the garment.

For *multiple cross-stitches,* make a row of diagonal stitches in one direction, and then stitch back over them in the opposite direction to form the cross pattern. Keep multiple cross-stitches small and evenly spaced if they'll be visible on the garment.

Bar tacks reinforce stress points such as pocket corners, placket ends, and buttonhole ends. The length of the bar depends on its location. For example, you need a longer one at the bottom of a fly zipper placket than you need at the ends of a buttonhole.

Secure the thread on the underside of the fabric. Then bring the needle through to the top. In the same place, make three or four stitches the length you want the bar to be. Beginning at the left end, make closely spaced blanket stitches over the bar, catching the fabric underneath as well. Secure the thread on the underside after you've covered the entire bar.

The *arrowhead,* which is stitched to have a diamond-shaped pattern in its center, is a more decorative reinforcement tack. If you use two or three strands of embroidery floss to make the tack, it can be an impor-

Tacking stitches

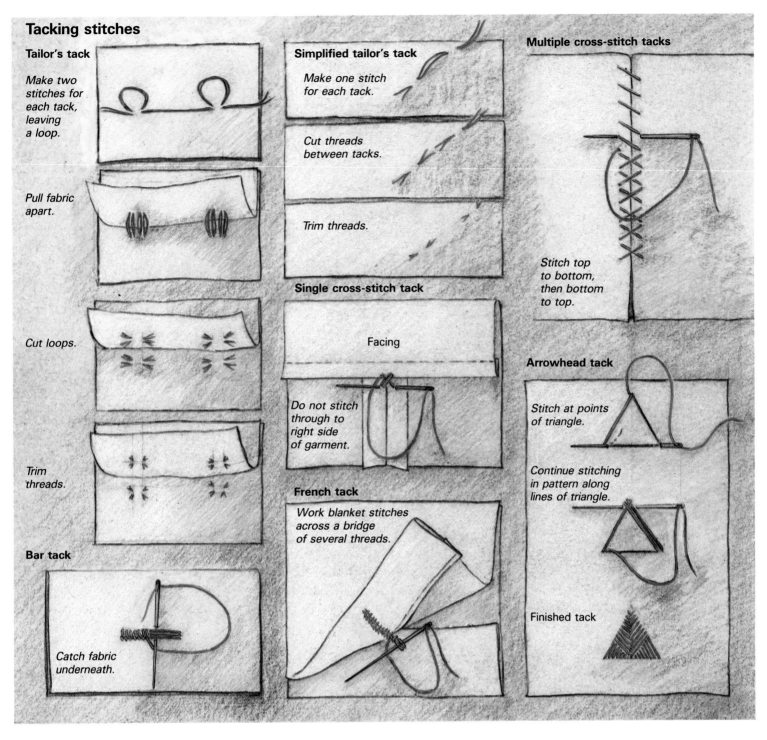

Tailor's tack

Make two stitches for each tack, leaving a loop.

Pull fabric apart.

Cut loops.

Trim threads.

Bar tack

Catch fabric underneath.

Simplified tailor's tack

Make one stitch for each tack.

Cut threads between tacks.

Trim threads.

Single cross-stitch tack

Facing

Do not stitch through to right side of garment.

French tack

Work blanket stitches across a bridge of several threads.

Multiple cross-stitch tacks

Stitch top to bottom, then bottom to top.

Arrowhead tack

Stitch at points of triangle.

Continue stitching in pattern along lines of triangle.

Finished tack

---

tant design element on such garments as Western shirts and other costumes.

Make all stitches from right to left within a triangle you have drawn on the fabric. Use the lines of the triangle as stitching guides; otherwise, it's almost impossible to keep the triangle edges straight. The triangle can be as small as ¼ in. or as large as 1 in., depending on how prominent you want it to be.

Draw the triangle where you want the arrowhead, using a ruler or seam gauge for accuracy. If you're going to make more than one, draw them all at once. Working on the right side of the fabric, secure the thread inside the lower left-hand corner of the triangle with three or four very tiny running stitches. Don't backstitch, as it may cause a small lump in your tack, especially if you're using thicker thread.

Bring the needle out exactly in the lower-left corner. Make a tiny stitch from right to left at the upper tip of the triangle, picking up only one or two threads. Then insert the needle in the lower-right corner and bring it out about one thread width to the right of the first stitch in the left corner. Continue, staying on the guidelines and stitching so the threads are side by side and barely touching. They should neither overlap nor have visible spaces between them. You'll notice that the stitches across the top of the triangle get longer as the stitches across the bottom get shorter. After you've completely covered the triangle, secure the stitching on the back side with three or four running stitches.

French tacks are used to hold sections of a garment loosely together to allow movement but prevent excessive shifting of the parts, such as when linings are anchored to garment bottoms. The French tack is actually a bar tack that forms a bridge between two pieces of a garment instead of being stitched onto one fabric's surface. Secure the thread on one garment section, and make a small stitch on the opposite section, leaving a length of thread between the two sections as long as you want the distance between the two sections to be. Make another stitch where the first one was anchored, and continue stitching back and forth across the space until you have four or six threads of equal length. Work closely spaced blanket stitches over this thread bridge, and inconspicuously secure the thread when you are finished. □

Grace Callaway is a frequent contributor to Threads *magazine.*

Coming to Grips with the Slide Fastener

Simple and effective methods for applying zippers

by Kathy Sandmann

ost of us fasten zippers every day without giving them a thought, unless, perhaps, as sewers, we're planning to put one into something, and then we usually consider them without much enthusiasm. It's true that there's rarely room for creative expression in zipper application—especially when fashion isn't calling attention to zippers, which is most of the time. It's equally true, however, that an inexpertly applied zipper can spoil the look of an otherwise perfect garment. These are exactly the reasons I feel that zipper application should be as simple and foolproof as possible. I've collected a number of methods that I think are as quick and easy as any you'll find.

The zipper was invented in the 1890s by a gentleman named Witcomb Judson, who devised a method of linking a series of hooks and eyes to create a long, continuous fastener, which he called the "C-Curity Placket Fastener." Not a total success, his idea nonetheless inspired others to improve on his device. One version, developed by the B.F. Goodrich Co. for its rubber boots, was sold with the slogan, "Just zip'er up and zip'er down," and the word *zipper* has been with us ever since. A company (later named Talon) started for the sole purpose of refining the slide fastener developed metal teeth to be used in place of hooks and eyes. Then Coats & Clark discovered a way to die-cast the zipper, attaching the metal teeth directly to a fabric tape and eliminating most of the early problems that had plagued the fastener. In the 1960s, the evo-

Claude Montana's up-front zipper was a hit last fall. On the left side, the zipper seam makes a sharp turn at the top to conceal itself under the overlap. (Photo by Ben Britt)

lutionary process went one step farther with the development of the coil zipper, a lightweight, flexible fastener that had almost unlimited versatility and that was every bit as strong as the metal zipper.

Although different zippers are available, all are basically the same—a chain or coil permanently attached to fabric tape. Coil zippers are usually made entirely of polyester and are the most flexible and lightweight. Chain zippers may be metal or plastic; they're generally less affected by heat (coils can easily melt under the iron) and are available in heavy-duty weights.

All zippers fall into one of three general categories: the conventional zipper, the separating zipper, and the invisible zipper. The *conventional zipper,* closed at one end, is the type most often required for dressmaking. The *separating zipper* opens at both ends and is ideal for jackets. The *invisible zipper* is designed so that only the pull tab shows when properly inserted. It enjoyed great popularity among home sewers after it was introduced in the 1960s, but it has since fallen out of favor, probably because it never caught on in ready-to-wear.

The best length for your project—If you have to make length alterations on commercial patterns, you may need to rethink zipper lengths. Zippers in the center-back seam of dresses look best when they end at the hipline. Zippers at the center-front or center-back seam on women's pants should not be so long that they extend into the crotch curve. They should start just where the curve becomes a straight line.

Purchasing a zipper an inch or two longer than your project requires can greatly simplify the installation process. If the zipper is long enough for the zipper pull to be completely out of the way outside the garment during application, you'll avoid having to stitch around it, which is hard to do neatly, and you won't have to move it out of the way as you stitch. You'll also eliminate the possibility of an annoying gap between the top of the zipper and the waistband on pants and skirts.

Shorten a zipper that extends beyond the garment by stitching cautiously across the excess when you apply the waistband; then trim the zipper, but be sure you've opened it before you trim it. It's painful to watch yourself cutting off the zipper pull after you've set in the zipper so carefully!

Zippers in openings that don't end in a waistband or neckband seam (such as faced openings or plackets that are closed at both ends) can be shortened from the bottom and cut off. Faced openings require a hook and eye at the top so that the strain is taken off the zipper teeth. To shorten a zipper from the bottom, whipstitch tightly around the chain or coil 10 or 12 times. Then cut the stitching between the teeth ½ in. or so below the stitching.

(continued p. 98)

From *Threads* magazine (February 1989) 21:30-33

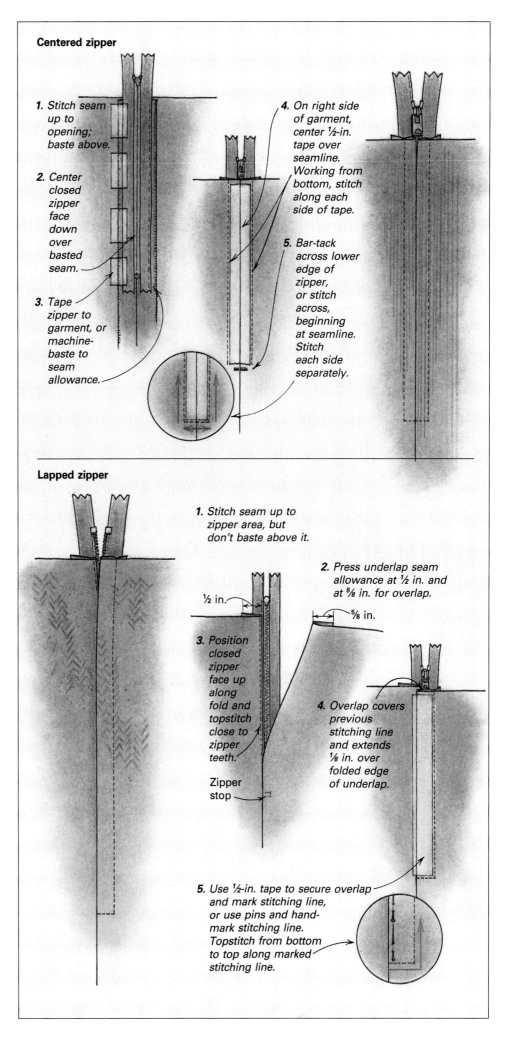

Centered zipper

1. Stitch seam up to opening; baste above.

2. Center closed zipper face down over basted seam.

3. Tape zipper to garment, or machine-baste to seam allowance.

4. On right side of garment, center ½-in. tape over seamline. Working from bottom, stitch along each side of tape.

5. Bar-tack across lower edge of zipper, or stitch across, beginning at seamline. Stitch each side separately.

Lapped zipper

1. Stitch seam up to zipper area, but don't baste above it.

2. Press underlap seam allowance at ½ in. and at ⅝ in. for overlap.

½ in.

⅝ in.

3. Position closed zipper face up along fold and topstitch close to zipper teeth.

Zipper stop

4. Overlap covers previous stitching line and extends ⅛ in. over folded edge of underlap.

5. Use ½-in. tape to secure overlap and mark stitching line, or use pins and hand-mark stitching line. Topstitch from bottom to top along marked stitching line.

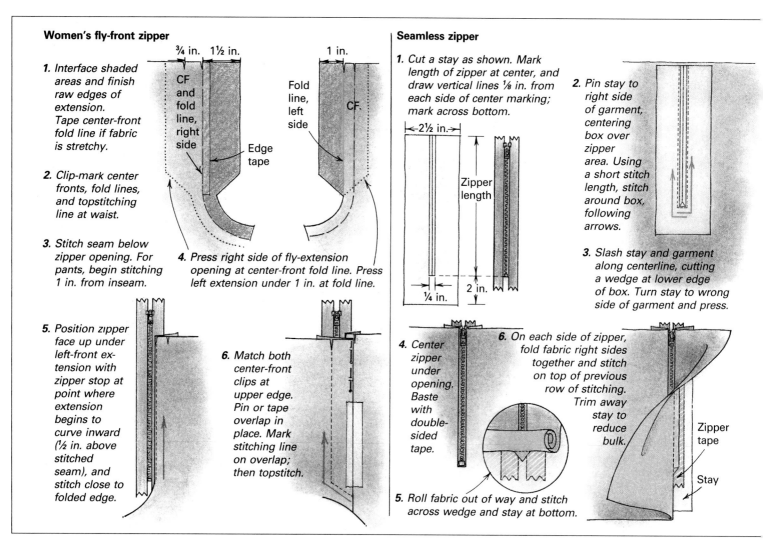

Women's fly-front zipper

1. Interface shaded areas and finish raw edges of extension. Tape center-front fold line if fabric is stretchy.

2. Clip-mark center fronts, fold lines, and topstitching line at waist.

3. Stitch seam below zipper opening. For pants, begin stitching 1 in. from inseam.

¾ in.   1½ in.

CF and fold line, right side

Edge tape

1 in.

Fold line, left side

CF.

4. Press right side of fly-extension opening at center-front fold line. Press left extension under 1 in. at fold line.

5. Position zipper face up under left-front extension with zipper stop at point where extension begins to curve inward (½ in. above stitched seam), and stitch close to folded edge.

6. Match both center-front clips at upper edge. Pin or tape overlap in place. Mark stitching line on overlap; then topstitch.

Seamless zipper

1. Cut a stay as shown. Mark length of zipper at center, and draw vertical lines ⅛ in. from each side of center marking; mark across bottom.

2½ in.

Zipper length

¼ in.   2 in.

2. Pin stay to right side of garment, centering box over zipper area. Using a short stitch length, stitch around box, following arrows.

3. Slash stay and garment along centerline, cutting a wedge at lower edge of box. Turn stay to wrong side of garment and press.

4. Center zipper under opening. Baste with double-sided tape.

5. Roll fabric out of way and stitch across wedge and stay at bottom.

6. On each side of zipper, fold fabric right sides together and stitch on top of previous row of stitching. Trim away stay to reduce bulk.

Zipper tape

Stay

Avoid pinning and basting—The easiest and fastest substitute for pinning and basting—on fabrics that can take it—is to stick your zipper in place with ordinary transparent tape. Tape is also an excellent guide for topstitching. Don't stitch through the tape, though, as the adhesive can coat the needle, causing stitching problems. If you can't use the tape, try using a water-soluble marking pen or a chalk wheel to mark topstitching lines.

Double-sided basting tape, and sometimes a glue stick, can both be very useful in securing zippers for stitching. Some zippers even come with a narrow strip of fusible tape along each side of the zipper (they're called "self-basting zippers"). When you're working with fabrics like plaids and stripes, which must be matched carefully, it's still a good idea to use hand- or machine-basting to ensure perfect placement.

Preparing pattern, fabric, and zipper—If you preshrink your garment fabric, preshrink the zipper at the same time. If the fabric isn't washable, pretreat the zipper by soaking it in hot water. Remove excess moisture by rolling it in a towel; then dry it. Press the zipper to remove creases, taking care not to let the hot iron rest on the coils.

A strip of lightweight fusible interfacing applied only to the seam allowance in the zipper area provides a neater finished effect on almost all fabrics and makes topstitching easier. When you're working with knit fabrics, fuse interfacing designed for knits to the seam allowance or staystitch ⅛ in. from the seamline to prevent stretching. One exception: If you're applying a zipper to an area where the fabric will be stretched during wear, such as the side seam of a knit skirt, put the garment on before positioning the zipper. Pin or baste the zipper in place before removing the garment. Although puckers may occur while the garment is flat, it will fit perfectly when you wear it. Stretch the fabric to fit the zipper as you stitch.

Keep in mind that it's easy to move the zipper on pant and skirt patterns. Even though patterns often advise side placement, there are advantages to moving the zipper to the center front or center back. Alterations, usually made at side seams, will be easier, and the straighter the seamline, the easier it is to insert a zipper.

Applications, from basic to couture— Zippers are generally inserted before facings, waistbands, and other details are applied to the garment. In the methods that are described and illustrated here, the machine stitching for all zipper applications is done with a zipper foot.

The *centered,* or *slot,* method and the *lapped* method are the most basic and the most common zipper applications. Both of these methods (drawings, p. 97) are used when the zipper is in the side and back seams of pants, skirts, and dresses and are interchangeable to some extent. The lapped method completely covers the zipper, so it's the best choice if your zipper isn't quite the right color. The centered method is frequently used on gathered garments. I find the overlapped method to be the easier technique. Usually, the overlap is on the left of a center-back-seam zipper and on the front of a side-seam zipper.

A hand-finished zipper is appropriate on couture garments. All you need to do is make the final topstitching on a centered or lapped zipper by hand-prickstitching. Depending on your fabric, use regular thread, silk thread, topstitching thread, or buttonhole twist.

A zipper placket that is closed at both ends is just a variation of either the centered zipper or lapped zipper and is constructed in the same manner. It is most frequently used in the side seam of dresses. A nice touch on the centered application is to bar-tack the ends, machine-stitching only along the sides.

Fly-front zippers (drawing above) are used at the center front of pants and skirts.

Separating zipper

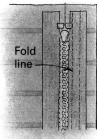

Fold line

1. After interfacing seam allowance (if desired), center zipper face down over center front and stitch to seam allowance with two rows of stitching, ¼ in. apart.

2. Fold seam allowance to wrong side; press the fold carefully.

Match points

3. Mark match points of patterned fabric on unstitched tape; then unzip. Attach loose zipper half in same way.

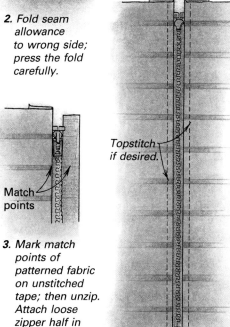

Topstitch if desired.

Separating zipper with 2-in. overlap

1. Apply left zipper half to left side of garment, centering teeth on center front, as for a normal separating zipper.

2. Add double width of overlap to right front only. Finish raw edge.

2 in. · 2 in. · ⅝ in.

Right front

Fold line

Original CF seam-line

3. To keep overlap away from neckline, turn right sides together on fold line, seam along top edge to seam allowance, clip, and turn. Do bottom edge in same way, if desired.

Clip here.

4. Center zipper teeth over seamline and stitch right zipper half to seam allowance only. Topstitch near center front, just inside zipper teeth.

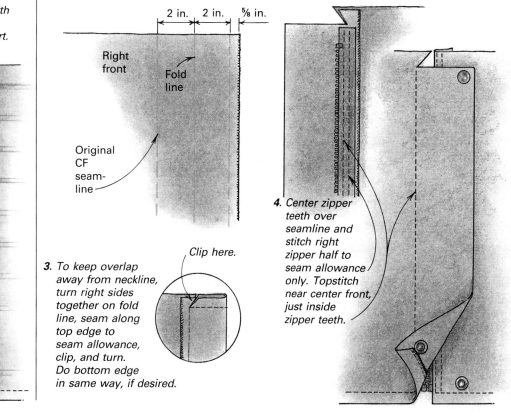

If you're working with a pattern that includes this type of zipper, transfer all markings from your pattern to your fabric. To add a front fly to a pattern or to simplify the one already there, add a 1½-in. extension at each center front, as illustrated.

I strongly recommend that you interface the fly extension from the outer edge up to the fold line for both the underlap and the overlap. If your fabric has a tendency to stretch, or if it doesn't take a crease well, you may also wish to stitch a narrow strip of twill tape or stay tape along the fold line for the overlap to provide extra stability.

The seamless zipper (drawing, facing page) is for garment areas that don't include a seam and is most often found at the neckline, usually at center back. Invisible application depends on a stabilizing backing or stay cut from a lightweight, firmly woven fabric (organdy, lining fabric), or from a nonwoven sew-in interfacing. The same method of insertion also works well for zippers that are closed at both ends, such as those that are placed in pocket slashes.

I find that the usual method of inserting *separating zippers* by topstitching is less than satisfactory in many cases, especially when I'm working on bulky fabrics, such as sweater knits and sweatshirt fleece. It's often difficult to prevent the zipper from shifting during topstitching, and it can be even more difficult to stitch neatly. In addition, the fabric fold between the topstitching and the zipper often curls back in an unattractive way. The method shown at left, above, eliminates all these problems.

A second type of separating-zipper application that is rarely seen in commercial patterns but is widely used in ready-to-wear is the lapped application, which is described at right, above. It's an especially good choice if you want to use a metal zipper in an outdoor garment, as metal zippers are often hard to operate when they're wet or ice-coated. You can add snaps or buttons to close the overlap, and the zipper doesn't have to go the entire length.

After inserting a zipper, check to see that the stitching is straight and inconspicuous and that the placket lies flat. Give the zipper area a final, careful pressing (don't iron it!).

Couture finishing treatments—A ribbon underlay is a special touch that protects the skin from the zipper teeth, a nice touch for zippers in close-fitting garments. Use a piece of ribbon wide enough to cover the zipper and long enough to cover the zipper tape from the lower edge up to the zipper stop, plus 1 in. Turn under and stitch ½ in. on each short end. Attach one long side of the ribbon to the outer edge of the seam allowance, either by hand or machine.

Catchstitch the lower edge of the ribbon to the seam allowance, and use a small snap at the upper edge of the unstitched side of the ribbon to fasten it in place.

A waistline stay is a good idea on fitted garments that include a zipper. Especially useful on dresses with skirts that are cut very full or from heavy fabric and on knit garments, the stay will help the waistline to hold its shape, and it will prevent the zipper area from gaping. It removes strain from the zipper in the waistline area and also makes it easier to close the zipper in garments that are very fitted. Use ½-in. grosgrain ribbon or stay tape cut to the waist measurement plus 2 in. Finish the raw ends and fold them under 1 in. on each end of the stay. Attach hooks and eyes to the folded ends of ribbon—the stay should now fit around the waist like a belt. Attach the stay to the garment by tacking it to the waistline seam allowance, or, if there's no seam, tack it to the darts and the vertical seam allowances. This extra touch will make a big difference in the longevity of your garment and in your pleasure every time you wear it. □

Kathy Sandmann writes and publishes the Sewing Sampler, *a monthly newsletter devoted to fashion sewing, available from her at Box 39, Springfield, MN 56087.*

The Jacket That Really Gets Around

How to re-create Patagonia's legendary fleece-lined top in any shape you want

by Rochelle Harper

baker, Oregon, was 20 miles ahead, and the wall of snow we were driving toward became flat, white sheets that swirled in front of the car. Just past Baker, the truckers started pulling off the road, and when we got out to strap on chains in the sleet, I put on my fleece-lined jacket. With only a sweater underneath and a felt hat tied around my head with a scarf, I faced the bitter wind and wet, but I stayed warm with my collar zipped high around my face and my bare hands dug deep in the fleecy pockets of my favorite jacket.

Modeled after Patagonia's shelled fleece jackets that redefined the sportswear top, the version I made has been a success in so many different weather zones and in such a variety of activities that I take it everywhere I go. The outer shell functions as a

Rochelle Harper faces all types of weather with calm in her customized version of Patagonia's famous shelled fleece jacket.

windbreaker and water repeller, but it's breathable to keep me from getting too hot. The fleece lining is cozy, but it's also highly breathable, and it wicks perspiration away from my skin. The ribbed cuffs and waistband prevent cold air from sneaking in.

I made the jacket in the photo below from DK Sports' Timberline Parka pattern, with a few variations: I shortened the collar 1 in., replaced the outer flap with an inner wind flap, and used welt pockets instead of flaps. It's a basic raglan, but you can use a drop-shoulder or set-in sleeve pattern and make it with the same techniques I used. The Rain Shed and The Green Pepper (see "Resources," p. 103) also have patterns that would work nicely. Just be sure to select a pattern with lots of ease, as the fleece will take up at least 1 in. of it.

Choosing fabrics—Patagonia's jacket shell is constructed of Taslanized nylon. Taslans use a textured, air-blown fiber that gives the fabric a soft, cottonlike look and makes it wear-resistant. Similar fabrics are sold under names like Supplex and Taslite.

When you choose your shell fabric, look for a high thread count and some percentage of nylon for water-repellency. Blended fabrics, such as poly/nylon or London Fog's poly/cotton, still work nicely but need some type of treatment, like Zepel or Scotchgard, to be really water-repellent. Avoid urethane-coated fabrics; they have zero breathability.

Waterproof/breathable fabrics can also be used for the shell layer: Goretex, Bion 11, Permia, Savina DP, etc., are expensive, but for skiing or wet-weather activities, the investment may be worth it.

You have fewer options for the pile lining, but why not choose exactly the same fabric that Patagonia developed for its world-class jacket: Synchilla, called Polar Plus when sold as yardage? Polar Plus is a true pile: The fibers stand up away from the inner knit layer and aren't matted down as in lesser fleeces, and the fabric doesn't pill. Fleece fabrics come in many weights, from

4 oz./sq. yd. to 16 oz./sq. yd. A good average for a jacket lining is about 6 oz.

Consider pocket linings carefully. The outer fabric will probably be too rough for pocketing, and if you're tempted to use your lining fleece, remember the double thickness that will be added right around the waistline. Look for some type of brushed or flannel fabric in a lightweight synthetic. Cotton absorbs moisture, and wet pockets will stay wet. Interfacing will be needed in the pocket welts and ribbing extension, and you'll need something that has some bulk because of the pile. Thermolab, a 3-oz. needlepunch batting, did the job for me.

You'll need to find a ribbing that's rugged enough to be compatible with your shell and lining fabric. Heavyweight nylon ribbing is the best, but you might also find brushed nylon and polypropylene ribbing that will work fine. Before you buy, test the return of the stretch. Pull a 4-in. section across the rib (not at the edge); then release it. It should immediately return to near its original shape. If it doesn't, it will probably stretch out quickly with wear.

Ask for fabrics and fiber content by name when shopping for your materials. There are many inadequate substitutes that won't give you the qualities of the fabrics I've mentioned. You can find them all at the places listed on p. 103, and you can read more about water-resistant fabrics in the article on pp. 104-109.

Notions, and the hot knife—The best thread for this project is a European long staple 100% polyester, like Metrosene or Molnlycke. Machine needles should be sharp or universal; size 9 works well on tightly woven nylons. If snagging or tension problems arise while you're working with the shell fabric, change your needle. Strong synthetic fabrics dull needles quickly.

YKK, Ideal, and Talon are the major zipper brands, and any of these would be serviceable in a sport weight, but Talon's OMNI style is the best choice because it's almost

From *Threads* magazine (October 1989) 25:52-55

impossible for a tooth to come loose from its zipper tape. Compared with most separating zippers, it's also easier to shorten to the exact length you need; buy a zipper at least 2 in. longer than you need if you can't find the exact length. The double-welt pockets also have zippers; buy ordinary nylon zippers about 6 in. to 7 in. long.

If you're using all-nylon fabric, you'll have to deal with the fabric's tendency to fray. One option is to cut out with a hot knife, an electrically heated woodburning tool that's available in hobby shops and from The Rain Shed. It has a sharpened, wedge-shaped tip, and it cuts and melts the raw edges at the same time, sealing them from fraying. You trace the pattern shapes onto the shell fabric. Then you lay the fabric on a surface that won't be marred by the hot tool, such as a glass window from a screen door or storm window. Before cutting, test a small corner of the fabric to see how fast or slow you'll need to move the tool in order to get a nice, even cut. For long, straight lines, use a piece of wood molding or a yardstick to guide the cut. This takes a little more time than cutting with scissors, but it saves you from finishing edges and fighting with fraying fabric.

If you don't have a hot knife, you can produce similar results by searing the edges of your nylon after cutting it out with scissors. Guide the cut edge of the fabric through the base of a candle flame at a steady rate; with a little practice on scraps, you'll learn how to avoid uneven edges. However you achieve them, don't trim the seared edges during construction; just clip into seams or across corners so you maintain the integrity of the seared edge. If you'd rather serge the edges, be sure to make your stitches as wide as possible; otherwise, they'll just pull off.

Garment pieces—For a typical pattern, you'll need the following parts:
- **Front:** Cut 2 outer shells and 2 linings.
- **Collar:** Cut 1 outer shell and 1 lining.
- **Back:** Cut 1 outer shell and 1 lining.
- **Sleeve:** Cut 2 outer shells and 2 linings.
- **Pocket welts:** Cut 4 shells the length of the opening plus the seam allowances by 1 ¼ in., and interface to fold line.
- **Pockets:** Cut 4 pieces of pocketing.
- **Wind flap:** Cut 1 each of shell and lining, the length of the finished zipper plus seam allowances and 2⅝ in. wide; measure the pattern pieces along center front (collar, front, and ribbing extension) inside of seam allowances to find the length.
- **Ribbing extension:** Cut 2 shells and interface to fold.
- **Waistband ribbing:** Cut 1 piece of ribbing as follows. Your pattern may include

A Patagonia customer out for a little air: Wing walker Lori Lynn Ross wears a shelled fleece jacket on the wing of Jim Franklin's Waco Mystery Ship. (Photo by John Sherman)

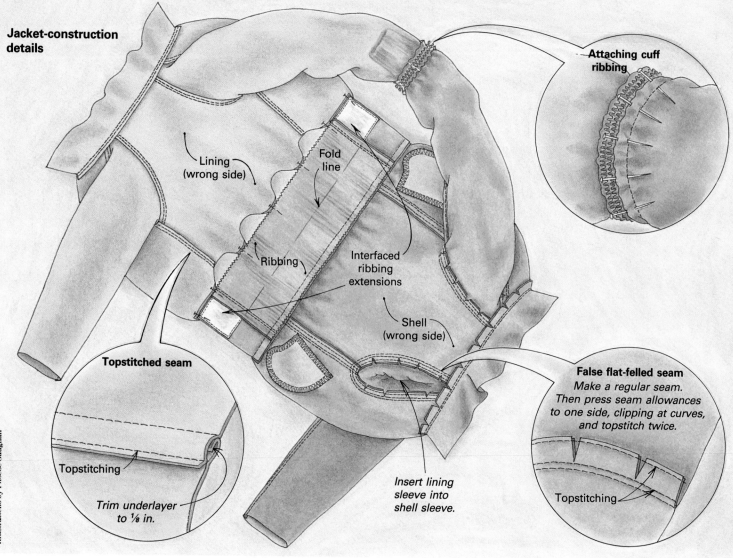

Jacket-construction details

Lining
(wrong side)

Fold
line

Ribbing

Interfaced
ribbing
extensions

Shell
(wrong side)

**Attaching cuff
ribbing**

Topstitched seam

Topstitching

Trim underlayer
to ⅛ in.

Insert lining
sleeve into
shell sleeve.

False flat-felled seam
*Make a regular seam.
Then press seam allowances
to one side, clipping at curves,
and topstitch twice.*

Topstitching

pattern pieces for ribbing, but this method is more accurate: Subtract 3 in. and twice the finished width of the ribbing extension from your body circumference at the place the waistband will fall. For example, my ribbing extension is 5 in. wide, so $5 \times 2 = 10 + 3 = 13$ in. Subtract this from your body measurement. The width is the same as the unfolded height of the ribbing extension; mine is 7½ in.

- **Cuffs:** Cut 2 rectangular pieces of ribbing the same width as the waistband ribbing and as long as the circumference of your wrist plus 1 in.; wristbands shouldn't be tight.

Flat-felled, false flat-felled, and topstitched seams are all options for this garment; I used the false flat-felled seam on mine because the curve of the raglan sleeve is difficult to flat-fell, and this looks just as good. For finishing seams on the fleece lining, I used a topstitched seam; both are shown in the drawing above. You can also use topstitched seams on the side and neck seams of the shell and false flat-felled seams only at the sleeve joints. The ribbing seams at hem and cuff are plain seams.

Each double-welt pocket has a zipper inserted so that the tab is at the bottom when it's closed (see pocket photo, facing page). Center the closed zipper between the welts

after you have stitched them and the pocket facing to the jacket front and have turned them through to the wrong side. Topstitch in the ditch around the outside of the welts, catching the zipper and the ends of the pocket opening. Then align the bottom pocket piece over the one attached to the jacket and stitch them together all around. Overcast the raw edges.

Construction sequence—The steps I took to make my jacket were based on a close look at Patagonia's construction methods. Construct the *shell* and the *lining* like two identical, separate garments, as follows:
- Join fronts to fronts of sleeves.
- Join backs to backs of sleeves.
- Join fronts, backs, and sleeves at sides.
- Join collar at neck.

The next step is to join the two parts at the hem and cuffs with *ribbing* (see drawing above). Interface the *ribbing extension* to the fold line, and stitch it to the ends of the waist ribbing, right sides together. Fold the seam allowances toward the extension and topstitch. Pin the extensions to the bottom edge of the front shell, right sides together, with a 1:1 ratio, but divide the ribbing in half and in half again and mark with pins. Do the same with the remaining bottom of the shell. Then pin together cor-

responding marks and stitch, stretching the ribbing to fit. Repeat for the other edge of the ribbing and the lining. Trim the fleece seam allowance to ¼ in.

Fold the *cuffs* right sides together along the ribbing, and stitch them with a ¼-in. seam. Turn them to the right side and fold them in half. Divide the cut edges into four equal parts and mark them with pins through both layers.

Fold the hem ribbing so that the lining and shell are wrong sides together, and insert the lining sleeve into the shell sleeve. Make sure that the lining is smooth and that it's not twisted inside the shell sleeve, which should mean that the underarm seams line up. Divide the edges together into four equal parts, marking the shell and lining separately with pins. Then pull the lining sleeves out of the shell sleeves until the wrist edges face each other. Center a cuff between the edges, with pins matching and seams together. Pin all the raw edges together and stitch through all layers around the cuff, as shown above. Then trim the fleece seam allowance to ¼ in.

Unzip and separate the *zipper*. With right sides together, put the left half of the zipper with the left side of the shell, teeth toward the shell and edges matching. The bottom of the zipper should be ¼ in. above

Shorten zipper to fit by folding it away from jacket and catching it in zipper seam. This forms an effective zipper stop at the same time. On top of zipper is wind flap; jacket is inside out so that lining can be attached by machine.

Pull jacket right side out through opening at zipper. Then topstitch to close opening.

Topstitch pocket zipper in place between welt lips; then attach pocket back to pocket facing, and overcast all around pocket.

the bottom of the jacket (ribbing-extension fold line.)

To shorten the zipper at the top, fold the excess length away from the shell (see zipper photo above), but don't cut off the excess until you've securely stitched it in place. Sew the zipper ⅛ in. from the teeth, stitching slowly across the teeth at the top. Cut off the excess zipper, leaving ¾ in. beyond the seam.

To make the *wind flap,* put shell fabric and lining pieces right sides together and stitch across the top, down one long side, and across the bottom. Trim the excess fleece from the seam allowance close to the stitching line, turn, and topstitch ¼ in. from the edge. Match the raw edge of the wind flap and the edge of the left front, with the shell fabric of the flap facing the zipper, and pin in place.

Next, refold the hem ribbing, this time bringing the shell and lining right sides together. The sleeves, inside out and attached at the cuffs, can hang below the hem. Line up the shell edge with the zipper/wind-flap edge and stitch through all layers along the zipper, using the previous stitching line on the shell side as a guide.

Turn the garment right side out, zip on the right half of the zipper, and match the center fronts. Using chalk or pen, mark the

free zipper tape where the neckline seam crosses it and where the top of the zipper needs to be. Separate the zipper, pin the right zipper to the right-front shell, right sides together, matching appropriate markers, and stitch in place. Turn the garment inside out again, and stitch the right zipper just like the left one, but this time leave about an 8-in. gap in the middle of the center front. Continue stitching across the top of the collar; connect it with the stitching for the left zipper. Trim the excess fleece from the seam allowances, except at the opening, and turn the garment to the right side through the gap in the zipper seam.

Fold under and pin the lining seam allowance at the opening. From the front, topstitch two rows of stitching (like a false flat-felled seam) along both sides of the center front and around the collar, catching the seam allowance at the opening.

Don't stop here!—Many of the techniques that I've discussed can be extended to other sportswear applications. The design of this jacket is basic, but the details you add, the colors you use, and the care you take in making it will give your jacket as much distinction as you want.

Here are a few variations that could be applied to this pattern:

• Use the hot knife to produce crisp appliqué designs, with nonraveling edges.
• Finish the jacket with a topstitched design through both layers for a quilted look.
• Block out the shell pattern with colorful, contrasting geometric shapes.
• Make brightly colored zipper pulls from scrap fabric.
• Sew a short separating zipper into the collar seam and make a hood that will attach in seconds.

Rochelle Harper of Portland, OR, is a freelance sportswear designer.

Outerwear patterns/fabrics/notions

DK Sports (Division of Daisy Kingdom)
134 N.W. 8th St.
Portland, OR 97209
(800) 288-5223
Catalog, $2.

The Green Pepper
941 Olive St.
Eugene, OR 97401
(503) 345-6665
Catalog, $2.

The Rain Shed
707 NW 11th St.
Corvallis, OR 97330
(503) 753-8900
Sells hot knives; catalog, $1.

Stalking the Perfect Raincoat

A survey of fabrics, patterns, and details essential for staying dry

by David Page Coffin

Why make a raincoat? The four big American pattern companies seem to have decided that there's little reason to do so; a careful search reveals precious few pattern offerings. It's true that you can easily buy a raincoat that does the job, without spending a fortune, but we sewers have our own logic. We can find plenty of reasons for making something we need: fit, fabric, fun, and getting just what we want.

I recently had the impulse to make a raincoat—my London Fog is 20 years old, though it doesn't look it. I've been hearing about Goretex, and Folkwear has a nice-looking pattern, so I decided to investigate the possibilities. I wanted something to wear to work and to the city, something that would travel well and that I could use year-round, rain or shine. I didn't want a poncho, a parka, or foul-weather gear.

State-of-the-art fabrics—To talk sensibly about rainwear fabrics, you must know what the terms *waterproof, water-repellent,* and *breathable* mean. *Waterproof* is the most clear-cut. Water, even wind-blown rain, won't come through waterproof fabrics, because it can't penetrate the surface. But neither can air. Some ingenuity is required to make truly waterproof garments comfortable. Keeping out the rain isn't much use if you're getting soaked by your own perspiration.

Water-repellent means that to some degree water will bead and run off the garment, rather than soak into and through the surface, but under pressure water will come through. Here's where another factor, water-resistance, comes in. Just how much pressure will it take before water does get through? That's the measure of resistance.

Usually, if water can come through, so can air. Then the fabric is said to be breath-

able. While the definition and tests for the designations *waterproof, water-repellent,* and *water-resistant* are well established, *breathability* is a more subjective term. There are no standards for breathability, and there's plenty of disagreement about how much is enough, especially regarding fabrics like Goretex, which claim to possess both breathability and waterproofness.

Fabrics become waterproof by being coated, usually with some form of rubber or urethane, or because they're nonwoven plastic to begin with. You can have your own fabric coated with clear vinyl if you have the time and money. You need to add holes to coated fabrics for ventilation; seal holes to prevent leaks; and treat the coating gently so it won't wear out, crack, or peel off. Adding grommets in the underarm area and using an open-weave or mesh fabric under waterproof flaps at the back and shoulders are good ways to add breathability to coated-fabric garments. Seams should be few, and carefully placed, and needle holes should be filled with seam sealants.

Goretex and Entrant are trade names for fabrics that use "microporous" coatings to release air and water vapor while blocking water droplets. Bion II is similar but claims to use molecular "gaps" instead of micropores. Reports vary on how successful these are, and the results seem to depend on how severely they're tested, but without exception these fabrics are expensive ($15-$20/yd.), come in limited colors, and are not known for their suppleness and drape. Goretex is also tricky to care for. Salt water, soap, mud, skin oils, and dry-cleaning fluids can reduce its effectiveness.

Lately, manufacturers have been trying to create fabrics that are structurally water-repellent so there's no finish to wear off or wash out, but that also have the drape and

feel of soft weaves and natural fibers. Supplex, Taslan, and Techtile are all 100%-nylon water-repellent fabrics whose yarns have been designed to feel like cotton but act like nylon. Savina DP is a brand-new fabric that rivals Goretex for high-tech chic. It claims an incredible density of ultra-fine yarns per square inch. The fabric is then tightly shrunk to achieve an almost microporous effect without a coating. The resulting fabric looks and feels like a heavy, high-quality lining fabric. It's available in subtle colors, but it's also expensive—nearly $17/yd. Samples of Savina DP and all the other fabrics shown on p. 106 are available from the suppliers listed in "Resources" on p. 109.

Is water-repellency enough?—For a general-purpose raincoat that may see more water in a single washing than in one season of dashing between buildings and cars, the need for such exotic fabrics is questionable. One look at a city street on a rainy day confirms that most people do fine in the poly/cotton standby of ordinary raincoat fabric. Comfort is every bit as important as protection, and water-repellent fabrics seem the perfect compromise. They are invariably tightly woven, often made of nylon (by nature water-repellent), sometimes with cotton and polyester added for more breathability and a softer hand. The more cotton and polyester, the more likely the fabric is to be chemically treated. The treatments, like Scotchgard and Zepel, can usually be renewed by the dry cleaner or by chemicals that can be applied at home.

I've scouted the more prominent mail-order fabric houses for the ordinary (but hard-to-find!) and less predictable fabrics and have found some interesting water-repellent ones in a wide range of prices. Another intriguing prospect is to treat ordi-

From *Threads* magazine (October 1988) 19:26-31

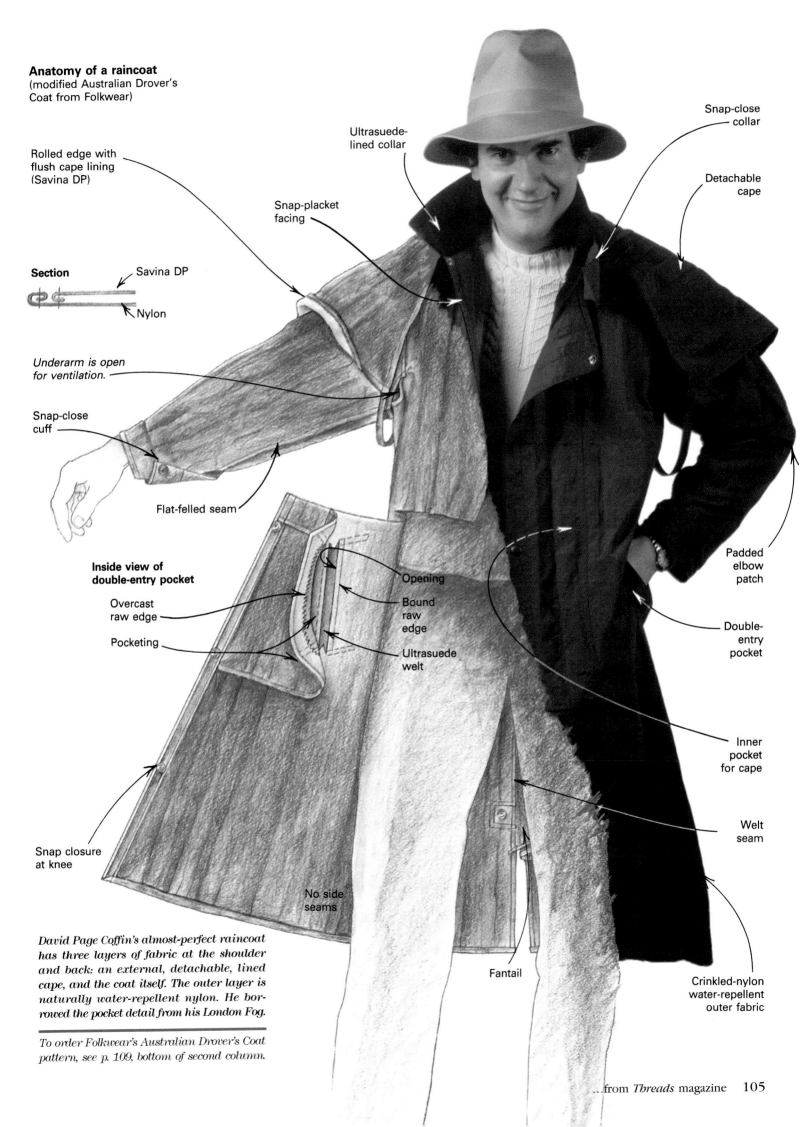

Anatomy of a raincoat
(modified Australian Drover's
Coat from Folkwear)

Rolled edge with
flush cape lining
(Savina DP)

Section   Savina DP

Nylon

*Underarm is open
for ventilation.*

Snap-close
cuff

Flat-felled seam

**Inside view of
double-entry pocket**

Overcast
raw edge

Pocketing

Ultrasuede-
lined collar

Snap-placket
facing

Opening

Bound
raw
edge

Ultrasuede
welt

Snap-close
collar

Detachable
cape

Padded
elbow
patch

Double-
entry
pocket

Inner
pocket
for cape

Welt
seam

Snap closure
at knee

No side
seams

Fantail

Crinkled-nylon
water-repellent
outer fabric

*David Page Coffin's almost-perfect raincoat
has three layers of fabric at the shoulder
and back: an external, detachable, lined
cape, and the coat itself. The outer layer is
naturally water-repellent nylon. He borrowed the pocket detail from his London Fog.*

*To order Folkwear's Australian Drover's Coat
pattern, see p. 109, bottom of second column.*

State-of-the-art rainwear fabrics (counterclockwise from right)—from Rain Shed and Green Pepper: Savina DP, microporous-coated Bion II, Goretex, Taslan, and Supplex (peach); from Britex: water-repellent, treated tight and crinkled weaves—cottons, rayons, and silks (these seven swatches vary in water-repellency); and from The Fabric Company: three home-treated cottons and a waterproof, vinyl-coated knit. The violet is a tightly woven nylon.

Testing for water-repellency

The official test for a fabric's water-repellency (according to The American Association of Textile Chemists and Colorists) is to put the fabric in an embroidery hoop, then to pour water on it through a watering-can-type nozzle held about 6 in. away, holding the cloth at a 45° angle to the flow. To test water-resistance, chemists stretch the fabric over a blotter on a clipboard held at a 45° angle and pour water on it, this time from 2 ft. away, through the same kind of nozzle. By weighing the blotter before and after, they can tell how wet it got. I replicated the water-repellency test more or less exactly, but for water-resistance I upped the stakes a bit and merely sprayed the fabric firmly in a hoop, holding the sprayer in my kitchen sink about 18 in. away.

I tested six cotton fabrics that I thought would make appealing raincoats: two weights of twill, a medium-weight poplin, blue-jean denim, and two tight plain weaves. I also tested swatches of Savina DP and the all-nylon fabric I'd bought for my own coat. Finally, I tested my London Fog, which had just been cleaned and treated for water-repellency with Dupont's Zepel. I had the cotton fabrics Zepel-treated at the same time, and I washed other samples of the same fabrics in Kenyon's Wash Cycle Water Repellent. I also tested the two fabrics that did the best in these treatments by spraying them with Scotchgard.

The obvious winner was Savina DP. It showed no wetting or penetration. The nylon was a close second, it's looser weave letting a few droplets through only after heavy spraying. Surprisingly, my old London Fog got very wet and even let some water through to the lining, showing that perfect water-resistance and water-repellency are not required from a successful raincoat, which the London Fog certainly is. With these standards established, I tested the treated fabric.

Without a doubt, for maximum water-resistance, tightly woven, smooth fabrics, like the fine twill or the plain-weave Japanese fabric shown at the bottom of the photo above are the best. Zepel, a surface treatment, was much more successful on lightweight fabrics. Kenyon's washed-on product worked best on thicker, heavier fabrics. Both products, and the Scotchgard I tried later, easily caused water sprinkled on all the fabrics to bead up, but when water was poured on continuously, most fabrics failed to stay dry. I concluded that I'd feel most confident in a lightweight Zepeled garment or a heavier coat washed in the Kenyon product, especially if it was lined.

What I found most interesting about the tests was observing that, even if a fabric resisted penetration well, if the surface held on to water (wasn't repellent), there was a good chance the water would eventually work through. Even if it doesn't, a wet surface certainly can't breathe, and it will stay cold and clammy until it dries. I'd prefer two layers of water-repellency to one layer of wet resistance. I'd also recommend that you do similar testing if you're interested in converting ordinary cotton into rainwear. —D.P.C.

Using a felling foot

Flat-felled seam

1. With right sides together, wider allowance folded over narrower, make a few stitches with foot on top.

2. Stop with needle down, and raise foot. Lift folded edge over blade. Finish seam.

3. Open seam and press flat.

4. Stitch second row same as first. Underside looks like welt seam.

Welt seam

1. With right sides together, match seam-lines and stitch, using regular foot.

2. Press seam allowances over, covering narrower allowance.

3. Use inside edge of felling foot as topstitching guide.

Illustrations by Jean Galli

Coffin's 20-year-old London Fog has an internal cape, or three-quarter lining, made like the loose external yoke of Style's pattern #1191. The effect is the same whether the extra protection is inside or outside.

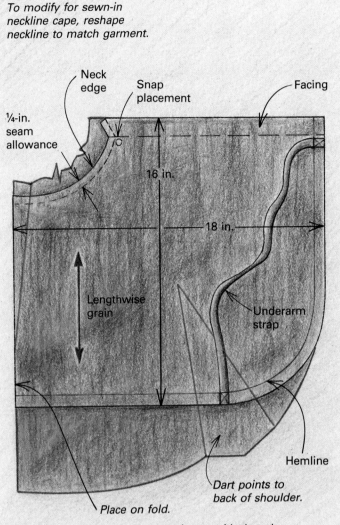

Folkwear's Drover Cape

To modify for sewn-in neckline cape, reshape neckline to match garment.

Neck edge

Snap placement

Facing

¼-in. seam allowance

16 in.

18 in.

Lengthwise grain

Underarm strap

Hemline

Dart points to back of shoulder.

Place on fold.

For a more elegant shape, experiment with darted variations, like one shown in red and blue.

nary fabrics to make them water-repellent, either at home or at the cleaners. I tested some of these methods and feel that they work well on tightly woven, smooth fabrics (see "Testing for water-repellency," facing page). If I hadn't found a crinkled nylon in the perfect color for my own coat, I would have used a treated all-cotton fabric.

Seams—Regardless of the fabric you decide on, choosing thread is easy: 100% polyester is the only choice for strength, stretch, and imperviousness to water. As for seams, French, felled, and welt seams are all ideal for raincoats. They're sturdy, attractive, self-finished, and easy to make on the machine. Most manufacturers use a ¼-in. flat-felled seam on straight seams. On the slight curves at shoulders and armholes of a lined garment, they frequently use the partially self-finished welt seam.

You can use either side of a felled seam on the outside of a garment, but to match a welt seam on the same garment, use the side with a single visible line of topstitching. It doesn't make much difference which di-

rection the concealed seam faces, but I like to point it to the back for looks and downward for water-resistance. My London Fog violates both these rules, and I've never suffered for it, but they still make sense to me.

A felling foot makes the outcome of either felled or welt seams a sure thing. It accurately folds over the felled-seam allowance and controls the feeding for perfectly parallel and identical topstitching (see drawing, facing page). If you can't get a felling foot from your dealer, check the "Resources" list. I wouldn't make a felled seam without one.

For either seam, you need two different seam-allowance widths, and I prefer to cut the garment out that way at the start, instead of trimming one seam later. In either case, base the allowance widths on the width of your felling foot. The outer allowance should be a little more than twice the width of the foot's opening, and the inner one should be the same width as the opening.

Start felling with right sides together and with the wider allowance on the bottom, seamlines matched. Fold the wider allowance over the narrow one, position both

layers under the foot, and make a few stitches. Stop, with the needle down. Then raise the foot and slip the folded edge into the foot, over the blade. Continue sewing, using the inside edge of the foot and the blade to keep a consistent width of fold as you stitch. Keep your eye on the narrow allowance to make sure you always catch its full width.

When you get to the end of the seam, open it and press the folded edge flat. Position the fold under the foot as before, and again make a few stitches before you stop, needle down, and raise the foot to insert the folded edge. From here to the end, the foot will guide the fold precisely for perfectly parallel topstitching.

For welt seams, use a regular foot for the first joining seam; then press the seam allowances over, covering the narrower allowance. From the right side, use the inside edge of the felling foot as a guide to topstitch the seam.

Working details—A fully equipped traditional trench coat still includes features that actually evolved in trench warfare, like

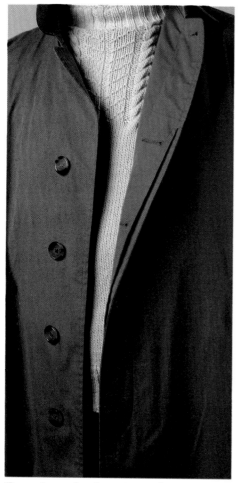

For a clean, simple, water-resistant closure, nothing beats the hidden button fly. See drawing at right for construction details.

Hidden-button fly front

An extra buttonhole strip and a buttonhole-strip facing lie between coat and coat facing. The buttonholes are made through coat facing and buttonhole strip.

1. Machine-stitch buttonhole strip to facing, right sides together.

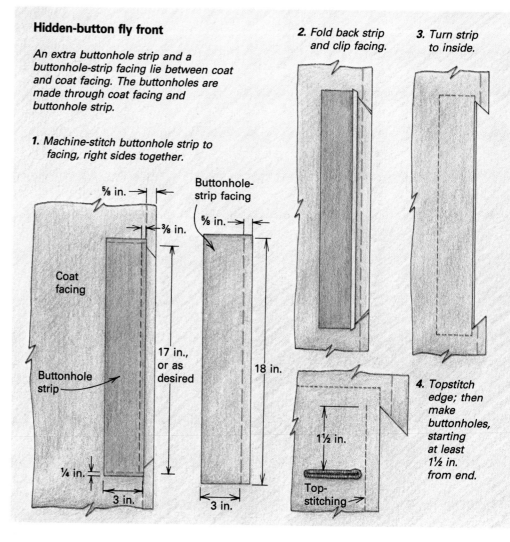

2. Fold back strip and clip facing.

3. Turn strip to inside.

4. Topstitch edge; then make buttonholes, starting at least 1½ in. from end.

Coat facing

Buttonhole-strip facing

Buttonhole strip

⅝ in.

⅜ in.

⅝ in.

17 in., or as desired

18 in.

¼ in.

3 in.

3 in.

1½ in.

Top-stitching

---

rings for hand grenades at the belt, but most trench-coat details remain eminently sensible. Strongly made opening epaulets do keep shoulder straps from slipping off. Belted cuffs and waist help control ventilation and retain warmth. A collar that buttons around the neck is more useful than a loose, flapping one.

Storm flaps may appear to be superfluous, but consider that they evolved from quarter-length shoulder capes and that the back and shoulders take the worst beating in a rainstorm. A second layer of water-repellency is an excellent idea; any moisture driven through the top layer by wind or rain will have a much harder time working through the second layer, and cooling from evaporation on the top layer will not be felt.

The detatchable cape of the Australian Drover's Coat (drawing p. 107) is probably the most functional version of the idea available on a current pattern because the entire shoulder is covered, and the shoulders extend like eaves beyond the arms to drain rain away from them. Wide shoulder pads, yoke flaps, and lined sleeves accomplish much the same thing, but the drover's cape could be easily adapted to other coats. It needn't be detachable; you can sew the cape to the neckline with the collar if you cut its neckline to match the coat's. You

may want to experiment with the shape; shoulder darts would be a logical addition.

If you plan a water-repellent design without an external second layer, consider an internal cape; i.e, a raincoat whose sleeves, back, and front are lined at least three-quarters of the way to the waist. Use self-fabric, a water-repellent lining, or a combination, as in my London Fog on p. 107. Savina DP might be ideal. It's as slick as regular lining, and for a fabric you've treated for water-repellency only, it would provide a fail-safe backup.

Raglan sleeves provide an easy, roomy fit. Their seams are all more or less parallel to the flow of water off the shoulder, so there are no grooves where water could collect. Raglan sleeves are also well suited to gussets, which provide extra upward reach and a place to put grommets. In most cases you don't have to make any changes to the existing pattern. Just insert a football-shaped bias-cut wedge into the underarm seam. (The wider the gusset, the greater the freedom of movement.) On my coat I left the sleeves and armholes unattached below the markings for maximum ventilation. I cut the armscye a little higher between the notches and scooped out corresponding curves on the sleeves.

After shoulders, knees get soaked most. Fashion raincoats that stop short of the

knees aren't worthy of the name, and coats that are long enough but don't button to the knee are almost as useless. I suppose the leg straps of the drover's coat are a bit of overkill, unless you plan to ride the range in the rain, but the idea is sound.

Besides the internal cape, my London Fog has a few other classic, but hidden, details that aren't included in any pattern I've seen. A single-breasted raincoat is perfect for a button-concealing fly front (see photo and drawing above). It looks clean, the buttons won't catch on things, and you don't have to spend time on fancy buttonholes. Since the fly stops at about mid-thigh, a single button tab has been provided to close the gap at the knee. The plain welt pockets, each with an opening through to the inside, provide access to pants (or skirt) pockets when the coat is buttoned.

Current patterns—Despite the poor showing from the major pattern companies, there's a reasonable assortment of patterns. McCalls' #2770 is an admirable one. It's a classic, lined raglan, with welt pockets and a button-in liner, suitable for rainwear and woolen fabrics. It's a Palmer & Pletsch "Personalized Instructions" pattern, and the instruction sheet is thorough and more informative about fitting and interfacing than most. An equally basic coat that's a bit

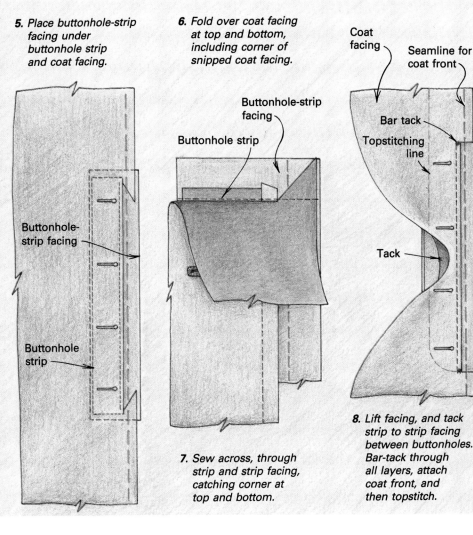

5. Place buttonhole-strip facing under buttonhole strip and coat facing.

Buttonhole-strip facing

Buttonhole strip

6. Fold over coat facing at top and bottom, including corner of snipped coat facing.

Buttonhole-strip facing

Buttonhole strip

Coat facing

Seamline for coat front

Bar tack

Topstitching line

Tack

7. Sew across, through strip and strip facing, catching corner at top and bottom.

8. Lift facing, and tack strip to strip facing between buttonholes. Bar-tack through all layers, attach coat front, and then topstitch.

more shaped is Stretch & Sew's #1094, not necessarily for knit fabrics. It has set-in sleeves, a belt, welt pockets, and a lining, but no button-in liner. Stretch & Sew's #1078 has a yoke and comes in two versions: a hooded, center-opening one; and one with an asymmetrical closure, puffed sleeves, and a ruffled collar. Both Stretch & Sew patterns are multisized; patterns and instructions are on heavy white paper. Simplicity's #8443 is a sporty slicker based on a big shirt, with drop shoulders, a shirttail hem, a wide two-layer yoke, and a plain stand-up collar. There's even a wide-brimmed floppy hat for a Christopher Robin look. This coat would be a good candidate for an add-on cape, although the yoke provides a small amount of extra protection.

For trench-coat details we have to look to the European pattern companies. Burda offers #5773, a modernized version with the requisite double-breasted, belted, and epauletted swagger; back yoke flaps; big shoulder pads; and wide raglan sleeves. It's lined and has welt pockets and a collar on a stand. Burda patterns are multisized and have no seam allowances, which is handy when you're planning felled and welt seams.

Style's #1191 is more traditionally cut, although the collar is only one piece. It has storm flaps all around, a lining, a belt, welt pockets, shoulder pads, and epaulets.

One last trench-coat option is Altra's kit #5435, which comes complete with precut poly/cotton fabric, all the necessary notions, from thread to care labels, and thorough instructions. If you think you'll be hard to fit, Altra will sell you the notions and yardage separately; you'll have to supply your own pattern, but the Style coat, for example, is very similar. The kit, or fabric, comes in four colors, and there are optional zip-in liner kits and even matching hood kits.

Less traditional options include two Folkwear patterns: #137, the drover's coat I chose (the only unisex pattern I found); and #230, a woman's "Model T" duster, in two lengths, unlined, loose-fitting, but shapely. Past Patterns offers a man's duster (#200).

Except for the man's duster, all patterns mentioned are explicitly suited to rainwear fabrics. Of course, you can adapt any coat pattern that suits your vision or mix and match those above to get the combination of features you want. It's also a good idea to check out ready-to-wear for inspiration.☐

David Page Coffin is an associate editor of Threads *magazine. You can order the unisex, multisize Australian Drover's Coat pattern for $14.95 (CT residents add 8% sales tax) plus $2.50 postage and handling from Folkwear, The Taunton Press, 63 South Main Street, Box 5506, Newtown, CT 06470-5506.*

Resources

Rainwear specialists
These stores have extensive catalogs ($1) of rainwear and outerwear fabrics, notions, and patterns; swatches available.

The Green Pepper
941 Olive St.
Eugene, OR 97401
(503) 345-6665

The Rain Shed
707 N.W. 11th St.
Corvallis, OR 97330
(503) 753-8900

Kits
These companies also sell the outerwear fabrics and notions used in their kits.

Altra
100 E. Washington St.
New Richmond, IN 47967
(800) 443-8714; Indiana: (317) 339-4653

DK Sports (division of Daisy Kingdom)
134 N.W. 8th Ave.
Portland, OR 97209
(800) 288-5223
Also offers a vinyl-coating service.

Mail-order fabrics
These stores carry a vast inventory and will send swatches to match your interests. They carry all three European patterns: Burda, Style, and New Look.

Britex Fabrics
146 Geary St.
San Francisco, CA 94108
(415) 392-2910
Has a very wide range of rainwear fabrics.

G Street Fabrics
11854 Rockville Pike
Rockville, MD 20852
(301) 231-8998
Good for basics; vinyl-coating service.

Occasional sources
The Fabric Company
197 Ethan Allen Highway
Ridgefield, CT 06877
(203) 431-8565
Has lots of designer-rainwear off-cuts. Send $3 and a list of what you want.

The Couture Touch
Box 681278
Schaumburg, IL 60168
(312) 310-8080
Stocks basics.

Fabrics Unlimited
5015 Columbia Pike
Arlington, VA 22204
(703) 671-0324
Stocks basics.

Left Bank Fabric Co.
8354 W. 3rd St.
Los Angeles, CA 90048
(213) 655-7289
Check for exotics.

Felling feet
The Sewing Emporium
1079 Third Ave.
Chula Vista, CA 92010
(619) 420-3490

Born to Shock

Elsa Schiaparelli's clothing designs from the '30s are innovative today

by Ilya Sandra Perlingieri

In the '20s and '30s, Elsa Schiaparelli blazed a new trail in fashion. She was an iconoclast, spirited and innovative. Despite her lack of training in sewing or design, Schiaparelli set off shock waves that are still being felt, nearly 100 years after her birth.

Elsa Schiaparelli (skap-a-rell-ee) entered the fashion world in the '20s through a chance shipboard meeting with Gaby Picabia, who knew the great French designer Paul Poiret. Poiret's luxurious designs (many lavishly embroidered) were the epitome of what the "new woman" of the early 20th century wore. Inspired by Oriental opulence and his passion for the theater and ballet, Poiret designed loose and flowing styles: swirling turbans with sprays of feathers, high waistlines, kimono tunics, harem pants, and hobble skirts. He created a look that was the complete opposite of the tightly corseted hourglass figure of 1900.

In 1922, Poiret invited Elsa's friend Gaby to one of his parties. Gaby could not afford a new gown, so Schiaparelli offered to make one for her, although she didn't know how to sew. It was a success; Poiret sent his compliments to the "designer." Word spread, and before she knew it, Schiaparelli was in business. Encouraged by Poiret, the leading figure in French fashion, and undeterred by her lack of formal training, she bought her first dress house in 1925.

The right place, the right time—Schiaparelli's combination of luck and talent was enhanced by the cultural and economic climate of Paris in the '20s. She was at the center of the artistic explosion that had started at the turn of the century; she could tap the imagination and skill of many Parisian avant-garde artists.

Where art had been staid and artists complacent, now there was an electricity in the air. Dada and surrealist artists were challenging the status quo. Often, they were out to shock—a word that became synonymous with Schiaparelli. The *Exposition des Arts Décoratifs et Industriels Modernes* of 1925 in Paris gave the name Art Deco to a design style characterized by bold, streamlined, rectilinear forms and the extensive use of plastic. Surrealism, a juxtaposing of ordinary, everyday images in an unnatural way to create fantastic effects, began as a literary movement; then, through painters and other artists, it gradually became part of the new direction in fashion.

Schiaparelli's ties to the surrealists opened haute couture to enormous possibilities. Surrealist painter and Dada exponent Man Ray, who did much of Schiaparelli's photography, got his start in fashion photography with Paul Poiret. A 1927 bra advertisement sums up his surreal approach: The classical Greek statue of Venus de Milo is

Elsa Schiaparelli (above, left) in 1937, by fashion photographer Horst P. Horst. (Photo courtesy of Horst P. Horst)

From *Threads* magazine (April 1988) 16:38-43

juxtaposed with the half torso of a mannequin displaying the commercial product.
Fashion photographer Horst P. Horst, with
whom Schiaparelli also worked (photo, facing page), often included trompe l'oeil effects (optical illusions on flat, painted surfaces that "fool the eye" into seeing great
depth) in his photos and considered his
work "done in the spirit of fun." Eventually
Schiaparelli would commission Raoul Dufy,
Salvador Dali, artist-writer Jean Cocteau,
and Marcel Vertès to design prints for her
well before designer prints were common.

By surrounding herself with the best artists, Schiaparelli was able to combine their
talents with her own innovative fashion
ideas. Even the great Balanciaga (see the article on pp. 80-85) said that "Schiaparelli was
the only true artist in Fashion." She was
also in the right place at the right time.

First designs—Women of the Jazz Age and
the Roaring Twenties were looking at new
directions for their careers and clothing as
more options opened to them. They were
tired of the simple, boyish look of the early
'20s. And, despite (or because of) the stock-
market crash of 1929 and the subsequent
gathering war clouds in the early '30s, wom-
en were abandoning themselves to frivol-
ity in fashion. Two fashion designers led
the way: Elsa Schiaparelli and Coco Chanel.

Chanel's styles were simple and elegant,
yet they were practical with a masculine
cut. She did much to promote the New
Sportswear look that she'd helped create.

Schiaparelli, on the other hand, approached
fashion playfully. In 1927, she showed her
first handmade sweaters. They had Art Deco
designs with matching jewelry and accessories. These custom-made knits used a
new stretch-wool fiber, which, when knit,
hugged the figure. Some of the sweaters
had metallic threads worked into the designs for a sparkly effect.

Essential to the success of these sweaters was Schiaparelli's discovery of Aroosiag
Mikaëlian, an Armenian refugee, who did
spectacular knitting. Schiaparelli hired her
"temporarily," and together they devised a
technique of knitting with two colors to
give a trompe l'oeil effect. The first design
"Mike" did for Schiaparelli was a black sweater with a large white scarf worked around
the neck and bow-knotted in front. She
followed these with sweaters with knit-in
images of handkerchiefs, ties, buckles, and
belts. Next, Schiaparelli ventured to shock
her customers by knitting a skeleton into a

*Schiaparelli had a real sense of fun and an
unconventional approach to embroidery. Artist Jean Cocteau designed this visual pun
profiles-and-urn motif for her 1937 blue
silk-jersey coat. The embroidery, by Maison
Lesage (see page 115) is in couched gold
threads, satin-stitched details, and roses of
pink silk ribbon folded and tacked. (Photo:
Philadelphia Museum of Art; gift of Mme.
Elsa Schiaparelli)*

The Cocteau jacket

Schiaparelli asked artist and writer Jean Cocteau to make drawings that could be translated into embroidered garments. In 1937 he sketched the image that was rendered in gold beading, couching, and sequin work on this coarse, light-gray linen jacket.

The jacket looks rather simple, with its collarless front, tapered sleeves, and square-cut bodice slightly fitted with shoulder and waist darts. But there is no sleeve-cap seam, so the lady's long golden hair can cascade uninterrupted down the right sleeve. The resulting bias sleeves are gusseted under the arms.

The jacket has no interfacing to support the heavily beaded bodice and sleeve. There is just the outer fabric and a light-gray China-silk lining. The side seams of the lining are machine-stitched, but the neckline, shoulders, sleeves, and hem are all slipstitched by hand. The jacket closes with a small, silk looped tab in the lining and a matching, silk-covered button.

Both the hand and the profile are couched cording with accents of silk floss in short and long satin stitches. The golden tresses are gold and clear-glass bugle beads interspersed with gold paillettes, outlined in bronze-wrapped, couched cording.

The simple design of this linen jacket, enhanced by beading and embroidery, is as contemporary today as it was in 1938, when it was created. (Photo: Philadelphia Museum of Art; gift of Mme. Elsa Schiaparelli)

sweater design. It did shock, but it sold—and was a precursor of today's punk.

The challenge of synthetics—The fashion world was experiencing severe economic changes. As raw materials, especially silk, the mainstay of French haute couture, skyrocketed in price in the late '20s, garments became more expensive to produce. The textile industry was looking for other kinds of fibers and discovering new manufacturing processes.

Schiaparelli took an avid interest in finding solutions. She didn't have a rigid way of viewing things, and her natural curiosity and innovative ideas helped pave the way for the production of new textiles. She traveled extensively to see how other countries produced their textiles.

Schiaparelli's most important contribution to solving the problem was her collaboration with Charles Colcombet, the head of a silk manufacturing company in Lyons, France. Colcombet had pioneered synthetic alternatives to silk. Schiaparelli was the first haute couture designer to make a fashion statement with synthetics. With her creative input, Colcombet's company developed most of the new synthetics to be used for haute couture. Rayon crepe became a pinafore evening dress and coat; cellophane (made with a secret formula developed by Colcombet and called "Rhodophane") was turned into a "see-through" glass cape (the forerunner of many of today's see-through fabrics). It also became silver and black evening hats and a cocktail suit of cellophane velvet. Rhodophane textured to resemble tree bark was made into a square-shouldered jacket. Other ideas included waterproofed, washable raincoats of linen, taffeta, and rayon crinkle crepe. In fact, Schiaparelli's consistent commitment to innovative approaches to fashion revolutionized the textile industry.

Natural fibers were also abundant in Schiaparelli's designs, and often unexpected: wool instead of silk for evening wear, lace with leather, wool crepe with polka dots and wool plaids for evening wear, evening capes of lamé wool tweed (with metallic fibers woven in). Her tree-bark crepes and velvets were forerunners of the crinkly cotton crepe and crushed velvet seen today.

Designer fabrics—As a surrealist fashion designer working with unusual shapes and fabrics, Schiaparelli let the world see that it was fun to design. An inverted shoe became a hat (right); she designed lounging "pajamas" (called palazzo pants in the '60s) and dresses with the skirts shaped like parachutes. A business-suit jacket had seven large rectangular pockets with buttons that looked like drawer handles. Inspired by Dali's "Venus de Milo with Drawers," it was called the Desk Suit. Her playful buttons came in every conceivable shape: animals, flying-trapeze artists, spinning tops, fish hooks, lollipops, safety pins, and paper clips.

By the 1930s, Schiaparelli had incorporated her playful approach into fabric design. Sketches by Dali, Vertès, and Cocteau were translated into silk-screened designs (the earliest examples of what we now call designer fabrics) and embroidery. Dali created a design with torn pieces of peeled tree bark that looked like rips in the cloth. It became the long, silk, cream-colored crepe dress with fitted bodice and split train shown at bottom right. A huge, "cooked" red lobster with parsley was painted across an evening dress (designed by Dali). It was another element of punk fashion, decades early. Vertès designed an allover animal print with swans, rabbits, bicycles, and prancing cows for a sleeveless evening gown of bright-blue crepe with matching hood and gigantic balloon sleeves in shocking pink. Jaunty Edwardian gentlemen sported beards on another Vertès-print dress splashed with vivid colors.

These bright, playful, and sometimes outrageous prints were the antithesis of what other designers were creating. Most haute couture designers in the '30s, including Coco Chanel, Madeleine Vionnet, and Jean Patou, who also exported their designs to America, were using small floral prints, polka dots, stripes, plaids, and lots of solids, mostly in natural fibers.

Haute couture and embroidery—In addition to pioneering designer prints, Schiaparelli was in a league by herself when it came to lavish embroidery in haute couture. Of course there is historical precedence for magnificently embroidered articles of clothing, in 16th-century Elizabethan England and 18th-century France, for example. Poiret, too, had numerous embroidered garments in his collections.

Schiaparelli was fortunate to have extremely talented embroiderers to decorate her garments. She worked closely with Albert Lesage, of Maison Lesage, who specialized in exquisite embroideries for haute couture (see "At the Lesage embroidery ateliers," page 115). Schiaparelli's bolero jackets, another of her hallmarks, were frequently covered with embroidery.

In 1938, Maison Lesage did the embroidery for a stunning black silk-velvet cape that Schiaparelli had designed. This simple

Schiaparelli's ultimate surrealistic joke: a shoe turned upside down makes a hat (above). This one is black felt. Salvador Dali designed textile prints for Schiaparelli (below). The trompe l'oeil torn-cloth design is echoed in the cut, lined, and reverse-appliquéd veil. (Photos courtesy of Fashion Institute of Technology; photographer, Michele Russell Slavinsky; top, collection of The Metropolitan Museum of Art, Costume Institute; bottom, collection of Philadelphia Museum of Art)

design is offset by lavish embroidery. The silk-crepe lined cape has a large black-velvet button at the left shoulder. The right front flares out considerably to leave room for the opulent embroidery. The decorative detail, Neptune in his chariot (left) was inspired by the bronze sculpture of Neptune in the Palace of Versailles garden.

Jean Cocteau's graphic style was perfectly suited to Lesage's delicate, linear embroideries. His sketch of a woman's profile, arm, and hand was translated into a woman's face and flowing hair embroidered on the right front bodice of a coarse, light-gray linen jacket (see photo, page 112). The jacket itself is cut elegantly simple: collarless, overlapping in the front, tapered sleeves, with the back bodice slightly fitted but still cut rather squarely. The lady's long golden hair, cascading down the right sleeve, is profusely embroidered in a combination of gold and clear-glass bugle beads interspersed with gold paillettes. The hair strands are outlined in couched bronze-wrapped cording.

Embroidery as a decorative element in Schiaparelli's fashions became a great deal more than mere surface design. Frequently there was an allusion to myth or fantasy or the illusion of jewels that turn out to be glass or magnificently worked satin stitches or couched gold threads. Many of these embroideries became themes for her seasonal collections.

During Schiaparelli's heyday in the '30s, she presented special-theme collections twice a year. In February of 1937, she showed her Music Collection. Summer dresses featuring prints of bees and birds were decorated with buttons shaped like musical instruments. Dresses had sheet music in couched gold thread for the bars with gold and silver satin-stitched musical notes. Others had musical bars made of ribbons "with roses for notes on white silk crepe."

The next year, Schiaparelli produced four collections, including the Circus, in February, featuring acrobats, trapeze artists, and animals galore (bottom photos). A pink twill

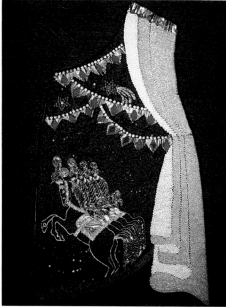

Maison Lesage made these samples for Schiaparelli's 1938 Circus collection. The trompe l'oeil couched curtain opens on prancing horses (left); above, satin-stitched elephants dance on bolero evening jackets. (Photos courtesy of Fashion Institute of Technology; photographer, Michele Russell Slavinsky)

jacket, darted and fitted with tapered sleeves, had buttons shaped like trapeze artists.

The embroidered bolero was a Schiaparelli hallmark. A white satin "ringmaster" bolero had tiny gathers at the sleeve cap and red cuffs and matching band at the bottom of the bodice front. Two sets of four white satin-stitched horses reared up on each side of the bodice front. Another short-sleeved bolero had elephants, done in gray-silk short and long satin stitches, standing on their hind legs on a row of barrels.

Schiaparelli's later years—Even as a child, Elsa had listened to a different drummer. Her intellectual and aristocratic parents had raised her in the cultural and artistic richness of Rome. Elsa considered herself very plain, especially in comparison to her older sister, Beatrice. One day she "planted" morning glory, nasturtium, and daisy seeds in her eyes, ears, and throat so that she would "blossom" into a beauty. An emergency visit from a doctor saved her from suffocation. That desire to compensate for her perceived plainness and her love for the vivid beauty and color of flowers reappeared in her shocking and vibrant designs. Before the outbreak of World War I, she and her father visited Tunisia, where she saw the gorgeous Oriental fashions, jewels, rich colors, and silver embroidery that she would also incorporate in her clothing designs. As a young woman, she visited Paris and New York before settling in the mid-'20s, after a brief marriage, with her daughter in Paris.

Schiaparelli's understanding of the '20s and '30s was her forte. She translated that understanding into a unique fashion statement, synthesizing the new trends in textiles, art, and design and often pioneering ideas that became trends.

Although she had many contradictory personality traits—she was difficult, autocratic, extremely reserved, shrewd, yet humble—she was fair and a very good boss. Her success in business was due in part to her knack for attracting the best talent in fashion. By 1934, she had a staff of 400. Through their insistence on excellence, these extraordinary embroiderers (including those from Maison Lesage), tailors, and seamstresses turned their craft into an art. "She had a keen insight into their capacities, respected them as artists and human beings, and tacitly signed a moral contract with them that neither she nor they ever dishonoured or broke," according to Palmer White (see "Further reading," at right). She may not have complimented them, but she was supportive of their needs.

Schiaparelli was generous to her staff long before it was mandated by any laws. Her wages were higher than those of other couture houses. There were paid vacations, extremely low-cost purchases of house designs, and in the event of illness, even hospital beds were available. When other designers, including Chanel, were having

problems with personnel, Schiaparelli did not have them. Many employees stayed with her until the business closed.

In the '40s, although Schiaparelli continued to design, the fashion scene changed drastically. During World War II, Schiaparelli was actively involved in her business; but when the Germans occupied Paris, she turned her house over to the Quakers for the benefit of refugees. She came to America and lectured on fashion, attempting to raise America's consciousness to the needs of the innocent people ravaged by war. Fashion was the second most important industry in France. Schiaparelli, the most well-known name in fashion, did much during the war to promote independent French fashion abroad.

After the war, in 1947, the mood was somber; fashion took an entirely different direction. Backed by the wealthy Boussac cotton firm, Christian Dior made fashion history with his "New Look." Schiaparelli's fashions were out of tune with the time, and her styles weren't selling well. For a while, she was assisted by the young Pierre Cardin, who was just getting his start. Later, Hubert de Givenchy joined Schiaparelli and stayed with her until he went into business on his own.

As innovative as Schiaparelli had been for 20 years, by the late '40s and early '50s, her career was over. She was persuaded to show her final collection in February of 1954. She spent her last years between Paris and the house she bought in Tunisia. She died on November 13, 1973.

Occasionally, a creative and innovative voice appears that transcends the fashion of the times. Elsa Schiaparelli was that voice. The echo is still heard today in fashion. □

Ilya Sandra Perlingieri is a contributing editor of Threads. *She has taught costume history and fashion design for 20 years.*

Further reading

(See page 78 for a review of Richard Martin's *Fashion and Surrealism.*)

Blum, Stella, and Louise Hamer, eds. *Fabulous Fashions: 1907-67.* New York: The Metropolitan Museum of Art, 1984.

Chierichetti, David. *Hollywood Costume Design.* New York: Harmony Books, 1977 (out of print).

De Marly, Diana. *The History of Haute Couture: Eighteen Fifty to Nineteen Fifty.* New York: Holmes & Meier, 1980.

Hall-Duncan, Nancy. *The History of Fashion Photography.* New York: Alpine Books, 1979 (out of print).

Schiaparelli, Elsa. *Shocking Life.* London: Dent, 1954 (out of print).

Vreeland, Diana, and Irving Penn. *Inventive Paris Clothes: 1909-39.* New York: Viking Press, 1977 (out of print).

White, Palmer. *Elsa Schiaparelli: Empress of Paris Fashion.* New York: Rizzoli, 1986.

At the Lesage embroidery ateliers

by Claire Shaeffer

I've always admired the Lesage embroideries on designs by French couturiers Balmain, Chanel, Dior, Schiaparelli, and American designers Bill Blass, Oscar de la Renta, and Mary McFadden. So, I welcomed the opportunity to visit François Lesage and his ateliers in Paris last fall.

The day before my appointment, I visited the Lesage boutique at 21 Place Vendôme. Once the Schiaparelli showroom, the boutique is in the midst of the world's foremost jewelers.

Maison Lesage—The most prestigious embroidery firm in the world, the house of Lesage was established in 1924 when the Lesage family acquired the house of Michonet, once the leading embroiderer for Napoléon III and his empress, Eugénie.

Albert Lesage saw the potential for decorative stitching in haute couture; his collaboration with his wife, Marie-Louise, and with Elsa Schiaparelli is frequently credited with reviving the art of embroidery. Schiaparelli often asked Lesage to design an embroidery around a theme; she then designed a garment to display it boldly. This was just the opposite of the traditional approach, in which embroideries were designed to decorate a specific garment.

François Lesage (photo above), the head of the firm and son of its founders, greets me in the small front office. He is an unusually generous man, whose eyes sparkle when he talks about his art.

Lesage grew up in the business. "I always drew," he explains. "After the war, I went to Hollywood and did some designs for the movie studios."

Recalled to Paris when his father died unexpectedly in 1949, Lesage began a new chapter in embroidery history when he introduced seasonal presentations of embroidered samples or prototypes for designers to draw from. "Each year we prepare three hundred to five hundred samples, which cost about one thousand dollars each. The samples are never sold. At the end of the season, they are stored flat in

Embroiderers at work in one of the Lesage ateliers. The base fabric is pinned to muslin and stretched on a simple four-piece frame.

large boxes. We have sixty thousand samples—twenty thousand collected by Michonet, twenty thousand from my parents' time [1924 to 1949], and twenty thousand since I arrived—a complete museum of embroidery history.

"About twenty percent of the ideas for samples come from the designers. Saint Laurent will call and say, 'I'm thinking of Marrakesh.' Karl Lagerfeld is most precise. He cuts photographs from books." Since Lagerfeld doesn't always know exactly how the embroideries will be used on the garments, the motifs are finished so they can be applied later.

The designs for the remaining samples are developed by Lesage and designer David Helman. Ideas come from everywhere: the samples in the firm's archives, Chinese porcelains, Italian mosaics, the artwork of Jean Cocteau and Christian Bérard, etc.

According to Lesage, "The challenge is to create something different by blending the same materials in a new way." To do this, he starts with mussel shells, gold, silver straw, mink, chenille, braids, cords, leather, hammered metal, pearls, Austrian rhinestones, Bohemian crystals, glass, mother-of-pearl chips, coral, tassels, pom-poms, fringe, paillettes, wood, jet, steel, and beads in every imaginable shape and color. He has developed special processes for painting the beads and sequins and for applying the materials.

In the workrooms—Every wall of each atelier is lined with shelves to store millions of beads, sequins, braids,

and threads. Embroidery frames with work in various stages are hung, stacked, and propped everywhere. The staff is always busy designing for the current collections or stitching next season's samples.

Most of the embroiderers are young women who have graduated from one of the three national embroidery schools in and around Paris. According to Lesage, each has an area of expertise. "This girl is better with flowers; this one is neater and more classical," he indicated as they worked. Most sit alone at their frames, but a few work in pairs. There is no idle chatter; embroidery requires meticulous precision.

The embroiderers fall into two broad groups: those who use needles to create fine thread designs and those who do beadwork or sequin designs with a tambour hook. The needleworkers use a small needle and silk threads in hundreds of shades, untwisted floss, gold and silver threads, or silk chenille to create elaborate decorations.

Tambour work derives its name from the French word *tambour,* meaning *drum,* because the background fabric or ground is stretched like a drum on a frame. A tambour hook is used to make a chain stitch and attach the beads to the fabric. Similar to a tiny crochet hook, it has a small notch above a sharp point. Generally worked with the fabric wrong side up, it is held in one hand while the other hand holds the string of beads beneath the fabric (center photo, facing page). The hook is inserted through the loop of the

last stitch into the fabric. It picks up the thread between the next two beads and pulls the loop to the surface through the previous stitch. The next stitch is made through this loop, as shown in the drawing below.

Development of a sample—Each embroidery design begins with a full-scale drawing about 20 in. by 24 in. After it is hand-colored, materials are selected. Sometimes the entire surface is covered with beads, sequins, or embroidery; sometimes the background fabric is an integral part of the design.

To make the first pattern, a draftsman traces the design onto a piece of parchment. Then all lines are perforated so the design can be transferred to the fabric. Lesage has two kinds of pricking machines. The one in use the day I visited is over 100 years old. On the end of an arm that's like an old-fashioned dentist's rig is a treadle-controlled, sharp-pointed brass rod. With the drawn pattern stationary on a felt pad, the operator holds and guides the pricker like a pencil, while pumping the treadle to move the rod up and down (top-left photo, facing page).

Applying beads with the tambour hook

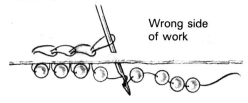

Wrong side of work

To transfer the design to the background fabric, a worker lays the pierced pattern over the fabric, then dabs over it with pounce powder, either black or white, and rubs it with a soft pad to force the powder through the holes (top-right photo).

The patternmarker stretches the fabric onto an embroidery frame (see photo, facing page) made of four pieces of hardwood. The frames can be adjusted for the fabric width but not its length. To stretch the work, the patternmaker pins a narrow piece of muslin to the end of the fabric, wraps it around the frame end, and pins it again. The strip is taken back and forth between frame and fabric until the full width of the piece is secured. The procedure is repeated at the other end.

Embroidering the garment—Each of the ten couturiers Lesage is currently working with selects several samples or prototypes from the Lesage collection and designs garments that will feature the selected embroideries. The garment patterns are taken to Lesage, who redraws the design to fit the individual garment. If the customer is too large or too small to fit the original garment, the design is "recreated to give the same impression" and prevent it from appearing too cluttered or too bald.

Garments are embroidered before the sections are cut out and sewn. A design is drawn onto the garment pattern to flow smoothly from one garment section to another, making seams and darts inconspicuous or invisible. The embroidery work does not extend into the seam allowances, darts, or facings.

When the design is transferred to the fabric, the seamlines, not the cutting lines, are marked. If two or more small garment sections are marked on one large fabric rectangle, several inches will be left between them for the seam allowances.

Each garment embroidered by Lesage has an identity card. Filed by designer, the card records the technical information needed to reproduce the garment, a fabric swatch, and the types and quantities of beads.

All this handwork isn't cheap. Embroiderers earn several times the minimum wage; and most garments cost $20,000 to $40,000.

A designer's designer, François Lesage is one of those rare individuals with the artistic talent to create magnificent designs and the practical know-how to make them work. His ideas and expertise have quietly influenced the history of fashion and decorative arts for over a quarter of a century.

Claire Shaeffer is a sewing expert specializing in adapting designer and ready-to-wear techniques for home sewers. She is the author of five books, including The Complete Book of Sewing Short Cuts *(Sterling, 1983). For more on Lesage, see Palmer White's* The Master Touch of Lesage: Embroidery for French Fashion *(Paris: Chêne, 1987). Photos pages 115-117 courtesy of Maison Lesage.*

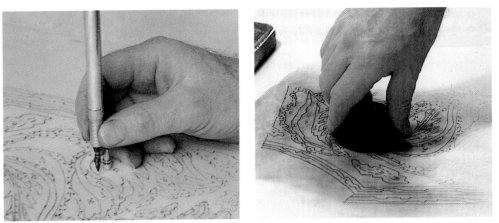

Parchment patterns are frequently perforated with a treadle-operated brass piercing tool (left). In order to transfer the image, a worker lays the pierced design over the fabric and then rubs it with pounce powder (right).

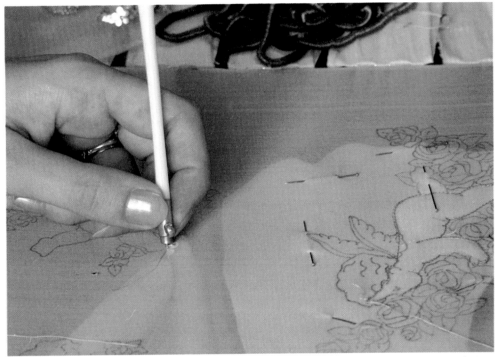

With the wrong side of the fabric face up, this embroiderer works with a tambour hook in her left hand. Her right hand supports the line of beads beneath the sheer fabric as she pulls crochetlike loops to lock the beads in place.

A left-handed embroiderer skillfully embellishes leaves with pink floss. The three-dimensional ribbon flowers are a Lesage hallmark.

Historic Chic

A vintage style gets a modern fit

by Nancy O. Bryant

Silk-georgette dress from about 1929

The shift style was fashionable, with no fitting in waist, bust, or shoulders. The hem dips longer in the back.

Shirring

Pleats

One-piece sleeve with inverted V is formed by an edge-stitched tuck.

Diagonal panels hang on bias, hugging hips.

Arrows indicate grain lines.

Placket opening has snaps set into bodice side seam and upper-diagonal panel edge.

Extra length, pleated for a blouson effect

Godets

Illustrations by Lainé Roundy

historic dress is a rich resource for style, pattern, and construction ideas for contemporary garments. Clothing in the collections at universities, museums, and historic societies contains many fine details rarely found in today's manufactured garments. Although you can't take these garments apart, you can translate a design you like into a pattern of your own, using the techniques I explain below.

I found a black silk-georgette dress from about 1929 (photo at right) that I wanted to adapt for myself. I liked the graceful flare of the skirt shaped by godets set between multiple vertical panels. Diagonal panels in the upper skirt create a close fit around the hip. Blousing at the lower back bodice balances the petal-shaped extensions of the V-shaped front neckline. The hem dips from just below the knee in front to below the calf in back, a nice finishing touch.

It's unlikely that an exact duplicate of a historic garment will fit a contemporary figure, because of changes in physique and the undergarments that are worn today. You may want to change the fit or modify the style. To avoid major fitting problems, I start by outlining basic pattern pieces on a tracing of my sloper, which fits my size and shape. If you don't have a sloper, you can make one by using a basic dress-fitting pattern. (Patterns are available from several pattern companies.)

Since a sloper is just a basic fitted shell, I have to build the style I want into my final pattern pieces. If I want pleats, for example, I add width or length to the piece.

Before I lay out the pattern pieces for cutting, I check the grain lines in the original garment. If I want to achieve the same drape as the original, I have to cut my pattern pieces on the same grain lines.

I usually check the fit, proportions, and construction sequence and techniques by making a muslin prototype. In this case I used a polyester crepe de chine for my muslin to mimic the silk I intended to use for the dress. Muslin prototypes can be constructed quickly and cheaply.

The original dress—The ideal woman of the 1920s had a boyish figure and tried to hide her curves. The original garment (drawing at left) has no darts for the bust, waist, or shoulder blades (the darts were "released," or a dartless sloper was used). The diagonal panels in the upper skirt were cut on the straight of grain but hang on the bias. The

Vintage garments fascinate Nancy Bryant, who wears her own version of the black silk-georgette dress (ca. 1929) on the mannequin. It hugs the hips because of eight diagonal panels in the upper skirt that hang on the bias. Twelve triangular godets set between twelve vertical panels form the skirt's flare. The hemline lengthens as it sweeps from front to back. (All photos by Roger Schreiber)

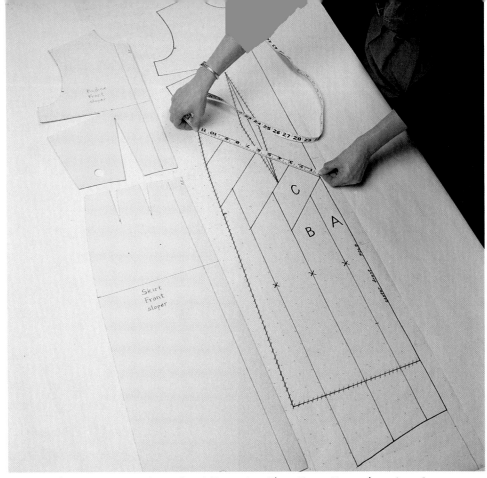

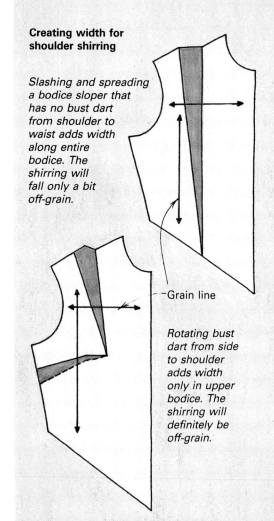

On a tracing of her dress-sloper front, Bryant outlines the pattern pieces based on proportions from the original. She has crossed out lines and darts she won't use. Diagonal panels cross the side seams in the skirt and will continue onto the back-sloper tracing. She has redrawn the hemline so the front is higher than the back and has marked positions for inserting godets with x's. The two darts on the skirt sloper were combined into one for the dress sloper.

back has 11 vertical pleats sewn closed near the neckline but released over the length of the back. The fullness is further enhanced by extra length in the back taken up by two tucked horizontal pleats at the side waist of the back bodice. The skirt has no side seams; the opening in the left side starts in the bodice side seam and extends along the edge of the topmost diagonal panel.

I decided to make my dress in the same proportion as the original but with a more contoured fit. Before I could use my sloper to make a pattern, I had to take measurements from the dress.

Taking measurements—I wanted to handle this dress as little as possible, so I put it on a mannequin. I sketched the shapes of all garment pieces on paper and recorded their measurements. This task was not easy, since the fabric had stretched over time. Pieces that should have been identical, such as the left and right skirt panels, were not, and I eventually decided to average the left and right measurements.

The grain of the fabric helped me determine the shapes of the garment and pattern pieces. The black fabric made it somewhat difficult to see the grain of each garment piece, although the georgette structure was helpful. Historic garments made from plaid fabrics make the task of measuring grain angles easier, since the plaid repeat can be used to measure the grain angles.

An area that was difficult to measure accurately was the front-shoulder shirring. I estimated the amount of shirring by observing the angles of the crosswise grain at the shoulder and armscye (drawing above). In this case I decided that the dressmaker had created the shirring by slashing the pattern from the shoulder to the waist and spreading the pattern rather than by moving the bust dart from side to shoulder.

Patternmaking with a sloper—Once I knew the grain, sizes, and shapes of the original garment pieces, I was ready to begin rescaling the pattern to my size. I needed to consider, though, how my sloper differed from the one used by the designer of the original dress. On a paper tracing of my dress sloper, which I had made by combining my bodice and skirt slopers, I drew lines defining the front and back bodice pieces, then continued with the skirt pieces (see above photo). To determine the widths of the vertical panels in the skirt, I divided my sloper hip circumference into 12 equal parts. I drew lines defining the sides of all vertical pieces. There are no side seams in the skirt; the front and back skirts slopers join in the center of one of the panels.

The diagonal skirt pieces were a bit tricky to draw, as they, too, crossed the side seams of the sloper tracings. I knew the angle at which the diagonal panels were set into the skirt and the length of the seamline that

joins the diagonal panels to the front bodice. To find the width of the individual panels, I divided the length of the seamline into four parts and then drew equally spaced, parallel lines at the proper angle to define the diagonal panels. Panels L and I (drawing, facing page) weren't complete yet; I still needed to refine the hip area.

Darts, ease, and godets—After drawing and separating the main pattern pieces, I began to modify individual pieces. The original garment doesn't have waist-fitting darts. I didn't include waist-fitting darts either, but I decided to incorporate the shape of the hip curve that my sloper provides. After drawing the diagonal panels onto my upper-skirt front and back-sloper tracings, I rotated the hip curve into the two uppermost panels, as shown in the drawing above. This produced a smoother contour at the side waist and fewer fabric gathers.

To add blousing to the back bodice, I added length at the bottom (top photo, facing page). I would pleat the extra length at the side-waist point before sewing the back bodice to the front bodice. I also slashed the bodice back vertically to create the width for the pleats. To allow the bodice back to fit the curve of my shoulder blades without looking any different in style from the original garment, I moved the shoulder-fitting dart from the shoulder seam to the back neckline. When sewn, the dart would be

Rotating the hip curve into the bias panels

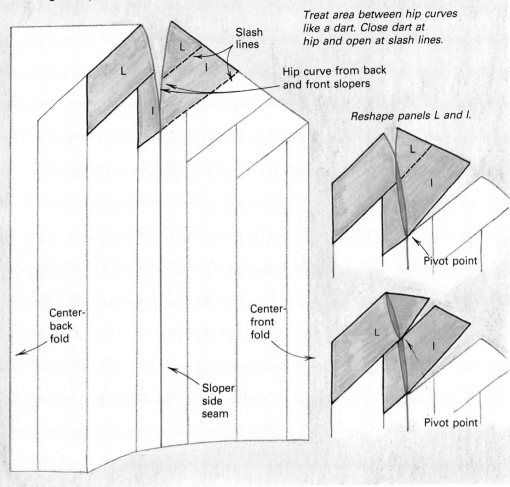

Slash lines

Treat area between hip curves like a dart. Close dart at hip and open at slash lines.

Hip curve from back and front slopers

Reshape panels L and I.

L

I

Pivot point

L

I

Pivot point

Center-back fold

Center-front fold

Sloper side seam

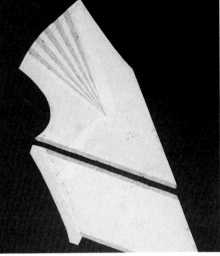

The back-bodice pattern (top) was slashed and spread to form pleats (gray vertical shaded areas) and lengthened for blousing. The shoulder dart (blue area) will be hidden. On the bodice front, Bryant rotated the bust dart from the side to the shoulder (above) before slashing the pattern into two parts. She spread the dart (shaded areas) for shirring.

concealed beneath the back neck pleat closest to the shoulder blade.

I provided fitting in the bust by rotating the bust dart from the side to the shoulder for shirring, as shown in the bottom photo at right. I also made a separate underlay pattern that's the width of the finished shoulder. When stitched to the shirring, the underlay would stabilize the gathers.

The hemline is longer in the back than in the front, but the godet insets all begin at the same distance from the hipline. This made each godet a different length. I also curved the bottom of each godet a bit.

Checking fit, construction, and fabric—
With a complete pattern, I sewed a prototype from polyester crepe de chine to test the fit and decide on the construction sequence before I worked on the final silk dress. The opaque polyester fabric revealed the dress details better than a sheer fabric.

When I sew, I like to work on the skirt, bodice, and sleeves separately and then join them, as smaller pieces are easier to handle. I followed this same construction sequence for my dress (see drawing, p. 122, for details). When joining pieces, I sew from the wider to the narrower end to keep the fabric grain from distorting.

I started the skirt by sewing the center-front panel to the adjacent vertical skirt gore, starting at the point where the godet insert begins and continuing to the top

edge. Next, I added the diagonal piece that lies above it (photo, p. 122). All the diagonal panels are oriented with their bias grains parallel to center front, but their long edges are on the straight of grain. These lengthwise grain edges stabilize the bias edges of the vertical panels.

After joining two vertical pieces and one diagonal piece, I inserted the corresponding godet, starting at the hemline on each side of the godet inset and ending at the point. I continued the construction sequence by alternately joining the next vertical panel, a diagonal panel, and a godet until the skirt was done. This sequence puts the least stress on the fabric.

I then worked on the bodice, sewing the pleats and the shoulder-fitting dart at the neckline of the bodice back. I shirred the front shoulders by pulling up parallel lines of stitches until the width of the shoulder matched the front-shirring underlay. I sewed over the gathering stitches to hold the shape of the shirring with the underlay.

After completing the decorative inverted V tuck of each sleeve's wrist placket, I sewed the underarm seams and set the sleeves into the bodice. Finally, I joined the completed bodice to the skirt at the waistline, while leaving an opening at the left side bodice for a snap opening.

The original garment had no elastic in the waistline, but I found that elastic helped to keep the blousing at my waist and con-

trol the waist fullness. I cut elastic the length of my waist measurement and sewed half of the length to the back-waist seam allowances with zigzag stitches. The front half of the elastic is unattached to the dress and fastens with a snap on the left side.

The diagonal panels stretch to fit snugly above the hips because they're on the bias, but they could have made the pattern too snug. (Bias pieces often stretch lengthwise and decrease in width.) I thought the pattern might have needed extra ease in the hip to compensate for the stretching, but when I tried on the prototype, the hip area fit well, and the only overall change I had to make was to add 1 in. to the length of all skirt pieces.

Final details—I'd originally hoped to find a dull silk fabric with woven stripes that would readily show the garment's cut. I settled on a solid-color, matte-finish silk with a nubby texture. Although I used only one color, the design would also look striking with white diagonal panels and the rest in black.⇨

Bryant sews a diagonal panel to the tops of two vertical panels in the final dress.

The neck trim on the original garment is a single layer of georgette, with three inset beige oval petals. All the edges of the trim and petals were hemmed by hand. To me, the oval shapes contradicted the straight lines of the dress, so I used diamond shapes. To support the neck trim and speed construction, I made the trim and the diamonds from two layers of material: silk crepe de chine for the top and dress material for the facing.

The original dress has a straight-grain, self-fabric belt. I used the sloper to make a contoured belt for a better fit.

My dress was a joy to make and is fun to wear. As I move, the silk moves fluidly, and the long hemline in back brushes my calves. A tremendous and satisfying learning experience awaits others who seek historic inspiration for a contemporary design. □

Nancy O. Bryant teaches apparel design at Oregon State University in Corvallis.

Seeking details

When it comes to allowing close-up inspection of their costume collections, museums and historical societies are torn between their desire to serve the public and their need to preserve their collections. Here are some guidelines for gaining access to them.

If you're professionally involved with garments or costumes, write to the curator of the collection, explaining what you would like to see and why. Be specific. You may need a preliminary appointment just to research what is in the collection.

Let the curator know if you'll be using the information for a nonprofit or profit purpose. Many organizations charge fees to commercially related ventures but waive them for researchers.

Consider requesting a showing for a small group. Curators see benefits to serving many people at once rather than devoting time to individuals.

Volunteer at the local museum or historical society to help with the costume collection. Each museum or society values volunteers differently; be prepared to go through a training period.

If you aren't near a collection and still need correct proportions and details, try one of the books listed below, which contain patterns drawn to scale. –N.O.B.

Arnold, Janet. *Patterns of Fashion: Eighteen Sixty to Nineteen Forty*, 1977; *Patterns of Fashion: Fifteen Sixty to Sixteen Twenty*, 1985. New York: Drama Book Publishers.

Hamilton, Margot Hill, and Peter A. Bucknell. *The Evolution of Fashion: Pattern and Cut from 1066 to 1930* (7th ed.). New York: Drama Book Publishers, 1981.

Payne, Blanche. *The History of Costume from the Ancient Egyptians to the Twentieth Century*. New York: Harper and Row, 1965.

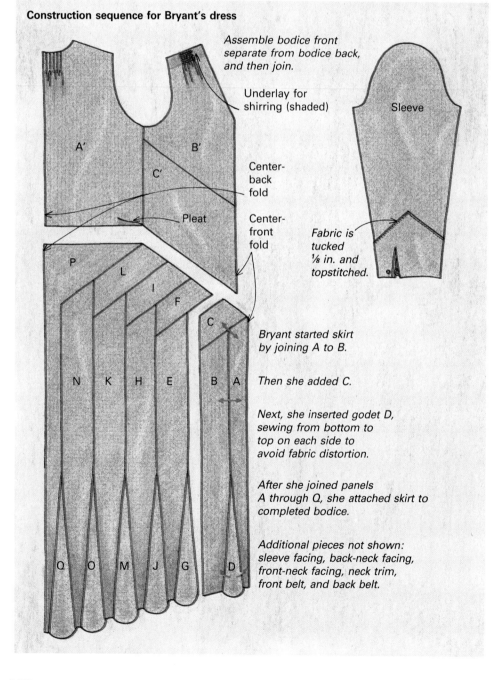

Construction sequence for Bryant's dress

Assemble bodice front separate from bodice back, and then join.

Underlay for shirring (shaded)

Sleeve

A' B'

C'

Center-back fold

Pleat

Center-front fold

Fabric is tucked ⅛ in. and topstitched.

P L I F C

N K H E B A

Q O M J G D

Bryant started skirt by joining A to B.

Then she added C.

Next, she inserted godet D, sewing from bottom to top on each side to avoid fabric distortion.

After she joined panels A through Q, she attached skirt to completed bodice.

Additional pieces not shown: sleeve facing, back-neck facing, front-neck facing, neck trim, front belt, and back belt.

Rei Kawakubo
This designer is reinventing fashion

By David Page Coffin

the clothes shown on these pages are the work of Rei Kawakubo, a 45-year-old Japanese woman who is as likely as anyone to be regarded by future observers as the premier designer of the 1980s. She calls her company Comme des Garçons (like the boys), and she's been delighting, and appalling, the fashion world since the early days of the decade.

I saw her work as part of the Fashion Institute of Technology's spring '87 show, *Three Women: Madeleine Vionnet, Claire McCardell, and Rei Kawakubo.* The show's thesis was, as the catalog states: "Each designer, in a separate era of the century, provided a new concept and vision of dress." Vionnet gave the woman of the late '20s the bias cut and freed her from stays and corsets; 20 years later, McCardell gave her sportswear: dresses with pockets.

I saw the show several times; Vionnet and McCardell were wonderful, but I needed a guide to ensure that I got the point—these women *invented* the images that now seem so characteristic of their times. Kawakubo I found astonishing.

Rei Kawakubo designs every aspect of the presentation of her clothing, from her spare and monumental boutiques, where often neither mirrors nor salespeople are visible, to the display and arrangement of the mannequins, and the mannequins themselves, at the FIT show. At first glimpse, it was hard to even enter the harshly lit Kawakubo gallery. The usual, safe separation of viewer from object was gone; something seemed to be going on in there, and I wasn't sure I wanted to be in on it. But once inside, I realized a fantasy had come true. I'd suddenly been able to freeze the action on a scene full of very curious clothing, and I

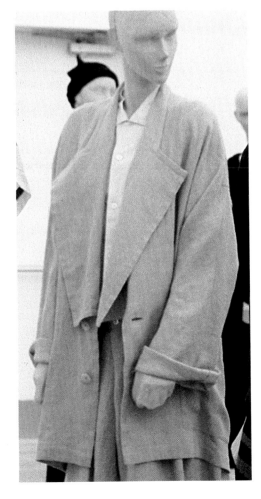

Wrap jacket, 1986 (right): Moving the eyes slowly down this ensemble from shoulders to ankles is like watching wit at work. The gabardine Mao jacket starts out in life with proper tailored dourness...but aren't the pockets off? ...Whoa! The spiral jacket hem conceals a distinctly mysterious skirt, atop...sweater-sleeve legs? The hat, straight out of a Van Eyck portrait, confirms the cultural circus.

Twist-back jacket, 1983 (left): Here's a plain muslin blouse under a plain linen jacket. Okay, the lapels are interesting. Wander around the back (above), and the piece explodes.

From *Threads* magazine (February 1988) 15:39-41

> **"If you want a well-designed pattern and good sewing, you don't need a fashion designer."**
> **—Rei Kawakubo**

could explore and examine to my heart's content. The forbidding atmosphere completely faded as I wandered among these strange creations. Each new garment seemed to dissolve another constraint: routine construction, fit, silhouette, choice of materials. They challenged every conventional fashion intention. It was like a Zen monk's Mardi Gras—a constant, silent surprise, all done in neutrals. Before I left, it had become totally exhilarating.

Kawakubo's clothes seem to suggest new ideas with every encounter: about fashion, about art, about art to wear, about feeling strong as opposed to looking good, about beauty as opposed to luxury, about what mere clothes could suggest or inspire. They struck me as an antidote to clothing as consumer goods, and fashion as make-believe. Kawakubo's clothes were entirely equal to the glare of the museum setting, but they were still *clothes.*

Admittedly, I wasn't being asked to actually wear any of them. But I enjoyed more and more the prospect of encountering real people in this sort of clothing. Fashion savants have been telling us for years that clothing is communication, but what does this stuff say? There's too much going on for the message to be simply, "This is new, I am fashionable." There's a surprising gentleness, a relaxing nonagression, and a good deal of humor behind this very high fashion, as if the clothes themselves are surprised at what they have been permitted to accomplish and what they've been freed from accomplishing.

The Japanese have always allowed everyday objects, like garments and textiles, to move beyond utility and aspire to the giddy heights we in the West reserve for fine art. Perhaps this freedom is why the Japanese entry into international fashion design has been so refreshing. □

David Page Coffin is an assistant editor of Threads *magazine. For more on Rei Kawakubo and other Japanese designers who are expanding boundaries about clothes, see Leonard Koren's* New Fashion Japan *(Kodansha International, 1984). The catalog for the FIT show is available for $10 from the Shirley Goodman Resource Center, FIT, 227 W. 27th St., New York, NY 10001. Photos by Brian Gulick.*

Index

If you enjoyed this book, you're going to love our magazine.

A year's subscription to *THREADS* brings you the kind of hands-on information you found in this book, and much more. In issue after issue - six times a year - you'll find articles on sewing, needlecrafts and textile arts. Artists and professionals will share their best techniques and trade secrets with you. With detailed illustrations and full-color photographs that bring each project to life, *THREADS* will inspire you to create your best work ever!

To subscribe, just fill out one of the attached subscription cards or call us at 1-203-426-8171. And as always, your satisfaction is guaranteed, or we'll give you your money back.

The Taunton Press
63 S. Main Street, Box 5506, Newtown, CT 06470-5506